830

THE SAILING RULES
IN YACHT RACING

START OF HINGHAM AND DETROIT 22 SQUARE METRE, INTERNATIONAL RATING CLASS. MIDSUMMER RACE WEEK. MARBLEHEAD, 1932.

(*Left to Right*)
Win-d-peg (*H*);
Kye-pol (*H*);
Gypsy II (*D*);
Dodo II (*H*);
Saga (*H*);
Goetass (*H*);
Fraeth (*D*)

Courtesy of "Boston Herald."

THE SAILING RULES IN YACHT RACING

Interpreted and Applied in Official Protest
Decisions of Yachting Tribunals of
Final Jurisdiction

REVISED EDITION

By

GEORGE E. HILLS

Former Chairman, Race Committee, Hingham Yacht Club
Member, Committee on Junior Yacht Racing
North American Yacht Racing Union

Foreword to First Edition by

CLIFFORD D. MALLORY

Honorary President, North American Yacht Racing Union

NEW YORK · LONDON
CHARLES SCRIBNER'S SONS
1940

COPYRIGHT, 1940, BY
GEORGE E. HILLS

Printed in the United States of America

All rights reserved. No part of this book may be reproduced in any form without the permission of Charles Scribner's Sons

AA

To

ERNESTINE AND EDWIN

PREFACE TO REVISED EDITION

Much water has flowed over the yacht racing dam since the publication of the first edition of this treatise seven years ago. Rules 29 (3) and 30 (1) were amended slightly at the International Conference at London, England, October 16–18, 1933. The former footnote to Rule 29 (6) 4 was ordered deleted at the Annual General Meeting of the North American Yacht Racing Union on November 20, 1936, for the reason that instead of being a clarification as had been hoped when the new rules were adopted in 1930, it had proved to be a complication. Never was it included in either the British or the International Yacht Racing Union Rules.

During the intervening years many leading protest cases have been adjudicated by the British Y. R. A., the New York Yacht Club Race Committee, the Committee on Racing Appeals of that Club, and the N. A. Y. R. U. These decisions have settled a number of formerly doubtful points of racing law. All such cases as were deemed pertinent and helpful will be found in this revision. The most recent decision cited is *Gleam* v. *Seven Seas* decided by the Committee on Racing Appeals of the N. Y. Y. C. in January, 1940. Included also are some cases which I was unable to examine carefully seven years ago on account of lack of time. Many requests were received that Rules 43 to 48, although strictly not a part of the Sailing Rules, be more extensively commented upon and cases pertaining thereto be cited if they could be found. My quest was successful. Much additional material relating to the interpretation of the yacht racing rules as a whole was acquired through correspondence and personal contacts with promi-

PREFACE TO REVISED EDITION

nent racing yachtsmen. All such data was carefully noted, filed and indexed for future reference.

Thirteen new diagrams have been added including that of the famous *Endeavor* v. *Rainbow* protest of September 22, 1934 and the somewhat analogous *Rainbow* v. *Yankee* case of August 15, 1936. The present volume contains over 180 separate references as compared with some 77 in the 1933 edition.

To enumerate all the yachtsmen who have been of assistance in relation to the added material contained in this revision would be too lengthy a task. I desire, however, particularly to thank the following:

> Philip J. Roosevelt, President, North American Yacht Racing Union.
>
> Edmund Lang, Chairman of the Race Committee of the New York Yacht Club for many years.
>
> Van S. Merle-Smith, Chairman, Committee on Racing Rules, N. A. Y. R. U.
>
> Alexander M. Orr, Member, Committee on Racing Rules, N. A. Y. R. U.
>
> J. Herbert Ware, Chairman, Appeals Committee, Southern Massachusetts Yacht Racing Association.

To my unnamed yachting friends who were of help my thanks also.

Chapters I–IV of the first edition are reprinted practically without change.

In Appendix I will be found certain of the present racing rules. In Appendix II will be found a few suggested changes, the most important of which relate to right-of-way during the preparatory period. I believe that they would very greatly lessen the number of protests, because

PREFACE TO REVISED EDITION

it is during those ofttimes hectic three or five minutes that the great majority of rule violations occur.

I have tried to conform even more closely to the method of interpreting the rules mentioned by Commodore Clifford D. Mallory in his Foreword to the first edition. Only in a few instances have I intentionally intruded my own opinion except by way of comment on decided protest cases.

GEORGE E. HILLS.

Boston, Massachusetts,
   February 15, 1940.

FOREWORD TO FIRST EDITION

It is with real pleasure and sincere appreciation of the compliment paid me that I have accepted Mr. George E. Hills' invitation to prepare a few words of introduction to this volume of interpretations of the Racing (Sailing) Rules,—specifically the "Right of Way" Rules, which he has assembled and commented upon.

Nearly all of the several interpretations contained herein have been taken from the Official Records of decisions rendered by the Yacht Racing Association of Long Island Sound, N. Y., the New York Yacht Club, the Yacht Racing Association of Great Britain and the North American Yacht Racing Union, and are based upon protests or appeals presented to them for adjudication.

The importance of this publication is greatly strengthened by the author's method of interpreting the Racing Rules. He has based such interpretation solely on the Official Decisions in so far as such precedents are available. Thus he has eliminated in great measure and wherever possible any personal or biased opinion.

The clarity with which these interpretations have been set forth in illustrating the various racing problems and the decisions regarding past breaches of the Rules will, I am sure, be helpful to the experienced racing yachtsmen of the present and to the keen racing men of the future.

Mr. Hills is to be congratulated upon this evidence of his devotion to the splendid sport of yachting and upon his clear and concise exposition of the subject matter recorded in this interesting and useful volume.

June, 1933. CLIFFORD D. MALLORY.

PREFACE TO FIRST EDITION

The skilful handling of a sailboat is an art which cannot be acquired from books but only by practical experience afloat. Parents are realizing more and more the benefits that children derive from small sailboat racing; that it makes not only for sound bodies, but develops initiative, alertness, concentration, good sportsmanship, good judgment and assumption of responsibility. As a result, each year more young people take part in yacht racing. Ten to twelve years of age is none too young to make a start, and in a *centreboard catboat*.

The Sailing Rules—Part II of the Racing Rules—comprise but a small part of the Racing Rules which in addition deal with entries, equipment, measurement, classification, etc. Year by year the Sailing Rules are more strictly enforced in all classes, both large and small; and yet, due to lack of knowledge of the *interpretation* of the rules, unintentional violations—infractions which spoil other yachtsmen's enjoyment of the sport—still are far too numerous.

A racing skipper not only should know the wording of the Sailing Rules—the rules which govern a race from the making of the preparatory signal to and including the finish,—but he should be conversant with their interpretation,—when and how they apply. Correct interpretation can best be learned by the study of protest decisions by yachting tribunals of final jurisdiction.

The Sailing Rules will be discussed, not in their numerical order as printed in the *North American Yacht*

PREFACE TO FIRST EDITION

Racing Union Year Book but in the order in which they apply from the making of the preparatory signal.

The reader will note references to decisions of the Council of the British Yacht Racing Association, together with a year date in each instance. References to such decisions prior to 1924, other than those examined in the Library of the New York Yacht Club, are taken from publications of British yachting writers of note, viz: Dixon Kemp's *A Manual of Yacht and Boat Sailing,* London, 8th edition, 1895; *An Exposition of the Yacht Racing Rules,* London, 1898; *Manual of Yacht and Boat Sailing and Yacht Architecture,* 11th edition, London, 1913, the last-named work edited by Major B. Heckstall-Smith and Linton Hope; and *Yacht Racing—A Text Book on the Sport,* B. Heckstall-Smith, London, 1923. These comprehensive treatises, which discuss not only the Sailing Rules but also the other Racing Rules, refer to the important decisions of the Y. R. A. from its organization in 1875 to and including 1923. I have no means of knowing whether the date appended to each such citation refers to the year in which the decision was handed down by the Council, or whether it refers to the Y. R. A. Year Book in which it may be found. Unless otherwise noted, each Y. R. A. reference beginning with 1924 is to the Year Book of the given year.

Why British references out-number American citations will be apparent after reading Chapter III.

Although most of the American cases cited antedate the adoption of the International Sailing Rules in November, 1929, each such decision would have been the same had the rules in force at the time of each protest been the present rules. Hence their value in interpreting the rules under which we now race.

PREFACE TO FIRST EDITION

References to protest cases include decisions of:

1. The Executive Committee of the North American Yacht Racing Union, to and including the Annual General Meeting of December 17, 1932.
2. The Executive Committee of the Yacht Racing Association of Long Island Sound, N. Y., to and including the Annual General Meeting of March, 1933.
3. The New York Yacht Club, to and including the Annual Meeting of December 15, 1932.
4. The Council of the Yacht Racing Association of Great Britain, to and including the Annual General Meeting of February 16, 1933.

The diagrams, from sketches by the Author, were drawn by Fred W. Goeller, Naval Architect, who collaborated with Addison G. Hanan in the design of *Josephine,* the sensation of Class "P" in 1913. They are *not* drawn to scale.

I desire to express my sincere thanks to the following yachtsmen for their valuable assistance in the preparation of this work:

> Clifford D. Mallory, President, North American Yacht Racing Union.
>
> C. Sherman Hoyt, Chairman, Committee on Racing Rules, N. A. Y. R. U.
>
> Johnston deForest, Member, Committee on Racing Rules, N. A. Y. R. U.
>
> Ernest Stavey, Corresponding Secretary, N. A. Y. R. U.
>
> W. A. W. Stewart, Vice-Commodore, New York Yacht Club.
>
> George A. Cormack, Secretary, N. Y. Y. C.

PREFACE TO FIRST EDITION

George Nichols, Former Commodore, N. Y. Y. C.
Major B. Heckstall-Smith, Secretary, International Yacht Racing Union, and Yacht Racing Association of Great Britain.

Included also, are a few topics which may be of interest to Race Committees. I hope such items may be of help to the men, Yes!—and women—for there *are* women on some Race Committees—who unselfishly give much time and effort to further the sport.

If, then, my endeavor to add to the sailing-rule knowledge of racing skippers shall result in fewer violations of the Sailing Rules, my time will have been well spent.

GEORGE E. HILLS.

Boston, Massachusetts,
   June, 1933.

CONTENTS

CHAPTER		PAGE
VIII.	RULE 29—DEFINITIONS	51
IX.	RULE 30—RIGHT OF WAY	64

    OVERTAKING:
        TO WINDWARD
        TO LEEWARD
        JIBING AND LUFFING BY OVERTAKEN YACHT
        JIBING AROUND MARKS
        THE FLORIDA CASE

X.	RULE 30 (CONTINUED)	107

    MEETING, CROSSING AND CONVERGING
    CLAUSES (D), (E), (F), (G) AND (H)
    CLAUSE (E)—"WHEN ANY REASONABLE DOUBT EXISTS THE STARBOARD TACK RULE MUST BE UPHELD"
    CLAUSE (F)—*Endeavour* v. *Rainbow*

XI.	RULE 30 (CONTINUED)	127

    ALTERING COURSE
    GATHER PROPER WAY ON NEW TACK
    OWING TO POSITION CANNOT KEEP CLEAR
    TACKING TOO CLOSE IN FRONT OF ANOTHER YACHT
    MISLEAD OR BALK (CLAUSE (K))
    PRESENCE OF MARKS DOES NOT AFFECT RULE 30

XII.	RULE 31—GIVING ROOM AT MARKS OR OBSTRUCTIONS TO SEA ROOM	153

    PURPOSE OF THE RULE
    REQUISITES NECESSARY TO INVOKE THE RULE
    DURATION OF PERIOD OF APPLICATION OF THE RULE

CONTENTS

	PAGE
Preface to Revised Edition	vii
Foreword to First Edition	x
Preface to First Edition	xi

CHAPTER
- I. Retrospect — 1
- II. Why This Book — 4
- III. Unification of the Sailing Rules — 6
- IV. Why So Many Disqualifications — 10
- V. Management of Races. Rule 1 — 13
  - General Authority of Race Committee — 13
  - Ordinary Customs of the Sea
  - Unfair Sailing

The Sailing Rules

- VI. Rule 14—When Amenable to Part 2 of the Racing Rules — 23
  - Bearing Away Before the Start
  - Yacht Racing Rules Supersede Rules of the Road at Sea
  - Rule 34. Marks of the Course
- VII. Start and Recall — 43
  - Required Number of Starters
  - Premature Start and Recall
  - Wrong Side of Starting Line
  - Right to Return and Make a Proper Start

CONTENTS

CHAPTER   PAGE

DEFINITION OF OBSTRUCTION TO SEA ROOM

FOUR SITUATIONS CONTEMPLATED BY THE RULE:

1. FIXED OBSTRUCTIONS
2. CRAFT UNDER WAY, INCLUDING ANOTHER YACHT RACING
3. MARKS OF THE COURSE OTHER THAN MARKS OF THE LINES OF START OR FINISH
   OVERLAP MADE IN PROPER TIME
   CUTTING IN AT MARKS
4. MARKS OF THE STARTING LINE:
   (a) BEFORE THE STARTING SIGNAL
   (b) AFTER THE STARTING SIGNAL
   BARGING

SQUEEZING THE INSIDE YACHT

LUFFING AND FOREREACHING PAST A MARK

OVERTAKING ALONG A SHORE OR SHOAL:

1. WEATHER SHORE
2. LEE SHORE

XIII. OVERTAKING—OBSTRUCTION TO SEA ROOM   196

THREE YACHTS INVOLVED

RULE 30 (A), (B), (C), (G) AND (K), AND RULE 31

WHICH OF THE TWO OUTSIDE YACHTS IS THE OBSTRUCTION

CASE 1. L (LEEWARD) AND W (WINDWARD) FIRST OVERLAPPED

CASE 2. M (MIDDLE) AND W (WINDWARD) FIRST OVERLAPPED

CASE 3. L (LEEWARD) AND M (MIDDLE) FIRST OVERLAPPED

CONTENTS

CHAPTER		PAGE

XIV. Rule 32—Close-Hauled, Approaching an Obstruction to Sea Room or a Mark — 218

REQUISITES NECESSARY TO INVOKE THE RULE

NOT MANDATORY THAT WINDWARD YACHT TACK

A HAIL IS A DEMAND FOR SEA ROOM ONLY

HAIL MUST BE GIVEN SEASONABLY

A YACHT IS RESPONSIBLE FOR HER HAIL

YACHTS MUST BE APPROACHING THE DANGER

Volunteer v. *Gracie*, 1891

XV. Rules 33, 34 and 35 — 234

RULE 33. FOULING OR IMPROPERLY ROUNDING MARKS

TRACK OF YACHT MUST INCLOSE MARKS

ESSENTIAL OR ORDINARY ABOVE-WATER PART OF A MARK

RULE 34. MARKS OF THE COURSE (SEE CHAPTER VI)

RULE 35. FOULING COMPETING YACHTS

The Bembridge Sailing Club, 1899

Lena v. *Countess*, 1924

Pilgrim v. *Maori*, 1935

YACHTING ETIQUETTE

XVI. Rules 36, 37, 38, 40 and 41 — 250

RULE 36. RUNNING AGROUND AND FOULING

OUTSIDE ASSISTANCE

CONTENTS

CHAPTER   PAGE

        RULE 37. ANCHORING
        RULE 38. PROPULSION
                       PROPULSION BY THE NORMAL ACTION OF WIND ON SAILS ALONE PERMITTED
        RULE 40. MAN OVERBOARD AND ACCIDENTS
        RULE 41. THE FINISH
                       VEERING ACROSS FINISH LINE WHILE ANCHORED

Protests, Disqualifications and Appeals

XVII. RULES 43, 45, 46, 47 AND 48   263
        RULE 43. PENALTY FOR INFRINGING RULES
        RULE 45. PROTESTS
                       FORM OF
                       REASONS FOR "PROMPTLY DISPLAY CODE FLAG 'B' "
                       JURIDICTION OF PROTEST
                       PROTESTS IN GENERAL
        RULE 46. HEARINGS BY RACE COMMITTEE
                       CONTESTANTS ENTITLED TO CROSS-EXAMINE WITNESSES
                       RACE COMMITTEE A COURT OF INQUIRY, NOT A COURT OF LAW
                       BURDEN OF PROOF
        RULE 47. DISQUALIFICATION WITHOUT PROTEST
        RULE 48. DECISIONS OF PROTESTS INVOLVING INTERPRETATION OF THE RULES SHOULD BE IN WRITING

CONTENTS

CHAPTER	PAGE
XVIII. COURTESY AND UNWRITTEN LAW	278

APPENDIXES

I. N. A. Y. R. U., CERTAIN RACING RULES	281
II. SUGGESTED CHANGES AND COMMENTS	304

INDEXES

CITATIONS AND REFERENCES ARRANGED BY RULE NUMBER	317
DIAGRAMS ARRANGED BY RULE NUMBER	327
GENERAL AND CROSS INDEX	329

THE SAILING RULES
IN YACHT RACING

Chapter I

RETROSPECT

Looking into the future, forty-five years seem almost interminable. Looking back over that period, it seems but a day. When I was a small boy and had learned to swim, my dad gave me a rowboat. After learning to row—after a fashion—I wanted to sail. My father said I was too young. Nothing daunted, I appropriated an umbrella from the household collection and bore it seaward. Again and again I rowed my heavy dory to the windward shore of the harbor of Hingham, Massachusetts, dry at low water except for a narrow, winding channel, unshipped the oars, opened my umbrella, and with an oar for a rudder ran down to leeward. Sometimes the wind was light, sometimes strong. As a result the family stock of umbrellas became depleted. One rainy morning my father could not find his pet umbrella. He made inquiries. The story of George Washington and the cherry tree was fresh in my mind. I confessed! Thereafter, umbrellas, as sails, were taboo. I had to resort to an oar, upright in the bow, blade square to the wind. Needless to state, my running time was slower.

The next year a centreboard was installed, a rudder and tiller added, also a spritsail. After capsizing a few times while trying to beat to windward, I mastered the rudiments of that art.

In later years came, first a fifteen-foot jib and mainsail craft, and still later a centreboard cabin sloop, thirty-six

THE SAILING RULES

feet over all, carrying over a thousand square feet of canvas. Subsequently the headrig was altered to a forestaysail and jib, which made her easier to handle.

We cruised along the coast from New York City to and into the Bras d'Or Lakes on Cape Breton Island, north of Nova Scotia. Almost every nook and cranny of the shore line was explored. There was scarcely a harbor in which we did not anchor at one time or another. I have not visited them for many years but they are still fresh in my memory. "The Basin," on the eastern shore of the New Meadows River, was one of our favorites. A tiny, landlocked haven with a narrow entrance just beyond the easterly end of Casco Bay, on the rock-bound coast of Maine. Quiet as a mill pond; the crows cawing in the tall pines; sometimes a radiant moon; care free. Nothing to do but enjoy the present and revel in the beauty of nature.

When at Hingham we thought nothing of sailing eight or ten miles to some point in Boston Harbor to enter a race. Sometimes we won. Sometimes we lost. But we had a wonderful time.

Only by mentioning individual instances which come under one's close observation may it be shown what can be accomplished by perseverance on the part of youngsters who love flying spray and are eager to learn and willing to work hard to attain success.

When my daughter was thirteen and my son twelve, they were given a one-design, fourteen-foot, centreboard catboat of the class known as Mighty Mite. After they had been taught to keep right side up, to reef, in what direction to move the tiller when in irons and gathering sternway, and last but not least, the three basic rules and three bits of advice, they were turned loose to race. They alternated as skipper. That season, of course, they fin-

THE SAILING RULES

ished at the foot of their class. But, oh! what a thrill when occasionally they finished ahead of one or more boats. Two years later they ended the season at the top of their class and the following year graduated into class "O," a centreboard jib and mainsail craft fifteen feet on the waterline, with spinnaker. In their second and third seasons in that class, 1930 and 1931, they sailed a total of sixty-one races, at Hingham, at other points in Boston Harbor, and at Marblehead during Midsummer Race Week, with an average number of twelve "O" boats in each race. Their average for the combined two years, with no disablements, withdrawals or disqualifications, was 94.83 per cent. In six years they did not miss a scheduled race.

Their record is mentioned solely in the hope that it may encourage other youngsters to take up sail-yacht racing; to persevere, and everlastingly keep at it. Not merely to profit by their own mistakes but also to learn by observing what the other fellow did which enabled him to come in ahead. *And* continually to work on their boats; to keep them in the pink of condition, deck, topsides, underbody, and standing as well as running rigging. Not to be discouraged when finishing last but confident that the time will come when some one else will view the stern of their boats at the finish. To respect the rights of competitors and to insist upon their own. To be fair sailers, cheerful losers and modest winners.

Chapter II

WHY THIS BOOK

The interest evinced by my children in sailing and racing led me, in 1927, to accept the Chairmanship of the Race Committee of my Club. This brought about contacts with officials in neighboring yacht clubs who also were interested in junior skippers, and resulted in the organization, in 1930, of the South Shore Junior Yacht Racing Association by representatives from a number of yacht clubs on the South Shore of Massachusetts Bay. Then followed an appointment in 1931, and again in 1932, as one of the three Judges at the National Junior Championship races for the Sears Cup held by the American Yacht Club of Rye, New York, and by the Beverly Yacht Club of Marion, Massachusetts.[1]

One thing leads to another. One day while searching for some authority on a certain topic connected with the Racing Rules, and purely by accident, I ran across a stray copy of the British Y. R. A. 1931 Year Book. I glanced through it. Toward the end of the book I discovered a number of protest decisions. Not only were the decisions reported in full, but in several instances the arguments on both sides, together with diagrams, were included. There is nothing more satisfying to a lawyer than to be able to back up his interpretation of a point of law by citing an

[1] It has been the Author's privilege to serve in that capacity ever since former Commodore Herbert M. Sears and the Eastern Yacht Club of Marblehead, Mass., placed the Sears Cup under the jurisdiction of the N. A. Y. R. U. in 1931.

opinion of a court of final jurisdiction and unquestioned authority. It occurred to me that if I could study the British protest decisions, together with official protest decisions of yachting tribunals of final jurisdiction in our own country, and classify them, opinions as to the interpretation of the Sailing Rules would be confirmed by authentic decisions of some of the world's supreme courts of yachting. I knew of no small treatise which discussed solely the Sailing Rules. No American book, so far as I was aware, cited recent official protest decisions of appellate yachting tribunals of final jurisdiction.

I wrote to Mr. Mallory, asking him what he thought of the idea. His reply was encouraging. Hence this book.

Chapter III

UNIFICATION OF THE SAILING RULES

The Sailing Rules, as is the case with the rules governing every competitive sport, are not of mushroom growth. They are not the result of theory alone but are the ripe fruit of practical experience of many years. Their growth is analogous to that of the English Common Law. Based, in the beginning, upon the Rules of the Road at Sea, they differ from them in so many respects that they well may be termed Special Yacht Racing Law.

This will be apparent when we realize that the International Rules of the Road are framed primarily to keep vessels at a distance from each other; not only to avert collision but to prevent the *slightest risk* of collision. In racing, yachts frequently are at close quarters. That is part of the sport. The Sailing Rules contemplate such close proximity when racing, and provide rights of way by which yachts approaching one another are required to keep clear.

In England there has existed a central yachting authority for more than sixty-four years. The British Yacht Racing Association was organized in 1875. Not until 1882, however, did the Royal Yacht Squadron, England's premier Yacht Club, founded in 1815 and located at Cowes on the Isle of Wight, together with the Royal Thames Yacht Club of London, founded in 1823, come within the fold. This was due largely to the benign influence of H. R. H. King Edward VII, then Prince of

THE SAILING RULES

Wales, Commodore of the Royal Yacht Squadron and later President of the Y. R. A. Since 1882 there has been national unity in British yacht racing. The Y. R. A. has member clubs in many parts of the civilized yachting world. An appeal, solely on a question pertaining to the interpretation of the Racing Rules, may be taken from the decision of a local Race Committee directly to the Council, the governing body of the Y. R. A. Annually the Y. R. A. publishes a Year Book in which, beginning with 1893, are reported the appeal cases passed upon by the Council. In many instances diagrams are included.

In October, 1907, the then Y. R. A. Sailing Rules, with a few minor verbal changes, were adopted by the International Conference at Paris, when the International Yacht Racing Union was formed. In 1912 a Committee of the Council drafted a series of explanatory footnotes to the Definitions and Right of Way Rules. In 1913, one footnote was added to Rule 31. On October 25, 1919, the Y. R. A. Sailing Rules, together with the footnotes of 1912 and 1913, were readopted by the International Conference at London.

Prior to 1925 there was no national yachting authority in North America. True, the Racing Rules of each Club were in most respects the same but there was no central governing body. In 1924 a number of prominent American yachtsmen with vision got together and in 1925 was born the North American Yacht Racing Union.

In November, 1929, an International Conference was held at London. For the first time North America could be and was represented. The result was the present code of International Sailing Rules; so that now, wherever a yachtsman may race, the Sailing Rules may be said to be uniform. With comparatively few exceptions the prior British Sailing Rules, plus most of the 1912 and 1913 footnotes, were adopted as the International Sailing Rules. It follows that the Council protest decisions, especially those from 1913 onward, are particularly valuable in interpreting the N. A. Y. R. U. Sailing Rules.

To no one is due greater credit for the 1929 unification than Major Brooke Heckstall-Smith, who since its foundation in 1907 has been Secretary of the International Y. R. U. and also of the British Y. R. A. since 1898. In 1919 he visited North America and as the guest of Mr. J. Pierpont Morgan, former Commodore of the New York Yacht Club, visited many yachting centres in the United States and Canada. Major Heckstall-Smith had long hoped and, until then, had striven in vain for uniform yacht racing rules between the two great English-speaking nations. Such unity was impossible until there should exist in America a central governing body on yachting with which all American and Canadian Yacht Clubs might affiliate. Not until that objective had been attained could any representative North American yachting authority meet with other national authorities to agree upon uniform Sailing Rules.

To quote from Major Heckstall-Smith's *All Hands on the Main Sheet,* London, 1921, page 192:

"A great object in my life has been to unite British and American yachting so that the two nations have the same rules in the sport and race under the same system. . . . I find in America a great many Clubs, and in Canada also, but no central body or central organization to which all Clubs are affiliated."

Six years after his visit to America a central governing body or national yachting authority on this side of the North Atlantic Ocean became a reality. Exactly a decade after his American and Canadian yachting tour, representatives from the central governing body of every civilized yachting nation met at London, and in November, 1929, adopted the present International Sailing Rules. Major Heckstall-Smith's long-cherished hope had become a reality. And best of all he has lived to see it.

Chapter IV

WHY SO MANY DISQUALIFICATIONS

Mr. William Waldron Swan, of the Larchmont Yacht Club, Long Island Sound, New York, an internationally known racing skipper and authority on all matters pertaining to yachting, stated in one of his lectures during the winter of 1931–1932 that during a recent yachting season, in a class of twenty yachts, there had been forty-one disqualifications. Observation of racing skippers, both Seniors and Juniors, leads the writer to say unqualifiedly that the racing skipper of today who tries to win a race by means other than fair sailing and superior speed and skill is almost non-existent.

Why, then, are there so many disqualifications? Is not the answer that most violations of the Sailing Rules are due to a lack of knowledge of their *interpretation* rather than to ignorance of their wording?

As a general rule a yacht is disqualified because at the time of the alleged violation she:

1. Was overtaking yacht, or
2. Was port-tack yacht, or
3. Was windward yacht, or
4. Tacked too close, or
5. Altered her course at a time when a competitor was too close to keep out of her way, or
6. Did not allow the inside yacht sufficient room at marks or obstructions to sea room.

THE SAILING RULES

A skipper may know by heart that "A yacht overtaking another shall keep out of the way of the overtaken yacht." But does he know *when* a yacht *ranks* as overtaking yacht? Again, he may know that by Section 2 of Rule 29 —Definitions, a luff is an alteration of course. But does he know *when* he has the right to luff, and *when* he has not that right?

Although there are over one hundred Racing Rules in the N. A. Y. R. U. Year Book, it is only with some fifteen of the Sailing Rules that a racing skipper need concern himself during a race. As a matter of fact even these fifteen boil down to three, viz., Rules 30, 31 and 32; and these in turn may be summarized in three sentences of four words each, together with three short sentences by way of Bits of Advice.

Three Basic Rules

1. OVERTAKING YACHT KEEPS CLEAR.
2. PORT-TACK YACHT KEEPS CLEAR.
3. WINDWARD YACHT KEEPS CLEAR.

Three Bits of Advice

1. DON'T TACK TOO CLOSE.
2. GIVE AMPLE ROOM AT MARKS.
3. ALWAYS AVOID A COLLISION.

The vital rules must be so thoroughly mastered by every racing skipper who is ambitious for success that his reaction to a given situation will be instinctive. It should be akin to that of a good seaman when the unexpected happens. For example: A shroud parts and the mast breaks. The good seaman instinctively puts his tiller *hard up* and bears away to leeward. As a result, the spar, sails and rigging fall harmlessly alongside.

THE SAILING RULES

Again: Some one falls overboard. The good seaman instantly throws over a life buoy, and *jibes*—no matter what the direction of the wind. Did he tack, precious minutes would be lost.

So with the few basic Sailing Rules. The true racing skipper is able instantly to apply the requisite rule. He *knows* instinctively; not only *how* but *why* it applies.

One skipper who is ignorant of the interpretation of the Sailing Rules may not only spoil a race for one or more unoffending competitors but may be the cause of serious damage not only to his own yacht but also to other and unoffending contestants.

Chapter V

MANAGEMENT OF RACES

Rule 1

GENERAL AUTHORITY OF RACE COMMITTEE

An internationally famous yachtsman once wrote us as follows:

"Disqualification under Rule 1 has always been considered disgraceful, which is unfortunate, as it is not necessarily so.

"The last sentence in Rule 1, as now written, expresses two totally unrelated ideas and might be improved by separating this sentence into two."

The last sentence reads as follows:

The decisions of the Race Committee shall be based upon these rules, so far as they apply, but as no rules can be devised capable of meeting every incident and accident of sailing, the Race Committee shall keep in view the ordinary customs of the sea, and discourage all attempts to win a race by other means than fair sailing and superior speed and skill.

It would seem that this sentence contained three separate ideas:

First, that no rules can be devised capable of meeting *every* incident of yacht racing;

THE SAILING RULES

Second, that in yacht racing the ordinary customs and practices of the sea as handed down through the years should always be kept in view, and

Third, it warns contestants not to use unfair tactics in maintaining or bettering their own standing or position.

This sentence clothes the Race Committee with what in law we would term broad equity powers. It seemingly gives the Committee the right to abrogate or change a rule. It is not intended to have that effect. It does, however, permit the Committee to rule that in the case of an extraordinary state of facts; in a situation which could not have been reasonably forseen by contestants; or in a situation in which a strictly literal interpretation of a rule would result in what was obviously an unjust decision or an "impossible" situation, equity, the square deal, common sense, and not the literal wording of the rule technically violated should govern.

The first rule of the sea is, "Avoid a collision." Suppose a yacht close-hauled on the starboard tack holds her course and deliberately runs into a yacht close-hauled on the port tack which refuses to get out of the way of the former. The port-tack yacht should be disqualified for violation of Rule 30 (E). Can there be any doubt that on the facts as stated the Race Committee also should disqualify the starboard-tack yacht under Rule I for deliberately violating an ordinary custom of the sea? If the starboard-tack yacht is not protested the Race Committee should initiate action against her under Rule 47.

Next to "Avoid a collision." there is no custom or practice of the sea better known to sailors than the unwritten law that you must not bear down upon another vessel to hinder her passing to leeward. Long before there were any established yacht racing rules, bearing down on a rival

THE SAILING RULES

when racing back to port to be the first to land a catch of fish was scrupulously avoided. Rule 30 was not intended to abolish time honored customs but to meet the incidents and necessity of close proximity when racing, and to make certain which yacht should keep clear in the various situations which continually arise.

The third idea is that of "fair sailing and superior speed and skill." Now-a-days skill in maneuvering and smartness in handling are of great importance. The old conception of yacht racing as a mere trial of speed is a thing of the past. Taking advantage of a skipper who has placed his yacht in a bad position is no more unsportsmanlike than is outmaneuvering him so as to force him into that bad position.

Now what constitutes "unfair sailing"? "The act of deliberately and wilfully sacrificing one's own chances or place in a race, thereby substantially injuring or improving the chances or place of others" is unfair sailing. A notable case is *Ace* v. *Whitecap* which occurred in the final race of the World's Championship of the International Star Class Y. R. A. at Newport Harbor, California, in 1935. The Governing Committee of the I. S. C. Y. R. A. not only disqualified *Whitecap* but suspended her skipper, for gross unsportsmanlike conduct, for the remainder of the year 1935.[1] This case resulted in the adoption by the I. S. C. Y. R. A. at a special meeting held in New York City on January 15, 1936, of a new rule from which the words quoted are taken, and which might well be adopted by the International Yacht Racing Union as Rule IA.

The N. A. Y. R. U. deemed this decision of sufficient importance to send a copy of the I. S. C. Y. R. A. "Investigation and Findings" to Union members under date of March 27, 1936.

[1] *Ace* v. *Whitecap*. "Starlights," November, 1935.

THE SAILING RULES

Now how about this case.

Diagram 1.

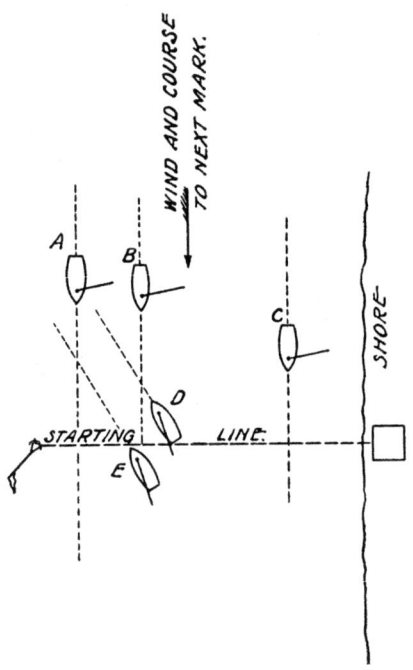

Yachts *A*, *B* and *C* are about to make a normal start straight on their course to the next mark. *D* and *E* have deliberately maneuvered on the wrong side of the starting line with the object of returning close-hauled on the starboard tack. *D* has already returned to the right side of the line. *E* will get there just before gunfire. Rule 30 (D) or (F) obliges *A* and *B* to keep clear of *D* and *E*. *D* and *E* claim that *A* and *B* should have foreseen this eventuality and should have borne away under the stern of *D*. In com-

THE SAILING RULES

menting upon this case Major B. Heckstall-Smith said: "Although all this argument is very sound law, I am not at all persuaded that D and E are not guilty of playing a dirty trick. So much do I feel this that if, after having disqualified A and B under Rule 30, the Sailing Committee were to turn round upon D and E and say, 'Now we are going to disqualify you two fellows also under Rule I for not keeping in view the ordinary customs of the sea,' I am not at all sure the Sailing Committee would not be supported by the Y. R. A."[2]

Such a maneuver might well result in a collision, especially in a narrow channel. In the case of large yachts it would be fraught with grave danger of injury to person and property.

Protest cases where Rule I is invoked or even commented upon are rare. We now cite two such cases. In the first, Rule I was invoked to prevent a miscarriage of justice. In the second case the Rule was not availed of.

Diagram 2.

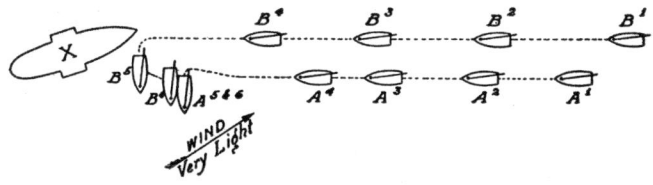

X was a side-wheel steamer which, through courtesy, had come to a standstill. A and B were fourteen-foot dinghies, beating to windward. The wind was light. B overtook A to leeward, and in Position 5, when very close to X, came about abreast and to windward of A. At that particular moment X started to back, and the wash from

[2]*Yachting World*, January 1, 1937, page 9.

THE SAILING RULES

her paddle-wheels threw *B* to leeward and against *A*. As windward yacht it was *B's* duty to keep clear of *A*. Ordinarily *B* would have to be disqualified, but in view of the unforeseen and unusual facts it would seem that under Rule I, the Committee should, in all fairness, have dismissed *A's* protest. Such was the decision of the Council.[3]

The second case was decided under Rule 37—ANCHORING—. *Lady Dainty* was fouled by another yacht and was obliged to tie up to the shore to mend a cross-tree pin sheared off by the collision. On appeal the Council upheld the decision of the Sailing Committee saying, " 'Lady Dainty' should be disqualified. She infringed Rule 37. The Council recognizes the fact that the case was very unfortunate for 'Lady Dainty'."[4]

Here was a case where a yacht was compelled to "make fast to an object" in order to repair damage directly resulting from the misbehavior of another yacht. We are in complete accord with Major B. Heckstall-Smith, who, in commenting upon this case said: "Personally I should have excused her on these grounds under Rule I."[5]

Every rule in the rule-book is there for a good reason—either to prevent collision or to prevent some form of unfair practice. Rule I gives the Committee full power to disqualify any yacht which has "misused the Rules"[6] or has been guilty of "foul sailing."[7]

Rule I is the most important of all the Yacht Racing Rules and should ever be uppermost in a skipper's mind. It is unsportsmanlike to take the point of view that because certain tactics are not *forbidden* by the rules they are legal and therefore ethical. We must never depart from the ordi-

[3]*Marjorie* v. *Sheila.* Y. R. A., 1929, Case 7.
[4]*Lady Dainty.* Y. R. A., 1939, Case 7.
[5]*Yachting World,* October 28, 1938, page 433.
[6]*Jade* v. *Bluebell.* Y. R. A., 1936, Case 3.
[7]*Tringa* v. *Susette.* Y. R. A., 1904, page 132.

THE SAILING RULES

nary customs and practices of good seamanship. Rule I is not a meaningless introduction to the Yacht Racing Rules.

In closing this chapter we may profitably quote again Major B. Heckstall-Smith:

"The incidents of seamanship, however, are so many during a yacht race, there may be accidents, gales, heavy seas or calms when the vessels holding or not holding right of way by the Y. R. A. rules may be out of control, so that every case must be judged upon its merits by 'Rule I' keeping in view the customs of the sea and the spirit of fair sailing."[8]

Fair play is the corner-stone of yacht racing.

[8] *Yachting World,* May 26, 1939, page 521.

THE SAILING RULES

Chapter VI

RULE 14

WHEN AMENABLE TO PART II OF THE RACING RULES

A yacht shall be amenable to Part II of the Racing Rules from the time the preparatory signal for her class is made, and shall continue so until she has finished and her entire hull and spars are clear of the finish line.

"The hull, gear, or spars set in a bona-fide manner is a part of the boat for the purpose of an overlap."[1]

Prior to the preparatory gun for her class a yacht is amenable only to the Rules of the Road at Sea which do not permit one vessel to alter course in order to hinder another.

Upon the firing of the preparatory gun for each class the Sailing Rules supersede the Rules of the Road at Sea, and gradual luffing is permitted. Here is the rule:

Before the starting signal is given there are no restrictions upon the manœuvring of the yachts other than the provisions of Rules 30, 31 and 32, and the yacht holding right of way may alter course in any reasonable manner (but a luff so sudden that it cannot be easily responded to would not be considered reasonable).

This paragraph expressly permits a leeward, right-of-way yacht to luff her opponent in a manner to which the latter can easily respond, even to the extent of forcing her across the starting line prematurely. Immediately the question will be asked whether a yacht overtaken to leeward, and after the overlap has been established, may bear

[1] *Yare and Bure Sailing Club.* Y. R. A., 1909, page 134.

THE SAILING RULES

down upon the non-right-of-way yacht in a manner to which the latter can easily respond, and force the latter also to bear away in order to keep clear. This brings us to a mooted question which was not settled authoritatively until the case of *Gleam* v. *Seven Seas* was decided by the Committee on Racing Appeals of the New York Yacht Club in January, 1940.

An intent on the part of the overtaken yacht merely to hinder her opponent might well be held to be contrary to the spirit of fair play in Rule I. Suppose, however, the reason for bearing away was to avoid crossing the starting line prior to gunfire or to better her starting position. What then? Prior to the making of the starting signal there is no "next mark" within the meaning of Rule 29 (7) —PROPER COURSE. It follows that there is no proper course prior to the start.[2] By a process of elimination it will be seen that with the exception of Rule 30 (K) which always is applicable, Rule 30 (A) alone governs. The *only* restriction upon the manœuvring of the overtaken yacht is that she shall not alter course in a manner that "cannot be easily responded to" by the non-right-of-way yacht.

The overtaking yacht will claim that because neither the quoted paragraph of the rule nor any other clause in the Sailing Rules expressly permits such a manœuvre it is illegal. Clearly this is far too narrow a construction of the Rules. A careful examination of Rule 30 will reveal that with the exception of Clauses (B) and (K) limiting to some extent the freedom of manœuvre of the right-of-way yacht, the other eight clauses specify what the non-right-of-way boat *shall* do, not what the right-of-way yacht *may* do. The overtaking yacht will claim also that such a manœuvre is contrary to the Rules of the Road at Sea.

[2]*Gleam* v. *Seven Seas*. New York Yacht Club, Committee on Racing Appeals, January, 1940. Y. R. A., 1935, page 170. Sir William Burton, President, Y. R. A., *Yachting World*, May 17, 1935, page 406.

THE SAILING RULES

Yachts racing or participating in squadron runs waive their rights against each other under the Rules of the Road at Sea and are governed solely by the Club Rules and by the Yacht Racing Rules from the time of the making of the preparatory signal for their class until they have crossed and are clear of the finish line.[3]

The American case was the outcome of a collision shortly after crossing the finish line in a racing run from New London, Connecticut, to Newport, Rhode Island, on an annual cruise of the New York Yacht Club. *A,* the plaintiff's yacht, although participating in the squadron run, did not compete in the race. Just how the collision occurred was not stated in the report of the case. The Appellate Court said, however:—"*A* was in advance of *B,* so that *B* was an 'overtaking vessel.' Both yachts were running free with the wind on the same side. It was, therefore, the duty of *B,* under the rules of navigation enacted by Congress to keep out of the way of *A,* except for the application of a rule of the Club. This rule is as follows: 'Yachts not in races—All yachts not racing must be kept to leeward, and out of the way of racing yachts.' We think this rule bound the plaintiff, as a member of the Club, and so the trial court properly held. We think it also clear that this rule applied, not only to the course from start to finish, but for a reasonable distance after the finish. . . . The learned trial court charged the jury that, while the navigation laws of the United States were imperative, they could be waived by persons who were willing to waive them, and, therefore, that the rule of the Yacht Club, as to its members, governed." So far as can be ascertained this case has neither been cited nor overruled.

---

[3] N. A. Y. R. U. Rules 14, 41 and 43, last sentence.
The *Satanita*. Law Times Rep. Vol. 72, page 316. Affirmed in the House of Lords Law Rep., App. Cas., 1897, page 60. *Clark* v. *Thayer*. 43 N. Y. Supplement, page 897. February 10, 1897.

THE SAILING RULES

Article 27 of the British Board of Trade Regulations is identical in wording with Article 27 of the United States "Pilot Rules for Certain Inland Waters of the Atlantic and Pacific Coasts, Etc.," and reads as follows:

"In obeying and construing these rules due regard shall be had to all dangers of navigation and collision, and to any special circumstances which may render a departure from the above rules necessary in order to avoid immediate danger."

By Article 21 of the United States Pilot Rules the right-of-way vessel "shall keep her course and speed." By Article 24 an overtaking vessel "shall keep out of the way of the overtaken vessel."

In reply to a question propounded by the Royal Singapore Yacht Club the Council of the British Y. R. A. replied: "The Board of Trade Regulations for the prevention of collision at sea are not relevant as between competitors sailing in a race under Y. R. A. Rules."[4]

It was claimed by those who opposed such a manœuvre that it was not an alteration of course in the "reasonable manner" specified in the paragraph quoted above and that, unless expressly permitted by the Sailing Rules, the "reasonableness" of a manœuvre should be based upon "the ordinary customs of the sea."

The Yacht Racing Rules allow a right-of-way yacht many manœuvres and changes of course prohibited by the Rules of the Road at Sea. The Sailing Rules neither expressly permit nor prohibit the manœuvre under discussion. By the Rules of the Road at Sea an overtaken vessel may neither luff nor bear away; "She shall keep her course and speed." During the preparatory period a non-right-of-way yacht should not only expect but must be on the alert for and respond to an alteration of course made "in any rea-

[4]*Royal Singapore Yacht Club.* Y. R. A., 1929, Case 4.

sonable manner" by her opponent. A dictionary meaning of "reasonable" is "moderate." The prohibition in Rule 30 (C) against bearing away after the start to hinder a yacht overtaking to leeward is believed to have been incorporated in the Sailing Rules more from the point of view of fair sailing than because it might be a potentially dangerous manœuvre.

It would seem to be beyond dispute that while still clear ahead, *A,* the overtaken yacht, may gradually bear away to leeward, even to the extent of jibing, because *B,* the stern yacht, can, if necessary, easily luff and pass astern of her opponent. It would seem equally clear that where *B* already has overlapped *A* to leeward, a jibe on *A's* part followed by a luff forcing *B* also to jibe in order to keep clear would be an unreasonable alteration of course.

Prior to the making of the starting signal yachts are just "milling around" so to speak, each skipper endeavoring to secure the most advantageous position at gunfire.

Gleam v. *Seven Seas*[5] is an interesting and instructive case for several reasons.

First, the foul took place during the preparatory or starting period when most rule violations occur;

Second, it involves the "twilight zone" between Overtaking and Converging;

Third, it establishes the doctrine that *before* gunfire any doubt as to whether yachts rank as Overtaking or as Converging must be resolved in favor of the existence of Converging conditions, whereas *after* gunfire, when as a rule yachts are sailing in the same general direction on the same leg of the course, the presumption should be otherwise and in favor of the existence of Overtaking conditions;

Fourth, it reaffirms the yacht racing law that there is no

[5] *Gleam* v. *Seven Seas.* New York Yacht Club, Committee on Racing Appeals, January, 1940.

"proper course" prior to the making of the starting signal;

Fifth, it states that "before the start, two points in smooth water is the *maximum divergence* of course which . . . can be construed as 'nearly the same course' " (Italics —the Author);

Sixth, it settles a controversy of long standing and establishes the right of a yacht overtaken to leeward during the preparatory period to bear away in a manner to which the other can easily respond; and

Seventh, but by no means least, it comments upon the important but rarely interpreted Clause (K) of Rule 30.

Gleam and *Seven Seas* are twelve-metre yachts some seventy feet in length overall. The foul occurred on August 14, 1939, shortly before the start of the race from Vineyard Haven to Mattapoisett, Massachusetts. "The starting line was laid at approximately right angles to the course to the first mark which was nearly dead to windward. There was a light breeze, a smooth sea and a strong tide setting across the starting line toward the first mark."

"Two minutes before the start *Gleam,* which had sailed away from the line, had jibed and was and had been for some time returning toward it, heading well to leeward of the further end of the line. At this time *Seven Seas* and *Nyala,* which had also sailed away from the starting line but on courses well to windward of that taken by *Gleam,* jibed. Upon the completion of their jibes they were between *Gleam* and the line, *Seven Seas* being the leading boat with *Nyala* between her and *Gleam*. At this moment, one minute and twenty-five seconds before the start, the three yachts were sailing free on the starboard tack with the wind approximately abeam, *Gleam* was somewhat to leeward of the course of *Seven Seas* and was about two hundred and twenty-five feet or three boat lengths astern of her and was holding her previous course well to leeward

THE SAILING RULES

of the further end of the line while *Seven Seas* immediately upon completing her jibe sailed a course toward the center of the line. Upon *Seven Seas* and *Nyala* completing their turns *Gleam* at once bore off slightly from her previous course and there was at least two points difference in their courses from that time until *Gleam,* fifty seconds before the start, had widened out to leeward and abeam of *Seven Seas* to a distance of one hundred and seventy-five feet. Thereupon *Gleam* hauled on the wind or nearly so and rapidly converged on *Seven Seas* which on reaching the starting line had borne off and commenced to sail down it. As the two yachts converged *Seven Seas* to windward held her course, and *Gleam* to leeward was forced to bear away to avoid a collision. The protest of *Gleam* was based upon this fact."

Seven Seas contended that she was overtaken to leeward by *Gleam*. *Gleam* claimed to be leeward, converging yacht. The decision continues:

"In our opinion, and upon the facts above stated, *Gleam,* when she bore away to avoid a collision with *Seven Seas,* had the rights of a leeward converging yacht as set forth in Rule 30, Clauses (D), (G) and (H), whichever of such Clauses may be, strictly speaking, applicable to the situation here presented, and the disqualification of *Seven Seas* by the Race Committee is sustained by us on that ground.

"This Committee is of the opinion that before a start when boats are constantly changing their courses and their relative positions, and there is doubt, as in this case, whether overtaking conditions have been established and have continued until the boats finally meet on converging courses, that doubt must be resolved against the assumption of the existence of overtaking conditions. After the start, however, where boats are sailing for considerable periods of time between the same marks on the same leg of a course,

THE SAILING RULES

we believe the presumption should be otherwise, and that in case of doubt it should be in favor of the existence of overtaking conditions. Before the start, two points in smooth water is the maximum divergence of course which in our opinion can be construed as 'nearly the same course'."

The Committee then performed a real service to racing yachtsmen by consenting to express its opinion as to the respective rights of the yachts if the facts had established Overtaking instead of Converging conditions. They said:

"The Race Committee and the owner of *Seven Seas* have requested this Committee that if it should find, as it has found, that converging and not overtaking conditions existed at the time the foul occurred, it would express its opinion as to the rights of *Seven Seas* and *Gleam* if we had found that *Gleam* had been the overtaking boat. With considerable reluctance but in the belief that this may be helpful both to the Race Committee and to the competitors in future races we have decided to do so.

"It appears that after *Seven Seas* bore away on reaching approximately the center of the starting line she sailed a course somewhat to leeward of the mark indicating the leeward end of the line. If she had not done so the strong tide running to windward would have put her across the line before the starting signal. Her right, upon the assumption that she was the overtaken boat, to take a course below the mark at the leeward end of the line was questioned by the Race Committee on the ground that by so doing she violated the provisions of Rule 30 (C) in that she bore away out of her 'proper course' to hinder an overtaking yacht passing her to leeward. In our opinion there is no 'proper course' before the start and prior to the making of the starting signal. Prior to the starting signal a yacht may sail towards the line, across the line, away

THE SAILING RULES

from the line, or take any course she may prefer provided only that in so doing she does not violate the rights of another yacht which is in the risk of collision zone. It is only after the starting signal that a yacht is required by the Rules to sail any particular course, namely a course 'consistent with the intention of crossing the line.' If we are correct in this it follows that when *Seven Seas,* twenty-five seconds before the starting signal, bore away on a course which would not cross the line but would take her to leeward of the leeward end thereof, she did not violate the provisions of Rule 30, Clause (C), since no 'proper course' then existed, and that Clause, by its express terms, is only effective where a 'proper course' exists. The right of *Seven Seas* as the overtaken boat having the right of way under Rule 30 (A) was only limited by the provisions of Rule 30, Clause (K). That Clause applies equally to all right-of-way yachts from whatever source the right of way may have arisen (special reference is made therein to rights given by Clause (B)).

"Clause (K) reads as follows:

> '(K) When by any of the above clauses one yacht has to keep out of the way of another, the latter (subject to Clause (B)) shall not alter course so as to prevent her doing so. Although the right-of-way yacht is not bound to hold her course, she must not so alter it as to mislead or baulk the other, in the act of keeping out of the way.'

This Clause has, we believe, rarely been interpreted and has not been given the very obvious importance which its subject matter requires. As applied to the situation before us, *Seven Seas,* if held the overtaken yacht, was not permitted under Clause (K) to alter her course 'so as to prevent' *Gleam* from keeping out of her way, but *Seven*

THE SAILING RULES

Seas by the last paragraph of the Clause was 'not bound to hold her course' but could not 'so alter it as to mislead or baulk' *Gleam* 'in the act of keeping out of the way.' Did *Seven Seas,* assuming that she was the right-of-way yacht, so alter her course as to 'mislead or baulk' *Gleam* 'in the act of keeping out of the way'? In our opinion she did not. *Seven Seas* did not alter course suddenly and only bore away slightly from her previous course and *Gleam* was easily able to respond to such change of course and keep clear of *Seven Seas.* It is true that *Gleam* was so close aboard of *Seven Seas* that if she had not altered her course she would have hit her, but we think it cannot fairly be said that in making a slight alteration of course which could easily be responded to, *Seven Seas* either prevented *Gleam* from keeping out of her way, or 'misled' or 'baulked' her in the act of keeping out of the way. If then *Seven Seas* had had the rights of an overtaken yacht we would have held that she was within her rights in bearing away as she did."[6]

At this point we feel that we should call the reader's attention to the case of *Yankee* v. *Rainbow* arising out of an episode just before the start of the race for the Astor Cups on August 16, 1934, shown in Diagram 21 and discussed in Chapter X. Although we now merely mention the case by name, it is nevertheless not only a leading decision on Rule 30 (E), port and starboard tack close-hauled, but is of paramount importance to manœuvres and right of way during the preparatory period.

May a yacht remain at her mooring[7] or made fast to a buoy, pier,[8] float, shore,[8] another vessel or other stationary object, after the preparatory gun for her class? No. It would be a violation of Rule 37—ANCHORING. She must either be under way or be lying to her own anchor,

[6]*Gleam* v. *Seven Seas. Ubi supra.*
[7]*Pelican* v. *Polly.* Y. R. A., 1934, Case 2.
[8]*Great Yarmouth Yacht Club.* Y. R. A., 1935, Case 11.

THE SAILING RULES

in which case she must weigh anchor and not slip or buoy the anchor-rode or chain.[9] Furthermore, the word "shore" is included in what is embraced by the words "or other object" in Rule 37.[8]

A clever skipper always hits the line under full headway, and thereby often forges through the lee of windward yachts in supposedly better positions, so that ten or fifteen seconds after the starting gun he is out ahead with his wind clear. A common occurrence is for a yacht to be too early. To kill time her skipper slacks off his sheets and lets his sails flap. Such a yacht is sailing "in the wind." She is sailing free. Although she probably will make a poor start and may be a source of annoyance to other yachts starting in a more seamanlike manner, we believe that until she loses all steerage way and becomes merely an obstruction, she is entitled to the rights of and is subject to the obligations imposed by the course she is sailing. We know of no rule expressly covering "parking on the starting line." We *do* know, however, that it is a prolific cause of "cussing," and justifiably so.

The only differences in the Sailing Rules during the preparatory period and those in effect after the starting gun are:

1. Before the start there is no proper course. After the start there is no proper course *unless* overtaking conditions exist, and the overtaking yacht attempts to pass to leeward of her opponent. In such case the windward yacht's proper course is defined by Rule 29, Section 7—Definitions.

2. During the preparatory period a yacht holding right of way may alter course in any reasonable manner but even if she ranks as overtaken yacht, she may not luff suddenly, because a luff so sudden that it cannot easily be responded to is not considered a reasonable alteration of

[9]*Royal Sidney Yacht Club.* Y. R. A., 1931, Case 3.

THE SAILING RULES

course. After the starting gun, however, a sudden luff is within the strict letter of the rules.

Whether a sudden luff, without warning, is sportsmanlike is quite another matter. It was not until the London conference of November, 1929, that it was prohibited prior to the starting signal. The reasons given for the continuance of this practice are that it is of ancient origin and tends to keep the overtaking yacht from passing too close aboard.

It is difficult to comprehend what pleasure or satisfaction can be had by suddenly and without warning putting down the helm and deliberately attempting to put a competitor out of a race. The only worth-while victory is that of superior speed and skill.

STARTING LINE MARKS

We now come to the time when in a few seconds the starting signal will be made. What about the marks of the startling line? These, we believe, would include any mark used in connection with the starting line, as for example, a distance buoy. This brings up for discussion at this point Rule 34—MARKS OF THE COURSE. We give it in full.

A mark is any vessel, boat, buoy or other object used to indicate the course but does not become a mark of the course until the preceding mark, if any, has been rounded or passed. The marks of the starting line are marks of the course from the making of the preparatory signal for each class, but there is no required side until after the starting signal has been made. Every mark rounded or passed remains a mark of the course until the next mark has been passed. A mark, until it becomes a mark of the course as above defined, shall be an obstruction to sea room.

To obtain a clearer understanding of the meaning of the

THE SAILING RULES

present rule a brief historical sketch may not be out of place. Prior to the International Conference in London on November 4 and 5, 1929, the American provisions in regard to marks were scattered among three separate rules. In the 1928 Year Book of the New York Yacht Club we find the following:

Rule X—Start and Finish—Section 1, second paragraph: *"The marks of the starting line are marks of the course from the making of the preparatory signal for each class and remain such until the finish of the race."*

Rule XII—Definitions—Section 6, Mark, first paragraph: *"A mark is any vessel, boat, buoy or other object used to indicate the course.";* paragraph three was practically identical in wording with the last sentence of present Rule 33.

Rule XX—Disqualifications—Section 1 was nearly identical in wording with the first two sentences of present Rule 33.

Now the British Y. R. A. rule was quite different. It read as follows:

"RULE 34—DEFINITION OF MARKS

"Nothing shall be considered a mark in the course unless specifically named as such in the Sailing Instructions, and until the preceding mark, if any, has been rounded or passed; otherwise it shall be an obstruction to sea room.

"Every essential or ordinary above-water part of any object named as a mark, counts as a mark for the purposes of this and the two preceding rules, but no part below water, nor any object accidentally or temporarily attached to the mark."

This rule had a footnote reading as follows:

"Y. R. A. NOTE—RULE 34

"Any mark used in connection with the starting or finishing line is a mark in the course, and every mark

THE SAILING RULES

rounded or passed remains a mark in the course until the next has been passed."

As will be noted in our discussion of Rule 30 (K) *infra*, the basis of the new International Sailing Rules was the British Rules in the 1929 Y. R. A. Year Book. Where the principle of the footnote was agreed to by the Conference, it was incorporated as an integral part of the new rule.

Present Rule 34 consists of four sentences. It was to all intents and purposes completely redrafted by the Conference. The first clause of the first sentence was part of the former British footnote; the second clause was part of paragraph one of former British Rule 34. The second sentence, to which especial attention is directed, was new. The third was part of paragraph one of former British Rule 34. The fourth and last sentence also was practically new.

Sentences two and four are of vital importance when two yachts before the start, and overlapped as defined in Rule 29 (4), are approaching a mark used in connection with the starting line.

It is an old and established principle of racing that when two yachts are overlapped as defined, the right-of-way yacht may luff or force her opponent the wrong side of a mark having a required side, or either side of an obstruction where there is clear water on all sides, *provided she goes with her*. On whichever side of the obstruction she elects to pass she must permit the non-right-of-way yacht also to pass. That this sound and ancient principle applies to marks of the course and obstructions to sea room within the meaning of Rule 31 which are encountered *after* the start, there can be no doubt.

We shall learn later that if two yachts overlapped, and without tacking, are about to pass an obstruction which requires the inside yacht to alter course to clear it, the

THE SAILING RULES

outside yacht, whether she be windward or leeward yacht, must "give room" to the inside yacht. If, on the other hand, the obstruction is small, such as a government buoy not a mark of the course, or an anchored row boat, passable on either side without an appreciable alteration of course, it would seem that the inside yacht is not entitled to room. Such a small object in the path of the inside yacht is not an obstruction to sea room within the meaning of Rule 31 because the inside yacht is in no real danger of fouling the object.[10]

Now how about the starting-line marks? Are they or are they not obstructions to sea room within the meaning of Rule 31 *prior* to the making of the starting signal?

From a casual reading, the first sentence of Rule 31 and the second and fourth sentences of Rule 34 would seem to be contradictory. Now how did the second sentence of Rule 34 reading "The marks of the starting line are marks of the course from the making of the preparatory signal for each class, *but there is no required side until after the starting signal has been made.*", (Italics—the Author), come to be incorporated in the rule? Furthermore, how has the British Y. R. A. interpreted it?

One of the American delegates to the Conference informed us that he had a very clear recollection of the reason for the inclusion of this sentence, and went on to say: "This particular sentence was included on the urgent suggestion of Mr. Johan Anker, representing Norway, who felt that it would prevent boats trying to cut in to windward and forcing an overlap over yachts slightly ahead of them and claiming room at a starting mark before the starting signal but after the preparatory signal. The clear intention of the Conference at that time was to prevent this practice. A year or two afterward, however, a famous case of this sort came before the British Y. R. A., which

[10] *Arcadian* v. *Margitta*. Y. R. A., 1920, Case 2.

THE SAILING RULES

really declined to follow the intention of the Rule as adopted by the Conference in 1929, and in order to make it clear that it did not propose to follow it, but without actually changing the wording of the Rule, inserted a footnote to the rule as follows: 'During this period, for the purpose of Rule 31, this mark ranks as an obstruction to sea room when racing under Y. R. A. Rules.' The insertion and wording of the footnote indicate very clearly that the British realized that they were not following the intent of Rule 34 and were calling specific attention to that fact to yachts which might be racing under the Rules of the British Y. R. A."

The "famous" English case referred to was *Cutty* v. *Nona* which resulted from a collision in a race off Cowes, Isle of Wight, on July 20, 1913. *Cutty,* yacht *B* in our diagram, was skippered by Captain R. T. Dixon; *Nona,* yacht *A,* by Lord Forster. Both gentlemen were members of the Council of the Y. R. A., and second to none as practical judges of the yacht racing rules.

The facts were as follows:

Diagram 3.

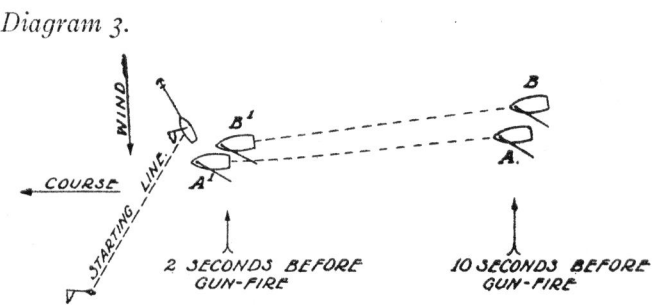

A and *B,* 8-metre yachts, overlapped, were reaching for the windward end of the starting line marked by a small flag-boat. *B* hailed for room. *A* refused to grant it. Two seconds before gunfire *A* had overlapped the flag-boat; *B*

THE SAILING RULES

had not. Immediately after gunfire *B* hit *A* and also the flag-boat. *A* protested *B* for infringement of Rule 30 (G). *B* protested *A* for not giving room under Rule 31. Lord Forster, the skipper of *A*, the outside yacht, said in argument: "*B* held the view that any mark, however small, is an obstruction to sea room within the meaning of Rule 31. I, on the other hand, consider this interpretation stultifies Rule 34 which expressly defines the mark or marks used in connection with the starting line. I have always believed that Rule 34 means what it says and whenever, as has happened, I have been luffed the wrong side of the mark before the starting signal has been made I have returned and restarted. . . . Moreover, the concluding paragraph of Rule 34, after defining the starting mark as a mark with no required side before the starting signal, deals with other marks in the course and says that until they come into use they shall be regarded as obstructions to sea room. This obviously does not apply to the mark on the starting line for if it did it would make the earlier portion of the rule of no effect. Rule 31 declares that when approaching a mark on the required side room must be given. Rule 34 declares that the mark on the starting line has no required side before the start. Therefore, the right-of-way yacht need not give room."

The Sailing Committee, with one dissentient, upheld *A's* protest under Rule 30 (G) saying: "Both *Nona* and *Cutty* were approaching a mark in the course which at that time had no required side (see Rule 34)." On appeal, the Council reversed the decision of the Sailing Committee and disqualified *A*."[11]

This case caused the Council at its quarterly meeting on November 18, 1931, "at which twenty-four members were present, the largest attendance in the history of the Y. R. A.", to add the above mentioned footnote to Rule

[11] *Cutty* v. *Nona*. Y. R. A., 1932, Case 3.

34. Whether American yachting tribunals would follow the Y. R. A. remained to be determined.

Five years later, to be exact, on July 22, 1936, occurred the American protest case of *Riptide* v. *Stella*. We were at Edgartown when this foul occurred and both skippers agree that *Stella's* course from Position 3 until she crossed the starting line was a straight line and that she did not bear away as indicated in the diagram on page 4 of N. A. Y. R. U. Bulletin No. 32 dated March 15, 1937. The only difference between *Cutty* v. *Nona* and *Riptide* v. *Stella*—and this "only difference" was the crux of the American decision—was that in the English case the outside yacht had overlapped the starting-line mark *before* gunfire, while in the American case the stem of *Stella,* outside, leeward and leading yacht "was still about three feet from the stern of the Committee Boat" at gunfire. To avoid colliding either with *Stella* or with the Committee Boat, and at practically the last instant, *Riptide* luffed, tacked, jibed and followed *Stella* across the starting line. She protested *Stella* under Rules 31 and 34.

The Executive Committee of the N. A. Y. R. U. upheld the decision of the Race Committee of the Edgartown Yacht Club disqualifying *Stella* and said:

"Before the starting signal, the right of the outside yacht, *Stella,* under Rule 30 (H), to decline to give the inside yacht, *Riptide,* room to pass between the Committee Boat, which had no required side, and the outside yacht, is unquestioned.

"After the starting signal, however, the outside yacht, *Stella,* could not divest herself of the obligation under Rule 31 to give the inside, overlapping yacht, *Riptide,* ample water to pass the Committee Boat, 'a mark,' on the required side, and she ought to have foreseen the conditions which arose and ought not to have been in a position

THE SAILING RULES

where she could not comply with the requirements of that Rule, the instant it became effective."[12]

The case hinged on the fact that at gunfire *Stella's* bow still was three or four feet distant from the stern of the Committee Boat. This was only a fraction of a second but it was sufficient to give the decision to *Riptide*. Lord Forster was right.

This case held that the duty to anticipate the changed situation that would arise at gunfire had she then not overlapped the mark lay upon the outside yacht. She should have foreseen that at that instant right-of-way shifted from her to the inside yacht because at that instant the Committee Boat or other mark of the starting line became vested with a "required side" on which it had to be passed by both yachts.

While the decision does not state expressly that a mark of the starting line ceases to be an obstruction to sea room within the meaning of Rule 31 when it becomes a mark of the course at the preparatory signal, as defined, it does say expressly that the inside, non-right-of-way yacht is not entitled to room prior to gunfire.

When a mark becomes a mark of the course it usually is considered to be both an obstruction to sea room and a mark with a required side. The *exception* is a mark of the starting line which by the second sentence of Rule 34 is *expressly* stated to have "no required side" during the preparatory period. This sentence would seem to "break down" the first sentence of Rule 31 into two distinct parts:

1. When two yachts overlapped, and without tacking, are about to pass "an *obstruction to sea room*," and
2. When they are about so to pass "a *mark on the required side*."

[12] *Riptide* v. *Stella*. N. A. Y. R. U., Appeal No. 5, Jan. 15, 1937.

THE SAILING RULES

If one reads the last sentence of Rule 34 "backward" so to speak, it would seem to mean that after a mark becomes a mark of the course as defined, it ceases to rank as an obstruction to sea room within the meaning of the first clause of the first sentence of Rule 31, and is governed only by the second clause of the first sentence of Rule 31 which pertains to passing "a mark on the required side." In other words, during the preparatory period a mark of the starting line is neither an obstruction to sea room within the meaning of Rule 31 entitling the inside yacht to room, nor has it a required side on which it must be passed. Any other construction would make the second sentence of Rule 34 meaningless.

Of course, if the inside yacht *insists* on being given room prior to gunfire, the outside yacht should give room in order to avoid a collision, and then protest for violation of Rules (G) or (H) and 34.

So clear are Rules 14, 33 and 34 to the effect that fouling a mark of the starting line during a yacht's preparatory period is cause for disqualification, that there is no American case on that point.

In Chapter XV, however, under the heading MARKS OF THE COURSE, we shall cite a recent English case where, during her preparatory period, a yacht's boom passed over the top of a starting-line flag mark but the drooping mainsheet fouled the flag causing her disqualification.[13]

[13]*Merlin* v. *Spray*. Y. R. A., 1939, Case 9.

Chapter VII

START AND RECALL

Although the N. A. Y. R. U. Sailing Rules prescribe that a yacht shall be timed at the start and at the finish when "any part of her hull, spars or other equipment" is "on the line," many yacht clubs in this vicinity take time by the mast as offering a smaller margin of error in close starts and finishes by a large class.

REQUIRED NUMBER OF STARTERS

Frequently the question arises whether the minimum number of yachts have started as required by the Race Circular. This is one of the many questions which trouble a Race Committee. For example: The circular requires six starters. Seven start. Before the yachts finish, the race is called off on account of a calm. In the resail only three start. Have the prescribed conditions been fulfilled? They have.[1]

Again: Six starters are required. One makes a premature start but not seeing her recall signal, keeps on. In this case also the prescribed conditions have been fulfilled.[2]

PREMATURE START AND RECALL

The last sentence of Rule 27, Section 5, reads as follows:
Failure of the Race Committee to give the recall signals above provided for shall not relieve a yacht which has

[1] *Little Hampton Sailing and Motor Club.* Y. R. A., 1926, Case 2, page 140.
[2] *West Mersea Yacht Club.* Y. R. A., 1928, Case 10.

THE SAILING RULES

made a premature start from the necessity of returning and recrossing the line.

It goes without saying that the Race Committee will make every reasonable effort to recall a yacht which has made a premature start. Often, however, conditions of wind and weather may make the giving of notice impossible. In other words, it is "up to you" to know whether or not you started correctly.

Now how about a yacht which starts prematurely, but not seeing her recall signal, continues in the race? She will, of course, be disqualified for violating Rule 27. But how about the right-of-way rules? Must she be treated as a competitor by other yachts in the race? Further, if she wins is she entitled to the gun? Let us first consider the second question. Although under Rule 47—Disqualification Without Protest—if the Committee see a yacht violate a rule, they may, after a hearing, disqualify her without a protest being made by a competitor, they must give that yacht the gun if she wins.[3] In the case of a premature starter winning the race it would seem, on the contrary, that she should not be given the gun.[4] The question of guilt is not debatable in such a case.

Reverting now to the first question, there can be no doubt that the other yachts must treat her as a qualified starter "until her intention to return is clear."[5] Or, as the Sailing Committee said in that case: "until she shows an obvious intention" to start anew, she is to be treated as still in the race.

[3] *The Vivacious.* Y. R. A., 1928, Case 8.
[4] *Jane* v. *Daphne.* Y. R. A. of L. I. S., 1932 Year Book, page 95.
[5] *Girleen* v. *Piccolo,* Y. R. A., 1902, page 110; discussed in Chapter X under Rule 30 (E).
Clymene v. *Noresca,* Y. R. A., 1927, Case 1. But see *Lena* v. *Countess,* N. Y. Y. C., 1924 Report of Race Committee, page 5, and *Pilgrim* v. *Maori,* N. A. Y. R. U., Appeal No. 4, Nov. 15, 1935, discussed in Chapter XV.

THE SAILING RULES

Sections 6 and 7 of Rule 27 are as follows:

(6) A yacht so returning, or one working into position from the wrong side of the line after her starting signal has been made, must keep clear of and give way to all competing yachts whose starting signal has been made.

(7) A yacht starting after the signal for the start of the next class has been made, shall, in starting, keep clear of and give way to yachts starting during their specified starting intervals.

Diagram 4.

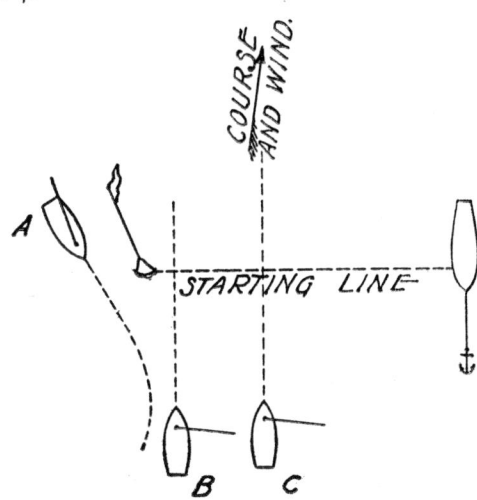

The diagram shows the position of the yachts just after the making of the starting signal. *B* refused to alter course; *A* was obliged to luff in order to avoid a collision. She protested *B* for violation of Rule 30 (D). *A* claimed that *B* should have borne away and permitted *A* to swing around the mark, leaving it to port as required. *B* claimed that *A* was "working into position from the wrong side of the line after her starting signal" had "been made," and, therefore, was subject to Section 6 of Rule 27. The decision hinges on the answer to the question "What waters comprise the 'wrong side of the line'?" Does that area comprise only the waters on the wrong side of the starting line between lines drawn through the starting-line marks at right angles to the starting line or does it include also the waters on the wrong side of the line of start extended beyond the marks at both ends of the starting line? The only reference we have been able to find is an opinion of Major B. Heckstall-Smith who in commenting on this case said: "If *A* was deliberately crossing the line the wrong way, *i.e.,* working into position from the wrong side of it, she must keep out of everybody's way (by Rule 29); but she is not here taking any such dangerous course."[6] (British Rule 29 is United States Rule 27.) In the case illustrated, *A* was "working into position" so as to cross the *continuation* of the line of start, and *outside* of the starting-line marks.

It is obvious, therefore, that in Major B. Heckstall-Smith's opinion the five words first quoted do not include the waters on the wrong side of the starting line *and such line extended beyond the starting-line marks*. If, therefore, a yacht were manœuvring not to cross in the wrong direction *between* the starting-line marks she would not be subject to Section 6 of Rule 27. After gunfire she "must sail a course consistent with the intention of crossing the line" from the correct side. Beyond this obligation she would be restricted in manœuvring only by the provisions of Rules 30, 31 and 32.

It makes no difference if a yacht:

    1. After a premature start, is working back into position to start anew;

[6] *Yachting World,* Nov. 9, 1934, page 388.

THE SAILING RULES

  2. On the wrong side of the line at gunfire, is working into position to make a proper start;
  3. Is starting after the signal for the start of the next class has been made.

In all three cases, even if she is close-hauled on the starboard tack, she must keep clear of and give way to all yachts which have started properly or are starting during their specified starting signals, even though such other yachts are running before the wind on the port tack.

Only as to yachts making *delayed* starts, that is, themselves starting *after* the starting signal for the class following that of such delayed starters, and when once more on the proper side of the line, is she again vested with her rights of way.[7]

Suppose, however, A and B have started prematurely. As to other yachts starting properly in their own class or in following classes whose starting signal has been made, delayed starters only excepted, they have no rights whatsoever until once more on the proper side of the line. But how about their rights and obligations as to each other? Rule 14 tells us that a yacht is amenable to the Sailing Rules from the time of the preparatory signal for her class, until she has finished and her entire hull and spars are clear of the finish line. In our supposititious case both A and B are amenable to the Sailing Rules. Each is equally guilty of violating them. It follows that as *between themselves* alone, A and B are entitled to the benefit of and are subject to the rights and obligations prescribed by the Sailing Rules. We know of no official decision on this point but it would seem to be a logical deduction.

[7]*Crouch Yacht Club.* Y. R. A., 1931, Case 6.

THE SAILING RULES

RIGHT TO RETURN AND MAKE A PROPER START

Diagram 5.

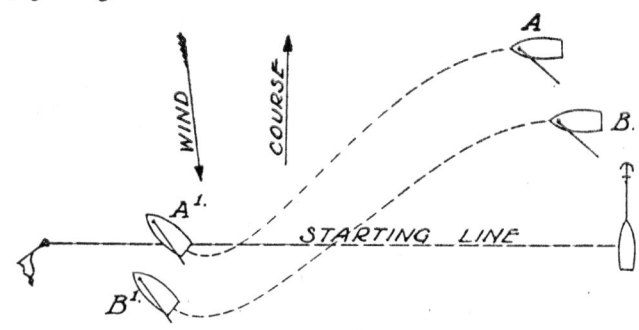

Both A and B have started prematurely. No overtaking is involved. As between themselves, A, as windward yacht, must keep clear. Is B under any obligation to grant A a safe return in order that she, too, may make a proper start? The answer would seem to be "No."

Neither before nor after she again gets back of the line need B consider A. If at the time B safely recrosses, A is still on the wrong side of the line, she can have no rights over B. Not only is B leeward yacht but she now is starting properly. If in recrossing, B goes so far back of the line that A safely recrosses also, B still is leeward yacht and holds right of way. In short, in returning to the proper side of the line it is not only incumbent upon A so to shape her course that she will be able always to keep clear of B, but, if wise, she will so manœuvre that B, once more back of the line, cannot block her.

We now come to a question which, until authoritatively decided in December, 1931, was the cause of much uncertainty and numerous fouls at the start of a race.

THE SAILING RULES

The third paragraph of "Meeting, Crossing and Converging" in Rule 30 commences thus:

As soon as the starting signal is given, yachts must sail a course consistent with the intention of crossing the line.

Prior to N. A. Y. R. U. Appeal No. 1[8] decided on December 11, 1931, and printed in full, with a diagram, in Bulletin No. 17 under date of January 20, 1932, it had been held quite generally that this sentence obligated a yacht to sail the most direct course to the line once the starting gun had fired, and that it abrogated some of the Right-of-Way rules until the starting line had been crossed. In other words, and assuming the first leg to be a reach on the port tack, that it was no longer legal to coast the line close-hauled on either tack and claim right of way over yachts to windward sailing free and making directly for the line and for the next mark.

Such an interpretation of the meaning of the words "consistent with the intention of crossing the line" was the cause of the foul out of which grew Appeal No. 1. This decision has clarified the situation and is "on all fours" with a dictum of the Council of the Y. R. A. pronounced at its Annual General Meeting on February 18, 1931. The Council said:

"The words did not interfere with the clauses of Rule 30, beyond prohibiting a leeward yacht after gunfire, deliberately luffing a windward yacht so that the latter could not cross the line."

N. A. Y. R. U. Appeal No. 1 decides in brief that to sail "a course consistent with the intention of crossing the line" means the right to head for any desired part of the line, not for the nearest part. The Executive Committee said:

---

[8] *Stranger* v. *Nutmeg III*, *Italia* v. *Nutmeg III*, N. A. Y. R. U., Appeal No. 1, Dec. 11, 1931.

THE SAILING RULES

"A yacht close-hauled, working to the weather end of the line, might, when the starting signal is given, actually be heading away from the line and still with propriety and right, so continue for so long as her so doing is consistent with an intention to cross the line at the weather end."

In other words, a yacht may once more coast the line close-hauled in order to cross at any desired point, and windward yachts, together with yachts sailing free, must give her right of way. She does not even have to be sailing a course which if projected in a straight line would carry her across the line.

"The generally accepted interpretation, abroad and in this country—never mind what the rule says—is that it means and all it means is that no yacht may luff another yacht the wrong side of a starting mark unless she goes there herself. That is practically what the British interpretation and our own interpretation mean."[9]

In the April, 1932, issue of *Yachting* will be found an interesting and historical discussion of this sentence, by Mr. C. Sherman Hoyt, then Chairman of the N. A. Y. R. U. Rules Committee. A careful reading of Mr. Hoyt's scholarly article will be found exceedingly profitable.

[9] C. Sherman Hoyt. N. A. Y. R. U., Bulletin No. 21, Jan. 28, 1933, page 19.

Chapter VIII

RULE 29—DEFINITIONS

Before discussing Rule 29 let us lay down a very important rule; a rule which, although not stated in so many words, is, nevertheless, a part, and a very important part, of the Sailing Rules. It is this:

Unless yachts are within Range of Risk of Collision, or, as we commonly term it, the Risk of Collision Zone, *no rules apply.*

When they draw within this range they become amenable to the Sailing Rules. The position of each yacht, together with the direction of her course at the time she comes within range of risk of collision, determine under which Rule and clause she *ranks*. She may be an overtaking yacht, an overtaken yacht, or she may be meeting, crossing or converging, or in the act of altering course. If *A* draws without the risk of collision zone with *B,* and later comes within it as regards *B, A* and *B* once again begin to *rank* under some clause of the Sailing Rules. The clause under which each yacht again ranks depends upon her new position and direction of course, and is in no way connected with the conditions which prevailed before.[1]

For example: If *A* and *B* are beating to windward, and occasionally approach within range of risk of collision, the question of how *A* and *B* rank must be judged separately for each tack without reference to the previous tack.

Immediately the reader will ask, "What is this Risk of

[1] *Surinam* v. *Elva.* Y. R. A. of L. I. S., 1932 Year Book, page 97.

THE SAILING RULES

Collision Zone?" It is set forth in Section 5 of Rule 29 and is of paramount importance.

RULE 29—SECTION 5—RISK OF COLLISION

The phrase "Risk of Collision" is used in the widest sense, and yachts must be considered to be "approaching so as to involve risk of collision" whenever either of two cannot with perfect safety be navigated without any regard to the proximity of the other.

For example, generally speaking, two yachts cannot be navigated without any regard to each other unless either or both can at any moment turn a complete circle with helm hard over either way without fouling the other.

When there is any doubt, risk of collision is to be presumed to exist.

Diagram 6.

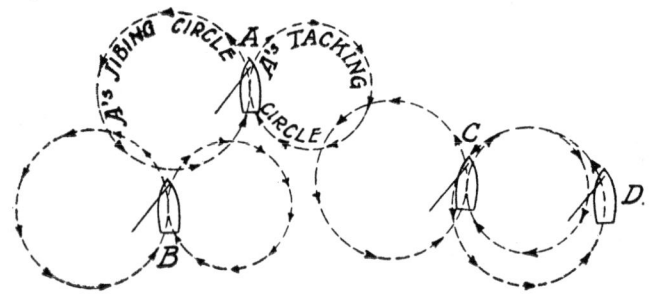

It is common knowledge that the radius of a yacht's tacking circle is shorter than that of a jibe. This is shown in Diagram 6. If, simultaneously, *A* and *B* jibe or if *A* jibes and *B* tacks, their paths will intersect. Also if *A* tacks and *C* jibes, their respective circles will intersect. Likewise if *C* tacks or jibes and *D* jibes.

But however *A* and *D,* or *B* and *C,* or *B* and *D*

THE SAILING RULES

manœuvre, their respective circles will not intersect. It therefore follows that:

A and B are		within	Range	of	Risk	of	Collision	
A " C "		"	"	"	"	"	"	
C " D "		"	"	"	"	"	"	
A " D "	not	"	"	"	"	"	"	
B " C "	"	"	"	"	"	"	"	
B " D "	"	"	"	"	"	"	"	

In other words, where two yachts are so situated that neither can be navigated without regard to the proximity or navigation of the other—so that if either or both, simultaneously or otherwise, *can* be navigated in such a manner that probability of collision may be involved—they are within the Zone of Risk of Collision, and the Sailing Rules apply. If they are beyond the Zone *no rules* apply. The sea is free; a yacht can sail where she wishes, luff, bear away, jibe, tack, cross ahead of another yacht—in fact do anything she desires.

If, however, it is a close question as to whether yachts are within the Risk of Collision Zone, Risk of Collision is *presumed* to exist, and the Sailing Rules apply. During the period between the preparatory and starting guns, yachts are constantly getting into and out of the Zone. Risk of Collision exists during the greater part of that period but after the start it exists only now and then.

Obviously a small yacht has a small Risk of Collision Zone, and a large yacht a large Zone. The rule, however, is the same for all—it is merely one of degree.[2]

Suppose a small yacht is right astern of and close aboard a large yacht; that both are sailing the same course; and that due to a light breeze or some other cause she is

[2]*Prestige* v. *Carolina*. N. Y. Y. C., 1927 Report of Race Committee, page 12.

THE SAILING RULES

keeping up with her larger competitor. Both yachts simultaneously can turn complete circles without colliding, the small yacht on the inside of the turning circle of the large one. According to the literal wording of the second paragraph of the rule it might be argued that they were not within the Zone. But can any one doubt that risk of collision exists? Suppose the larger yacht should strike a mud bank. A rear end collision would inevitably follow. There being doubt, "risk of collision is to be presumed to exist."

Now let us discuss the other sections of Rule 29.

Section 1. Close-hauled and Free

(a) *Close-hauled. A yacht is close-hauled when sailing by the wind as close as she can lie with advantage in working to windward.*

(b) *Free. A yacht not sailing close-hauled as defined above, and not in the wind, is sailing free.*

This section needs no comment except to say that a yacht's course in relation to the wind, and not the trim of her sails, is the criterion which decides whether she is close-hauled or free. Her sails may be sheeted in flat but if she is not pointing as high as she can to obtain the best results in working to windward it is incorrect to say that she is sailing close-hauled.

Section 2. Luffing

A yacht is luffing when she so alters her course as to sail a course more nearly into the wind.

It should be remembered that a luff is an alteration of course within the meaning of Rule 30 (K). But of this, more hereafter.

Section 3. Clear Ahead and Clear Astern

A yacht is clear astern of another when all her hull and equipment is abaft all the other yacht's hull and equipment,

THE SAILING RULES

judged by the course which the two yachts are sailing. The other is clear ahead.

Only a few words need be said concerning this section. The skipper of the leading yacht will now and then glance at the yacht behind him to see if she is still clear astern— better by far is it to have the main-sheet man do this. He must mentally divide the angle made by the courses of the two yachts and take the line across his own boom end or counter—whichever of the two extends farther astern —at right angles to the dividing line of that angle—be the angle large or small. If the bow of the stern yacht is behind that line, she is clear astern. A skipper does not "square off" from his own course. He "squares off" from the average course of the two yachts.

Section 4. Overlap

An overlap between two yachts exists when they are sailing approximately the same course and neither has her bowsprit end (or stem if she has no bowsprit) abaft the other yacht's boom end or counter, judged by the course which the two yachts are sailing.

The word "overlap" is a much misunderstood word. By this is meant that just because two yachts are converging on somewhat different courses so that if they keep on they will make contact, and just because shortly before colliding the bow of one is ahead of the other's stern, does not cause them to be overlapping within the meaning of the definition. To be overlapping they must be sailing "approximately the same course." The word "approximately" means "very nearly but not absolutely."

Formerly it was held that if two yachts were sailing within three compass points (33.75°) of each other, and neither was clear astern, they were considered overlapping. This leeway or variation between their respective courses

THE SAILING RULES

made for many fouls and consequent protests. This confusion arose from the former wording of the rule—"nearly the same course." The substitution of the word "approximately" for the word "nearly" has done away with the three-compass-point argument zone and the phrase "approximately the same course" is held to mean "approximately parallel courses." Of course the two courses do not have to be *exactly* parallel but a slight variance between the courses of the two yachts will make them non-overlapping.

The concensus of opinion seems to be that the divergence of course should not exceed one compass point ($11\frac{1}{4}°$). It should be easy and useful to set into the deck or cockpit immediately in front of the steering wheel or tiller a small brass plate the two sides of which form an angle of $22\frac{1}{2}°$. A "sight" astern along either side of the "∧" would determine at a glance whether the two yachts were legally overlapped.

Section 6. Overtaking

Of two yachts sailing the same or nearly the same course one which is clear astern of the other begins to rank as overtaking yacht as soon as she comes anywhere within range of risk of collision and continues so to rank until she either—

1. *Draws clear ahead; and then she begins to rank as overtaken yacht.*
2. *Draws clear abreast by widening out beyond range of risk of collision.*
3. *Falls astern beyond range of risk of collision.*
4. *One or both of the yachts tack.*

The obligation of proving that she has drawn clear lies on the late overtaking yacht.

No question of overtaking can arise unless the yachts are sailing approximately the same course (A luff by one

THE SAILING RULES

of the yachts under Rule 30, clause (B), does not count as a difference of course in this connection).

The first point to remember is that for overtaking conditions to exist the yachts must be sailing "approximately the same course."

Second, that they must be within the risk of collision zone.

Third, that at some point on that particular tack one yacht must have been clear astern of the other.

Fourth, that overtaking conditions are not carried over from one tack to another.

Fifth, that overtaking conditions are not necessarily cancelled by a jibe on the part of one of the yachts.[3]

Sixth, that the burden of proving that she has drawn clear ahead lies on the late overtaking yacht.

Here is an interesting protest decision on the point that overtaking conditions are not carried over from one tack to another.

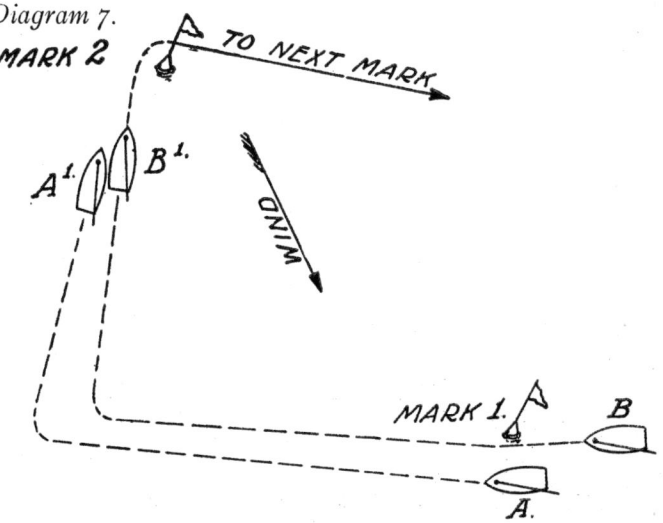

Diagram 7.

[3]*Forelle* v. *Seagull.* Y. R. A., 1939, Case 2.

THE SAILING RULES

At Mark 1, *B* was in fact overtaking yacht. Shortly afterward they came about onto the port tack and were then nearly abreast. Before they weathered Mark 2, they collided. *A* was disqualified under Rule 30 (H). On the tack where the foul occurred neither had been clear astern. They were approximately abreast, and converged. It was the duty of *A*, as windward yacht, to keep clear.[4]

To summarize Overtaking.

No question of overtaking arises unless:

1. Both yachts are sailing "approximately the same course."
2. The overtaking yacht is or comes within the risk of collision zone.
3. At some point on that particular tack one yacht is or has been clear astern of the other.

Section 7. Proper Course

During the existence of overtaking conditions the proper course is prima facie nothing to leeward of full and by if on a wind, or of the next mark if the wind be free; but there may be conditions of tide or circumstances, other than the desire to hinder the competitor overtaking to leeward, which justify a more leeward course, in this case the responsibility for proving the justification for such a leeward course would lie upon the weather yacht.

The question of proper course arises when the starting gun fires but *only* if and when overtaking-to-leeward conditions exist.[5] Prior to the start there is no proper course because by Rule 34 there is no required side to the starting-line marks until after the starting gun.[6]

[4]*Ananké* v. *Banshee*. Y. R. A., 1909, Case 6, affirmed in *Talisman* v. *Ivanhoe*. Y. R. A., 1934, Case 5.
[5]*Alerte* v. *Freida*. N. A. Y. R. U., Appeal No. 2, Dec. 12, 1932.
[6]*Gleam* v. *Seven Seas*. N. Y. Y. C., Committee on Racing Appeals, January, 1940. Y. R. A., 1935, page 170; Sir William Burton, President, Y. R. A., *Yachting World*, May 17, 1935, page 406.

THE SAILING RULES

It may be helpful briefly to discuss the doctrine that *even after* the start there is no proper course *unless* overtaking-to-leeward conditions exist. For example:

Diagram 8.

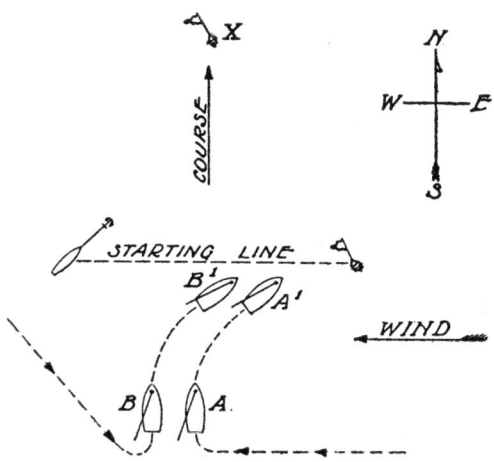

Shortly before the start A comes in from the Eastward, B from the Northwest, and the yachts assume position A, B. Just prior to the start B is gradually luffing A in order to work up to the windward end of the starting line. At gunfire the yachts are in position A^1, B^1—nearly close-hauled, and heading Northeast. No question of overtaking is involved for the reason that at position A, B, the yachts were overlapped, and neither clear astern.

A 1912 footnote to the British Meeting, Crossing and Converging rules, adopted by the 1919 International Conference at London, sanctioned the disqualification of a yacht *after* the start, which obstructed another yacht by steering a course "unreasonably wide of her own proper course for the next mark, taking wind and tide into consideration."

No rules in force in America "ever made any mention whatsoever of 'proper course' . . . the New York Yacht Club, . . . continued, when deciding protests, to refuse to recognize that 'proper course' was an integral or even an inferred part of the American rules."

"At the 1929 London Conference some concessions and compromises were admittedly necessary. The Americans conceded the application of the proper course principle in overtaking conditions, in that an overtaken yacht should not bear away from her proper course to the next mark to hinder another yacht from passing to leeward, and accepted the current European definition of 'proper course.' They were most reluctant, however, to agree to the 'proper course' principle elsewhere and, eventually, the other interests graciously consented to the deletion of 'proper course' from the contentious footnote to the International Rules on Meeting, Crossing and Converging."[7]

Under the International and British rules prior to the 1929 London Conference, in the case illustrated in Diagram 8, at gun-fire B would have been obliged to slack off her sheets and sail a "proper course" for X.

In America there was no such rule and not only could B continue to sail on her Northeast course as long as she pleased but she had the right further and gradually to luff A. As leeward yacht, B held right of way, and so long as she did not alter course in such a manner as to prevent A from keeping clear she could sail where she wished.

This is the American Yachting Law today and will be

[7] C. Sherman Hoyt. *An Ambiguous Racing Rule, Yachting,* April, 1932, page 71.

THE SAILING RULES

discussed more fully in Chapter XI in commenting on Rule 30, Clause (K).

The same is true in the situation illustrated in the following diagram.

Diagram 9.

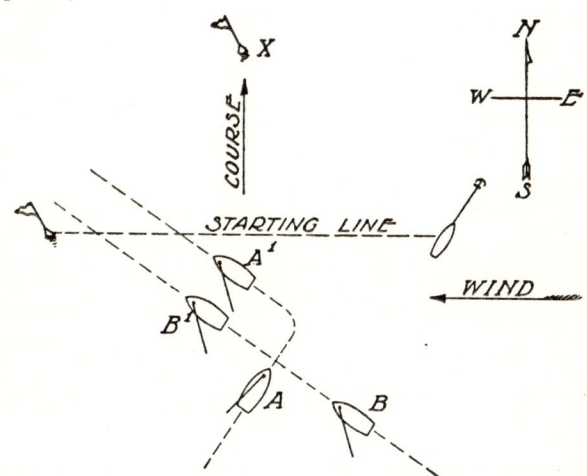

Before the start *A* crosses ahead of *B,* and then bears away, to windward of and overlapping *B;* both yachts heading Northwest. To avoid a tide, they cross at the leeward end of the starting line. As leeward yacht *B* holds right of way, and both before and after the start may luff *A* gradually. *B* may not luff sharply because she does not *rank* as overtaken yacht. Only if *B ranked* as overtaking yacht, would the question of *A's* proper course arise. In that event, but *only after* the start, Rule 30 (C) would obligate *A* to sail a proper course as defined by Rule 29, Section 7.

THE SAILING RULES

To illustrate:

Diagram 10.

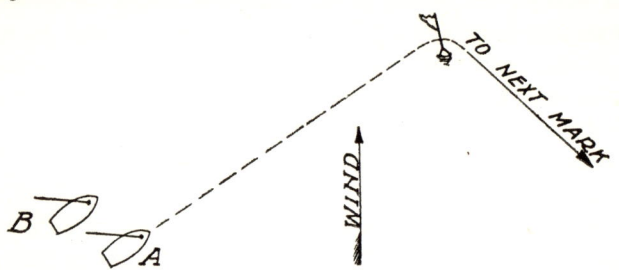

B overtakes *A* to leeward. *A's* proper course is the dotted line. If, however, there is a lee bow tide, or more wind to leeward of that course, or if *A* has some other valid reason, she may sail a more leeward course.

REACHING A YACHT BEYOND A MARK

We often hear this phrase. To many it means little or nothing. Perhaps a diagram will make it clear.

Diagram 11.

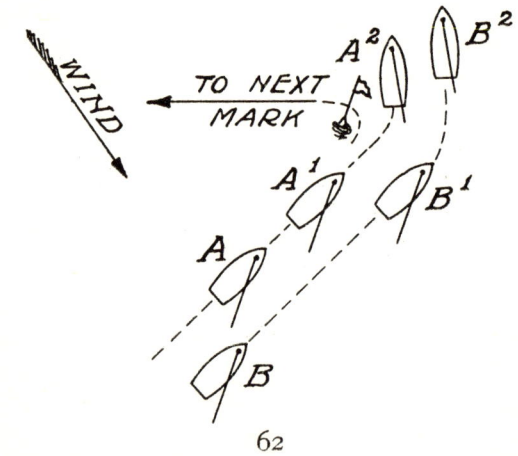

THE SAILING RULES

B overtakes *A* to leeward. When *A* reaches the mark, she may continue on the same tack. *B* cannot tack without fouling *A*. There is no rule compelling *A* to come about and head directly for the next mark,[8] *but* as soon as *A* has reached the mark, she must haul on the wind in order to avoid a protest by *B* under Rule 30 (C). On the wind her proper course is full and by, and if *A* is then on that point of sailing, *B* cannot object. If *A* does not haul on the wind as soon as she passes the mark she will in effect be bearing away below her proper course for the next mark, and the net result will be to hinder *B*. If *B* does not wish to be carried beyond the mark she must ease her sheets, drop astern, and tack.

It will be noted that Section 7 refers to "conditions of tide," etc., which justify a more leeward course to the next mark. Also that the rule says "the responsibility for proving the justification for such leeward course lies upon the weather yacht."

It is suggested, therefore, that if a skipper feels obliged to sail a course to leeward of the next mark, he make note of other yachts in his immediate vicinity in order that in the event of a protest by his leeward, overtaking competitor he may be able to offer testimony of other witnesses to corroborate his own as to the necessity for such leeward course.

[8] *Gem* v. *Maud*. Y. R. A., 1884.

Chapter IX

RULE 30—RIGHT OF WAY

The first point to be noted not only in connection with Rule 30 but also with all the Sailing Rules is that in a protest case the decision is pretty apt to be in favor of the yacht having right of way under the rule claimed to have been violated, *unless* the non-right-of-way yacht can offer corroborative testimony that she was not at fault.

By far the greatest number of protests are based on Overtaking, Clauses (A), (B), and (C). This entire chapter will, therefore, be devoted to that topic.

OVERTAKING

Clause (A)

A yacht overtaking another shall keep out of the way of the overtaken yacht.

This clause contains the first basic rule of yacht racing:

OVERTAKING YACHT KEEPS CLEAR

Now when does a yacht *rank* as an overtaking yacht? The *requisites* are three in number:

1. The yachts must be sailing "approximately the same course."
2. They must be or have come within range of risk of collision.
3. At some point on that tack one is or has been clear astern of the other.

THE SAILING RULES

If the foregoing three *requisites* are or have been fulfilled the yacht which is or has been clear astern *ranks* as overtaking yacht and continues to rank as such until:

1. She draws clear ahead. She then begins to rank as overtaken yacht.
2. She widens out abeam beyond range of risk of collision.
3. She falls astern beyond range of risk of collision.
4. One or both yachts *tack,* not jibe.

Dismiss the notion that the stern yacht must be overhauling or catching the yacht ahead. It is not an essential part of overtaking for the purpose of the rule. Yachts often sail for a considerable distance at nearly equal speed. If while they are so sailing, *requisites* one (1) and two (2) are fulfilled, and if three (3) is or has been fulfilled, then the yacht which is or has been clear astern *ranks* as overtaking yacht.

Let us illustrate.

Diagram 12.

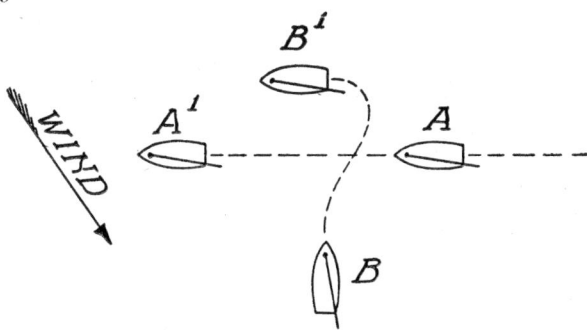

A and *B* are beating to windward. *B,* on the port tack, crosses astern of *A*. *B* then comes about onto the starboard tack, clear astern and slightly to windward of *A*.

They sail along at the same speed. *B* is not overhauling or catching *A*. Nevertheless *B ranks* as overtaking yacht because:

1. They are sailing "approximately the same course";
2. They are within range of risk of collision;
3. When *B* came about onto the starboard tack she was clear astern of *A*.

It has been argued that in order to rank as overtaking yacht, *B* should have come into the range of risk of collision from clear astern and while "sailing the same or nearly the same course." To put it another way, the yacht astern must have been outside the Zone and sailing "nearly the same course" *just before* coming within the range of risk of collision. Upon what authority, therefore, do we base the statement that in Diagram 12, *B ranked* as overtaking yacht the moment she tacked and filled away on her new course?

In 1900, British Y. R. A. Rule 29—OVERTAKING, LUFFING AND BEARING AWAY—read that *"A yacht overtaking another shall keep out of the way of the overtaken yacht; and a yacht may luff as she pleases to prevent another yacht passing to windward, but must never bear away out of her course to hinder the other passing to leeward,——"*

At that time the Y. R. A. Rules contained no definition of what constituted an overtaking yacht. In the absence of a definition it was assumed apparently that an overtaking yacht was one which came within our "three requisites."

In 1907 at Paris, France, the I. Y. R. U. Conference adopted the following definition of Overtaking:

"Of two yachts sailing the same or nearly the same course, one which is clear astern of another when ap-

THE SAILING RULES

proaching her so as to involve risk of collision, is said to be an overtaking yacht, and she continues as such after the yachts overlap, until she has again drawn clear."

It would seem evident that this did not change the 1900 conception of what constituted an overtaking yacht.

In 1912 the Y. R. A. added the following footnote:

"BEGINNING OF OVERTAKING

"When one yacht is clear astern of another she begins to rank as overtaking yacht as soon as she comes anywhere within the range of risk of collision while still remaining clear astern."

Was this footnote intended to change the definition so as to bar out a yacht that came into the range of risk of collision on a different tack; or was it intended merely to designate a point at which a yacht coming up from astern on the same course would herself become subject to the rights and obligations of an overtaking yacht? We do not believe that any one would seriously urge the first proposition. Note carefully the title to the footnote. A yacht that enters the Risk of Collision Zone on a different course and tacks astern as shown in Diagram 12 would not have to ask when she began to rank as overtaking; she would know that overtaking conditions commenced when she straightened out on her new course. But where a yacht is overhauling another from a considerable distance astern, it is of vital importance to both skippers to know just when overtaking conditions commence. This question was settled by the 1912 Y. R. A. footnote.

Then came the revision of November, 1929. We doubt if there was any intention of changing the former definition. The intent was to simplify it by combining it with the footnote and to specify four states of fact the happening of any one of which would terminate overtaking.

THE SAILING RULES

Would that a fifth had been included as urged by the delegate from Holland, Mr. H. C. A. van Kampen. But of that more anon when we discuss "The Florida Case."

The first paragraph of Rule 29, Section 6, has always seemed to be somewhat hazy. It seems to be merely a description of a special case. It does not exclude, as a proper definition should, every case not intended to come within the classification. It does not contain the elements of the 1907 definition. It merely states *when* a yacht overhauling another from astern *begins* to rank as overtaking yacht. In short, it would seem to be nothing more nor less than the 1912 British footnote. Does it not seem that instead of consolidating the 1912 footnote with the 1907 definition, the 1929 conference in reality, but doubtless unintentionally, obliterated the definition and merely perpetuated the footnote. In other words, since 1929 the yachting world has had no definition of an overtaking yacht.

In 1900 the Council of the Y. R. A. handed down a decision which as far as we can ascertain was the first recorded and reported case establishing the *three* requisites necessary to constitute overtaking conditions. It is illustrated in Diagram 13.

Tringa v. *Ceres* was a case of cross tacking during a beat to windward by two yachts twenty-four feet overall. At position 1, B forced A to tack. Shortly thereafter A tacked to port and crossed under the stern of B. At position 2, A forced B to tack. Shortly afterward B tacked to port and passed astern of A. Between positions 2 and 3 the yachts were over half a mile apart.

At position 3, instead of bearing away and passing under B's stern, A tacked to starboard two lengths ahead and three lengths to leeward of B. B could foot faster than A but could not point as high. B began to overhaul A but at the same sagged down upon her. Soon she estab-

THE SAILING RULES

lished an overlap upon *A's* weather quarter. *A* luffed sharply and *B* struck her as shown at position 4.

Diagram 13.

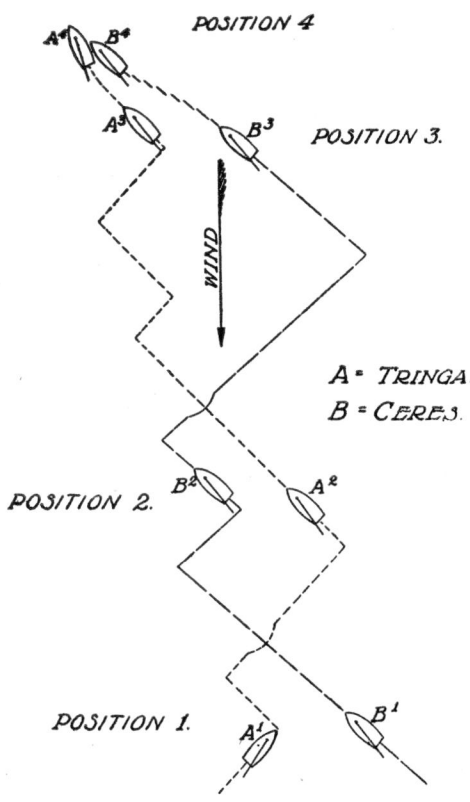

  B claimed that because at position 2 *A ranked* as overtaking yacht she must be considered still so to rank at position 3, for the reason that had she then borne away

THE SAILING RULES

under *B's* stern instead of tacking on *B's* lee bow, she, *A*, still would have been clear astern and would have continued to rank as overtaking yacht; and that therefore she must be considered to rank as such at the time of the foul.

The Sailing Committee was not misled by *B's* ingenious but fallacious reasoning and decided that at position 4 *A* was the overtaken yacht, was entitled to luff, and that *B* had to keep clear.

"The Council decided that *A* had the right to luff, *in consequence of the position she occupied after both boats were on the starboard tack* (see position 3), and that the decision of the Sailing Committee is so far upheld."[1] (Italics—the Author.)

Of like tenor are the three other cases also cited under reference No. 1.

In terms of the present day Sailing Rules the meaning of *Tringa* v. *Ceres* is this:

That if two yachts are sailing approximately the same course, one clear astern of the other as defined by Rule 29, Section 3, and are within range of risk of collision, it matters not what courses they were sailing when first they came within the zone. If thereafter they remain within the zone and sail approximately the same course the yacht clear astern *ranks* as overtaking yacht. Emphatically does it disprove the theory that a yacht cannot rank as overtaking yacht unless she was clear astern outside the zone and sailing approximately the same course *immediately before* coming within range of risk of collision.

Clause (B)

If the overtaking yacht steers a course to pass the over-

[1] *Tringa* v. *Ceres*. Y. R. A., 1901, page 140. *Shamrock* v. *White Heather*. Y. R. A., 1910, Case 2. *Mignonette* v. *Pariah*. Y. R. A., 1912, Case 8. *Indra* v. *Nike*. N. A. Y. R. U., Appeal No. 6, February 10, 1937.

THE SAILING RULES

taken yacht on the side opposite to that on which the latter then carries her main boom, the latter may luff from her course, head to wind if she pleases, to prevent the former passing her to windward, until she is in such a position that her bowsprit end, or stem if she has no bowsprit, would strike the overtaking yacht abaft the main shrouds, after which she may maintain her course, but may luff no further.

In cases of doubt as to the right of the leeward yacht to luff, the windward yacht must respond to the luff, and protest if she thinks fit.

Prior to the adoption of the present Sailing Rules in November, 1929, at London, when the luffing rights of a yacht overtaken to windward terminated, viz.: when further luffing would cause her bow to strike the overtaking yacht abaft the latter's main shrouds, the English rules obliged the overtaken yacht to resume her proper course for the next mark. The American rules did not—not even by inference.

Under present Clause (B) a yacht overtaken to windward may attempt to repel the attack of the overtaking yacht by luffing from her course *"head to wind if she pleases"*—and she may then *"maintain her course"* or luff. She may head into the eye of the wind and come to a standstill—even gather sternway—if she pleases. If while the overtaken yacht is at a standstill or going astern, the overtaking yacht has sufficient momentum to carry her leeward, main shrouds sufficiently far forward so that the right of the overtaken yacht further to luff has terminated, still the overtaken yacht is under no obligation to resume her former course, and woe betide the overtaking yacht if any part of her hull, spars or gear touches her opponent. She will be doubly at fault. She is not only overtaking but also windward yacht. She must keep clear until she

THE SAILING RULES

has drawn clear ahead and herself ranks as overtaken yacht. Both yachts must be careful not to fill away on the other tack because in such event an entirely new situation will arise. A safe rule for the overtaking yacht to follow is to keep not less than one and a half boat lengths of open water between herself and her competitor.

How is the first paragraph of Clause (B) to be interpreted in reference to bluff-ended, pram-bowed vessels such as many modern dinghies? In boats of that type the leeward boat's stem may often be well forward of the point where contact would be apt to occur.

Diagram 14.

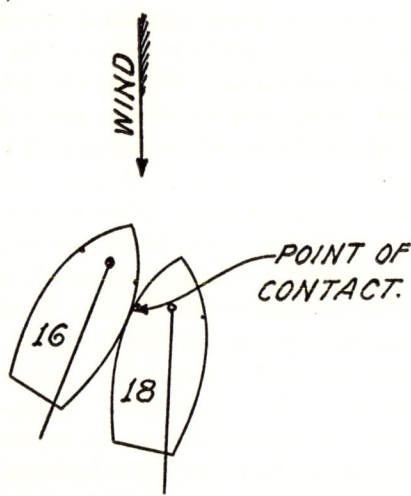

Dinghey No. 16 overtook No. 18 to windward. Several luffing matches ensued. Shortly before the collision and at a time when the bow of No. 18 still was well ahead of that of No. 16, No. 18 luffed almost head to wind. The

THE SAILING RULES

point of contact first occurred at a point eight to twelve inches *forward* of No. 18's weather shrouds and two to three inches *aft* of No. 16's leeward shrouds. No. 18 protested No. 16 for violation of Rule 30 (B). The defense of No. 16 was "that if No. 18 had struck her with her stem it could not possibly have been forward of my main shrouds." The Sailing Committee disqualified No. 18 for the reason "that in his final luff 'No. 18' left it until too late." On appeal to the Y. R. A., the Council reversed the decision and disqualified No. 16, the weather boat, saying: "The stem must be forward of the main rigging or not abaft the main rigging at the time of contact."[2]

Clause (B) was framed for yachts with bowsprits or sharp-pointed stems. In those days bluff-bowed dinghies were not as numerous as they are today. This Y. R. A. case would seem to hold that in the case of yachts having no bowsprit, the correct modern interpretation of Rule 30 (B) is that if at the instant of contact the STEM of the leeward boat is not "abaft the main shrouds" of the overtaking boat, then the actual point of contact is immaterial; the overtaking, weather boat will be held to be at fault.

The second paragraph of Clause (B) prescribes what the overtaking yacht *must* do even after she *thinks* her opponent's luffing rights have terminated. If her opponent continues to luff she must "take steps to keep out of the way under Rule 30." She must respond to her opponent's "dying kick" even if "the last luff of the overtaken yacht was too late."[3] In this case the Council disqualified both yachts; the overtaken yacht for continuing to luff after her right to luff had terminated, and the overtaking yacht for failing to respond to the last luff of her opponent.

[2]*Royal Dart Yacht Club, Dinghy No. 18* v. *Dinghy No. 16.* Y. R. A., 1935, Case 9.
[3]*Moonfleet* v. *Ajax.* Y. R. A., 1938, Case 15.

THE SAILING RULES

SUDDEN LUFFING WITHOUT WARNING

We trust we shall be pardoned for commenting briefly on this topic. For many years the luffing rule corresponding to present Rule 30 (B) provided that when a yacht was overtaken to windward she *"may luff as she pleases"* to prevent her competitor from passing to windward.

As amended at the 1929 I. Y. R. U. Conference in London, Clause (B) provides that the overtaken yacht *"may luff from her course, head to wind if she pleases, to prevent"* etc.

In international diplomacy the change of a single word may be of deep significance. Why then the change in wording? Was it intended to curtail the practice of sudden luffing without warning which in some countries had become more and more savage and less and less frowned upon since the beginning of the twentieth century? As we have stated heretofore, sudden luffing *prior* to the start was outlawed by the second paragraph of the meeting, crossing and converging parts of Rule 30 adopted by the 1929 Conference.

In more than 350 reported protest cases arising under the former as well as under the present rules, we have not found a decision which sanctioned ferocious and sudden luffing without warning, *luffing certain to result in a foul*. That smart and quick luffing to *prevent* an opponent passing close to windward—luffing to which an alert and skilful opponent *should* be able to respond and keep clear—is ethical as well as legal seems too obvious for argument. It is the only weapon available to repel the attack of the overtaking yacht which is voluntarily assuming a double obligation to keep clear. Luffing in a manner *certain to cause a foul* seems to us, however, to be a very different proposition.

THE SAILING RULES

The following excerpts from the pen of Major B. Heckstall-Smith, Secretary of the I. Y. R. U. Conference of 1929, and written very soon after its adjournment may be of interest. He wrote:

"Some critics say that whilst the old Rule permitted a 'sudden' or 'savage' luff because of the words 'the latter may luff as she pleases,' the new Rule does not permit 'sudden' or 'savage' luffs.

"The new rule is evidently very carefully worded; it says 'the latter may luff from her course, head to wind if she pleases,' to prevent the other from passing.

"Now, the words of the new Rule exactly follow the oldest customs of yacht-racing seamanship. They allow the overtaken yacht to luff up into the wind and, if she pleases, to luff up so far from her course as to be actually head to wind. This is exactly what all people who sail all kinds of boats have done for fifty, sixty, seventy or eighty years. Some people, however, in the last thirty years have read into the words of the old Rule 'luff as she pleases,' not merely a permission to luff head to wind, but also a permission to shove down the helm so ferociously and suddenly, or in any way the helmsman pleased, even to doing this in a manner certain to make a foul. This reading of the old Rule has been upheld by a great many influential Sailing Committees of Clubs in the past. I am not quite sure whether the Y. R. A. ever upheld it. I do not think this VERY sudden luffing is justified by the words of the new Rule. If it is not, all the better. I think we can generally luff quickly, smartly and sufficiently head to wind and still not luff obviously to make a foul. I therefore greatly prefer the words of the new Rule no matter what their interpretation may be. In my opinion the new words make no difference to the old fair sailing customs."[4]

[4]*Yachting World,* November 29, 1929.

THE SAILING RULES

Is it "fair sailing" within the intent of Rule 1 to luff suddenly, savagely and without warning and in a manner *certain* to cause a foul? Furthermore, granting that legally it was within the *letter* of the former rule, is it legal according to Clause (B) as now worded?

Clause (C)

A yacht must never bear away out of her proper course to hinder an overtaking yacht passing her to leeward. The overtaking yacht, if to leeward, must not luff so as to interfere* with the windward yacht or cause her to alter her course, until she ranks as an overtaken yacht. The lee side shall be considered that on which the leading yacht of the two carries her main boom at the time she ceases to be clear ahead.

**'Interfere' is used in the sense of interference through actual contact.*

This clause has been the cause of much controversy. When may it be said that a yacht is bearing away out of her proper course to the next mark to hinder an overtaking yacht passing her to leeward? When she clearly is *without* the Risk of Collision Zone she may do so because no rules apply. When she clearly is *within* the Zone she may not. How about such a manœuvre when there is *doubt* on that point? The phrase "Range of Risk of Collision" must be interpreted in its *broadest,* not its narrowest, sense. Remember the last sentence of Section 5, Rule 29: "When there is any doubt, risk of collision is to be presumed to exist."

The prohibition against bearing away to hinder applies from the time the overtaking yacht comes within range of risk of collision.[5] In *Juno* v. *Zoe* the Council said:

"Clause (B) of Rule 30, ... gives the overtaken yacht

[5]*Juno* v. *Zoe.* Y. R. A., 1936, Case 6.

THE SAILING RULES

a great advantage. Clause (C) of Rule 30, under which the overtaken yacht must never bear away to hinder, compensates the overtaking yacht for the disadvantage she suffers under Clause (B)."

If in doubt, therefore, don't bear away to leeward unless conditions of tide or circumstances other than the desire to hinder a competitor overtaking to leeward make such course desirable. And lastly, a word of warning to the overtaking-to-leeward yacht. She must have drawn clear ahead before she starts to luff. If she luffs too soon, and the overtaken yacht is obliged to alter course, even a wee bit, to avoid a collision, the former will be disqualified on protest.[6]

JIBING AND LUFFING BY OVERTAKEN YACHT

We already have seen that overtaking conditions are not necessarily terminated by a jibe on the part of one of the yachts.[7] In *Forelle* v. *Seagull* the overtaken yacht did not perceptibly alter course when she jibed. Neither was the jibe a part of a gradual turn as in the case of *Rainbow* v. *Yankee* illustrated in Diagram 15. The latter case is interesting also from the point of view of manœuvres during the preparatory period discussed in Chapter VI.

The Race Committee found the facts to be as follows:

A few minutes before the start of the race on August 15, 1936, both yachts were sailing away from the starting line. *Rainbow* was three-quarters of a boat's length directly astern of and sailing the same course as *Yankee*. *Yankee* bore away to leeward, and jibed with the intention of returning to the starting line. *Rainbow* followed *Yankee* but on the inside of the latter's turn, keeping between *Yankee* and the starting line and shortly established an overlap. As a result of this manœuvre the yachts nearly

[6]*Thistle* v. *Felma*. Y. R. A., 1927, Case 2.
[7]*Forelle* v. *Seagull*. Y. R. A., 1939, Case 2.

Diagram 15.

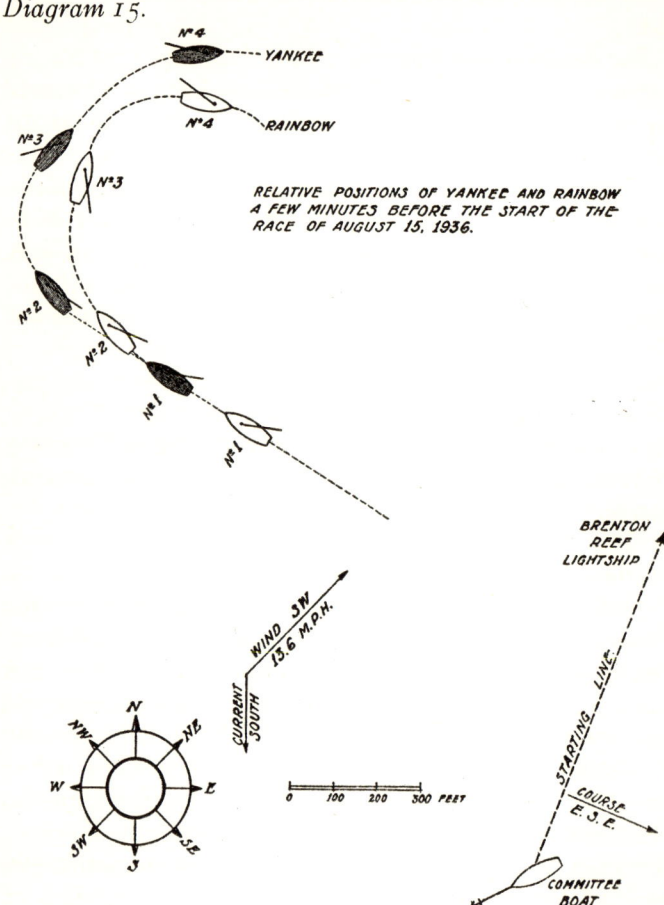

THE SAILING RULES

collided and *Yankee* was obliged to bear away to avoid a collision. The Race Committee dismissed *Rainbow's* protest.[8]

The decision was appealed to the Committee on Racing Appeals of the N. Y. Y. C., which unanimously sustained the decision of the Race Committee. In its opinion the Committee on Racing Appeals said:

"At the commencement of the jibe (by *Yankee*) *Rainbow* was, therefore, the overtaking and *Yankee* the overtaken boat, and *Yankee* had the right of way subject, however, to the limitations imposed by Section (K) of Rule 30 upon the yacht holding the right of way, and the provision of Rule 30 that the yacht holding right of way may before the starting signal 'alter course in any reasonable manner' from which it may be inferred that at least before the starting signal a yacht, although holding right of way, may not alter course in an unreasonable manner.

"The first question, therefore, for our decision is whether *Yankee* in jibing contravened the provisions of Section (K). The Race Committee has found that *Yankee's* alteration of course in the act of jibing did not require any alteration of *Rainbow's* course. Upon that finding it is clear that *Yankee's* alteration of course did not 'prevent' *Rainbow's* keeping clear of her, nor did it 'mislead or baulk' *Rainbow* 'in the act of keeping out of the way.' We find, therefore, that under the situation which existed here Section (K) did not apply to *Yankee's* alteration of course for the purpose and in the act of jibing, and also that it is not an unreasonable alteration of course for the overtaken yacht to jibe where at the commencement of the jibe the overtaking yacht is clear astern in her wake and such jibe does not require any alteration

[8]*Rainbow* v. *Yankee*. N. Y. Y. C., 1936 Report of Race Committee, page 10. Affirmed on appeal by the Committee on Racing Appeals, N. Y. Y. C., January 22, 1937.

of course by the overtaking yacht. *Rainbow,* however, did not elect to maintain her course and thus go clear of *Yankee,* but, as found by the Race Committee, voluntarily chose to follow *Yankee* on the inside of her turn keeping between her and the starting line and shortly establishing an overlap. As a result of this manœuvre by *Rainbow* she, still on the port tack, nearly collided with *Yankee* after *Yankee* had jibed and was on the starboard tack and *Yankee* was compelled to bear away to avoid a collision. In view of this fact *Yankee* had clearly the right of way under Rule 30, Section (F), at the time a collision was averted by her bearing away to avoid it. But even if the situation had been otherwise and before *Yankee's* jibe both boats had been on the starboard tack so that when *Yankee* jibed she was on the port tack and *Rainbow* still on the starboard tack, our decision would have been the same since, as we have held above, *Yankee* had the right to jibe under the circumstances which existed in this case and *Rainbow, having at all times followed* generally the course of *Yankee* (Italics—the Author), continued to be the overtaking boat and was required to keep out of her way [Rule 30, Section (A)]. It is not to be inferred from this decision, however, that an overtaken boat may at any time jibe and then have the right to an unimpeded course back to the starting line. If in any instance the overtaking conditions should cease to exist, either through such an alteration of course of the boats involved that overtaking conditions no longer continued or through the occurrence of one or more of the conditions specified by Rule 29, Section 6, then the overtaking rule ceases to cover the situation and the rights of the yachts when converging must be determined under the 'Meeting, Crossing and Converging' provisions of Rule 30 as modified by Sections (I) and (K) of that Rule."

THE SAILING RULES

It will be apparent after studying the protest case of *Endeavour* v. *Rainbow* concerning an incident that took place on September 22, 1934, shortly prior to the start of the fourth race for the America's Cup, discussed *infra* under Rule 30 (F), that the last two sentences quoted above intimate clearly what would have been the decision on Count One of that internationally famous protest had it been heard by the Race Committee of the New York Yacht Club.

Diagram 16.

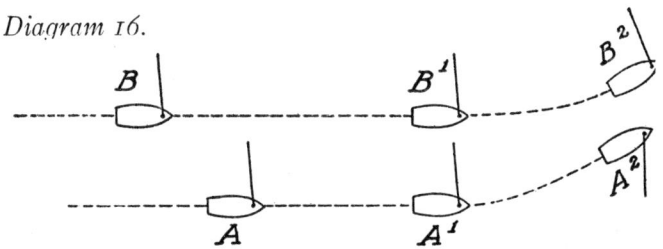

B overtook and attempted to pass A to leeward. *After* B had established an overlap A jibed and then luffed. On protest, A was disqualified.[9] A had no right to starboard her helm *after* jibing, as this constituted bearing away out of her course to hinder B passing to leeward.[10]

In none of the above cases was there what might be termed a radical alteration of course on the part of the overtaken yacht nor was any turning mark involved. In the following case, although the jibe occurred in the open sea, it involved a radical change of course.

A and B were running before the wind on the starboard tack, B endeavoring to overtake A to windward in order to obtain the inside position at the next mark which had to be left to starboard. A luffed, B did likewise. The

[9] *Nyria* v. *White Heather*. Y. R. A., 1922, Case 6.
[10] *Su Su* v. *Endrick*. Y. R. A., 1908, page 153.

THE SAILING RULES

prolonged luffing match carried the yachts well to windward of the straight course to the mark. *A* jibed while still clear ahead. The jibe was over 90°. *B* jibed also and overtook *A* on the latter's port (then windward) side. *A* luffed sharply and *B* collided with her. The Sailing Committee dismissed *A's* protest. The Council reversed the decision and disqualified *B* saying: "It is admitted that *B* was at one time astern. If the Sailing Committee do not consider it proved that she was subsequently clear ahead, it was their duty to disqualify her for not keeping clear of *A*."[11]

Now let us discuss two cases both of which involved a radical change of course, consisting of a jibe followed by a luff around a turning mark, of over 90°. In each case the jibe and subsequent luff by the leading yacht were parts of the normal manœuvre of rounding the mark. Therefore, any claim under Rule 30 (K) by the yacht clear astern that she was misled or balked is without foundation because she should have anticipated just such a manœuvre by her opponent.

The facts in the English case, *June Mary* v. *Flying Cloud*,[12] were nearly identical with those in the American case, *Aileen* v. *Canvasback*.[13] The only difference was that in the English case (1) both yachts had been running on the port tack, and (2) when *A, June Mary,* the leading and overtaken yacht, jibed around the mark leaving it to starboard, *B* collided with her; whereas in the American case (1) both yachts had been reaching broad on the starboard tack and (2) when *A, Canvasback,* the yacht clear ahead, jibed to round the mark, leaving it to port, *B* chose to hit the mark instead of colliding with *A*.

The English case was a protest by *A* under Rule 30

[11]*Viola* v. *Camelia.* Y. R. A., 1904, page 115.
[12]*June Mary* v. *Flying Cloud.* Y. R. A., 1931, Case 1.
[13]*Aileen* v. *Canvasback.* Y. R. A. of Long Island Sound, N. Y., October 27, 1933; N. A. Y. R. U. Bulletin No. 24, March 10, 1934.

THE SAILING RULES

(A). She made no claim that when she jibed Clause (A) ceased to apply and that Clause (F) then came into effect. She based her protest solely on the grounds that (1) she ranked as overtaken yacht, (2) when she reached the mark B was clear astern and therefore could not invoke Rule 31, and (3) that a jibe not being a tack within the meaning of Rule 29, (6), 4, she had a right to jibe and luff around the mark unhindered by B.

B contended that (1) A was not entitled to jibe around the mark regardless of B's proximity, and (2) A had no right so to jibe unless she was so far ahead that she could carry out that manœuvre without interfering with B. Clause (K) was not referred to in the report of the case.

The Sailing Committee disqualified B. The Council, without comment, affirmed the decision.

In the American case both yachts had been reaching

Diagram 17.

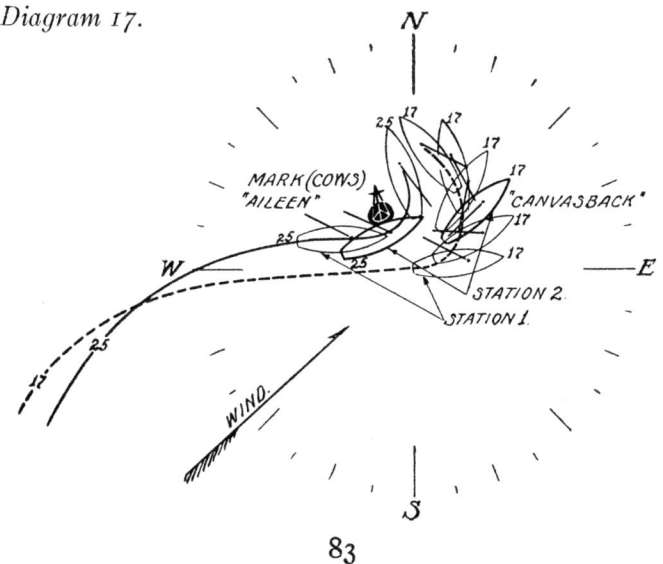

THE SAILING RULES

broad on the starboard tack for a mark to be left to port, the next leg being a beat to windward. *Canvasback, A,* was slightly to windward and from six to eight feet clear ahead when she reached the mark and altered her helm to jibe around it and haul on the wind on the port tack. *B, Aileen,* called for room to jibe around the mark inside of *A*. *A* held to her course and in the endeavor to secure the inside and weather berth on the next leg, *B* fouled the mark.

Under the provisions of Rule 33, *B* "must immediately abandon the race or hoist a protest signal." She chose the latter alternative. Her original protest was based on Rule 30 (F)—both yachts free on opposite tacks, neither overtaking, port tack keeps clear. The Race Committee found as a fact that when *A* reached the mark and altered her helm to jibe around it and haul on the wind on the port tack, *B* still was from six to eight feet clear astern. It ruled that *B* "was the overtaking yacht, having fulfilled the necessary requisites to rank as such." It dismissed the protest and disqualified *B* for fouling the mark without justification.

In her appeal to the Executive Committee of the Y. R. A. of Long Island Sound, New York, *B* contended that Rule 30, Clauses (C), (G) and (K) and Rule 31 also were pertinent to the case.

She contended:

1. That when *A* jibed she lost her status as overtaken yacht and Rule 30 (F) governed the situation;
2. That the word "tack" in the first line of the third paragraph of Rule 31 included the word "jibe."

The appellate tribunal affirmed the decision of the Race Committee. We quote a few passages from the opinion of the Executive Committee:

"Rule 30 (F) and (G) can have no bearing, since by their terms they apply only to situations when 'neither (yacht) can claim the rights of a yacht being overtaken,' unless an entirely new relationship developed just previous to the alleged foul. . . . As no one of these conditions" (the four conditions enumerated in Rule 29 (6) "occurred, it is held that overtaking conditions continued up to and including the time of the alleged foul."

As regards the second sentence of Clause (K) the Executive Committee said:

"In the open sea, this sentence of Clause (K) might have justified a protest by *Aileen*," (B), "provided the overtaken yacht, hard on a jibe, had so unexpectedly and rapidly altered her course by luffing that the overtaking yacht was misled and was not given reasonable opportunity to keep clear. Under the existing facts, however, since *Canvasback's*," (A's), "luff after jibing was part of the normal manœuvre of rounding a mark, it is held that *Aileen*," (B), "cannot be heard to claim that she was misled or baulked, for she must have anticipated just such an action on the part of *Canvasback*," (A).". . . Because of reasonable anticipation that *Canvasback*," (A), "would alter her course to round the mark, the Committee considers that neither under Clause (K) of Rule 30 nor under the express provisions of the second sentence of paragraph 1 of Rule 31, which is later discussed, can *Aileen*," (B), "be justified in intentionally placing herself in a position where she may reasonably anticipate she would not be able to keep clear of *Canvasback*," (A), "without fouling the mark."

As to *B's* second contention that the word "tack" in the first line of the third paragraph of Rule 31 included the word "jibe," the Committee said:

"It is clear that considered with the preceding para-

THE SAILING RULES

graph" (wherein was quoted the second paragraph of Rule 31), "and the conclusions we have reached as to the application of Rule 30 to a situation such as the one herein involved, the word 'tack' means what it says and is not intended to include the word 'jibe.'"

The two English cases and the American case last cited

Diagram 18.

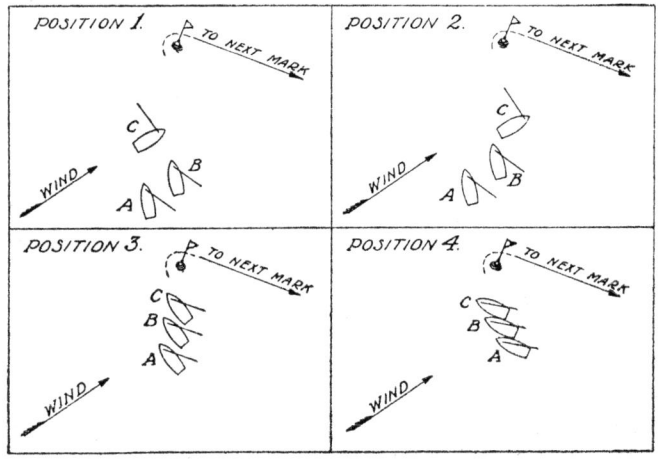

clearly hold that even in the open sea an overtaken yacht still clear ahead may jibe and make a radical alteration of course, and not lose her status as an overtaken yacht, provided that her jibe and alteration of course is not so unexpected and rapid that the stern yacht is misled or is not given reasonable opportunity to keep clear. (See discussion of Clause (K), *infra.*) Especially is this true if the manœuvre is one that should have been foreseen or reasonably anticipated by the yacht clear astern; and pro-

THE SAILING RULES

vided always that the second sentence of Clause (K) is not contravened by the right-of-way yacht.

Now let us turn for a moment to a three-boat situation. It is inserted at this point because the Council decided it under Rule 30 (A), and because it deals with jibing and luffing by a yacht overtaken to leeward. (Diagram 18.)

"*Position 1. A* and *B* had been running with booms to port; *A* overtaking *B*. Both *A* and *B* jibe *after A* establishes an overlap on *B*. *C* with her boom still to port is overtaking both *A* and *B*.

"*Position 2. C* crosses ahead of *A* and *B,* and gets to leeward of both. *C,* now being unable to fetch the mark without jibing, and being blanketed by *A* and *B,* is being rapidly overhauled by both yachts. *B* is on the point of establishing an overlap on *C,* on the same side that *C* is carrying her boom.

"*Position 3. C* now jibes and luffs out to windward of the mark in order to get her wind clear, *B* establishing an overlap on *C* immediately *after C's* boom goes over to starboard.

"*Position 4.* The three yachts collide."

The Race Committee found as a fact that *C* jibed just in time to prevent *B* from establishing her overlap while *C's* boom was still to pòrt.

On appeal the Council held :[14]

1. *C* had the right to jibe *and* luff *B* as she jibed *before B* established an overlap.
2. *B* should not be disqualified, as she was prevented by *A* from keeping clear of *C*.
3. *A* was disqualified under Rule 30 (A).

In our opinion *A* should have been disqualified for violating Rule 31, *not* Rule 30 (A). After *C* jibed, she

[14]*Widgeon* v. *Chittabob*. Y. R. A., 1931, Case 2.

ranked as an obstruction to *B* by virtue of the last sentence of the first paragraph of Rule 31. *A* and *B* were overlapped. *B* was inside yacht. Both yachts "without tacking" were "about to pass an obstruction to sea room," namely *C*. Rule 31 temporarily superseded Rule 30. It was the duty of *A* as outside yacht to "give room" to *B,* "the yacht in danger of fouling such ... obstruction." *A,* and *A* alone, was to blame for the foul.

We now draw nigh to the protest case of *Doris* v. *Seagull,* better known to yachtsmen as "The Florida Case." It occurred on the east coast of Florida during the early spring of 1934. Unfortunately the decision of the Race Committee was not appealed to the Executive Committee of the N. A. Y. R. U., so that a golden opportunity to have determined an interpretation of Clauses (A), (B), (C), (G) and (K) of Rule 30, and also Rule 29, (6), 4, was lost.

In our brief discussion of the history or evolution of the definition of Overtaking, Rule 29, (6), we bemoaned the absence of a fifth condition or manœuvre which would terminate overtaking conditions.

At the I. Y. R. U. Conference in November, 1929, the fourth condition for the termination of overtaking (*i.e.,* one or both of the yachts tack") was added at the suggestion of Mr. H. C. A. van Kampen, the delegate from Holland. He also proposed a fifth point: "If one of the yachts alters course so that the courses are no more approximately the same." Mr. van Kampen's fifth point was not adopted because it "was met by Major B. Heckstall-Smith who argued that this point was already dealt with in the definition of 'Overtaking.' "[15] In our opinion the last paragraph of Rule 29 (6) would have been less ambiguous had it been worded as follows: "No question

[15]*Yachting World,* October 26, 1934, page 341.

THE SAILING RULES

of overtaking can arise *or continue to exist* unless the yachts are sailing approximately the same course," etc.

Mr. van Kampen's "fifth point," however, would not have covered the anomalous situation which arose in "The Florida Case." That situation perhaps would have required another "point" or condition which also would terminate overtaking.

Commodore Harold S. Vanderbilt has made some pertinent comments on Mr. van Kampen's "fifth point." He said: "Surely Mr. van Kampen would not have made this excellent suggestion if, in his opinion, the subject matter had already been covered by the overtaking definition. Apparently, the 1929 Conference was in accord with the substance of his suggestion, but did not adopt it, because it was argued that the subject matter was already covered in the definition. But is it? When we have four numbered clauses which specifically state how overtaking conditions terminate, must we not infer that no other terminating clause exists? Is it not reasonable to assume that, in a supposedly carefully drafted set of rules, all terminating clauses are grouped together? The clause which has been interpreted to mean that overtaking conditions terminate when two yachts cease to sail approximately the same course, reads: 'No question of overtaking can *arise* unless the yachts are sailing approximately the same course.' This clause is the 'joker' in the overtaking rule. . . . Note that the 'joker' clause uses the verb 'arise,' not 'continue' or 'exist.' Clearly 'arise' deals with the inception, not the termination, of a set of conditions. But necessity is the mother of invention, and it was necessary to interpret the definition as it has been interpreted, to avoid a series of impossible situations in the application of the overtaking rule. But who, reading this definition, could possibly fathom its interpreted meaning? Certainly no one can be blamed

THE SAILING RULES

for construing the definition literally. . . . There is no doubt that Mr. van Kampen was right. . . . If Mr. van Kampen's advice had been followed, and the meaning of the rule made clear in 1929, I am confident that three important international protests would have been avoided in 1934, namely, the first count of *Endeavour's* protest in the fourth race, . . . ; *Rainbow's* protest at the start of the last race; and *Endeavour's* protest at the start of the last race. While the last two protests were both withdrawn and, consequently, never heard, they were made following a situation which competent observers, including Major B. Heckstall-Smith, agreed closely resembled the one at the start of the fourth race, and involved the identical interpretation of the overtaking definition already discussed."[16]

Mr. Vanderbilt's remarks in regard to what he terms the "joker" in the overtaking rule caused us to wonder how it happened that after the present rules were adopted in November, 1929, the British Y. R. A. continued to interpret the overtaking rule in the same manner as it had done theretofore. Through further research we found that at the Annual General Meeting on February 23, 1912, the Y. R. A. adopted eleven footnotes to Rule 30. One of the footnotes read as follows:

"Y. R. A. NOTE—RULE 30
"OVERLAPPING AND CLEAR AND OVERTAKING

*"No question of overtaking can arise **or continue to exist** unless the yachts are sailing approximately the same course; and a new set of conditions arises if either yacht changes her tack. (A luff by one of the yachts under Clause (b) does not count as a difference of course in this connection.)"* (Heavy italics—the Author.)

[16]*On the Wind's Highway*, pages 208–209.

THE SAILING RULES

We already have mentioned in Chapter VI that where the principle of a Y. R. A. footnote was agreed to by the 1929 Conference it was incorporated as an integral part of the new rule. We shall learn also in our discussion of Clause (K) that in the final printing and typographical set-up of the new rules in England an error was made in Clause (K) which escaped notice until the spring of 1933.

Mr. Vanderbilt speaks of the 1929 Rules as "a supposedly carefully drafted set." Can it be doubted that the Conference intended to retain the principles of the Y. R. A. 1912 footnote to the overtaking rule? To retain those principles it was necessary that the wording of the last paragraph of Rule 29 (6)—Overtaking—should be practically identical not only with the first clause of nineteen words of the 1912 Y. R. A. footnote but also with the last sentence of that footnote, the sentence in parentheses. The principle of the second clause in the footnote reading "and a new set of conditions arises if either yacht changes her tack" is identical in meaning with that of Clause 4 of the present overtaking rule reading: "4. One or both of the yachts tack."

Does it not seem reasonable to believe, therefore, that the very important words *"or continue to exist"* were omitted from the text on account of the oversight or inadvertence of some individual. We know of *one* mistake in printing the Rules. Is it unreasonable to believe that it was not the only mistake made? Incidentally, in the 1929 Racing Rules of the New York Yacht Club, "Rule 36. Definitions 3. Overtaking," will be found a footnote entitled "Overlapping and Clear and Overtaking" which contains the words *"or continue to exist."*

It should not be overlooked that, as adopted in 1929, American Rule 29, (6), 4, had an asterisk after the last word in the line "tack.*" This asterisk referred to a foot-

THE SAILING RULES

note reading as follows: "*A jibe is not a tack within the meaning of this rule."

Neither the British nor the I. Y. R. U. Rules contained this footnote. It was deleted from the American Rules at the Annual General Meeting of the North American Yacht Racing Union on November 20, 1936, and by the New York Yacht Club at its Annual Meeting the following month.

In the 1937 *Year Book* the N. A. Y. R. U. inserted a pink slip reading as follows:

"The action of the Delegates of the North American Yacht Racing Union in deleting that footnote was not intended to have any effect whatsoever upon the meaning of the rule. After the conference in London in 1929, at which meeting our Racing (Sailing) Rules were brought into conformity with the sailing rules of other nations, the footnote was inserted at the request of a distinguished American yachtsman as it was believed that the meaning of the rule would be clarified thereby. When the footnote was inserted it was not intended that our Rules should differ in any way in their meaning from the Racing (Sailing) Rules of other countries. After some years it has become increasingly clear that the footnote instead of being a clarification has in fact proved a complication and the footnote was therefore deleted for that reason and for that reason only."

Course triangular; all marks to be left to port. First leg a beat to windward; second leg a broad reach on the starboard tack; third leg a reach on the port tack. Wind steady and true. No tide. *A's* proper course if any between Marks 1 and 2 and 2 and 3 is a straight line from mark to mark.

In a fleet of yachts *A* rounds Mark 1 closely followed by *B, C, D,* etc. After rounding Mark 1, *A* ranks as over-

THE SAILING RULES

taken and *B* as overtaking yacht, the three requisites to constitute such condition having been fulfilled. On the broad reach to Mark 2, *B* gradually overhauls *A* and establishes an overlap to leeward. The yachts then rank under Rule 30 (A) and (C). Both yachts jibe around Mark 2

Diagram 19.

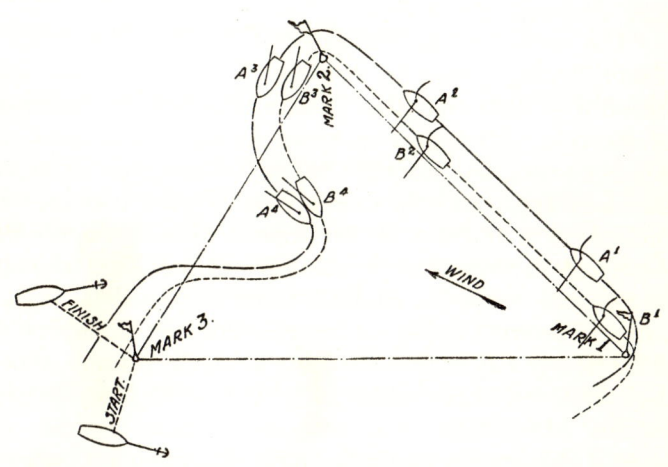

THE FLORIDA CASE—
DORIS V. SEAGULL

simultaneously, *A* still being slightly ahead as they square away on the reach to the finish line. *B* commences to gain. *A* luffs gradually at first. *B* responds. *A* then luffs sharply. *B* responds again. By this time the yachts are well to windward of the straight line between Mark 2 and Mark 3 at the windward end of the finish line. *A* continues to luff. Fearing that further luffing will permit *C, D,* etc., to finish ahead, *B* refuses to luff further, and the yachts touch, *A's* stem still being forward of *B's* main shrouds. After the

THE SAILING RULES

foul the yachts bear away for the finish line, the order of finish being *C, B, A, D,* etc.

B protests *A* for violation of Rule 29 (7) Proper Course, and Rule 30 (C), in that by luffing to windward of the straight line between Marks 2 and 3, *A* technically bore away out of her proper course for Mark 3 to hinder *B* passing to leeward.

A protests *B* for violation of (1) Rule 30 (A) and (B), in that *B,* being overtaking yacht to windward, did not keep clear; (2) Rule 30 (G) in the event that at the time of contact the yachts no longer ranked under the Overtaking Rule; and (3) "the ordinary customs of the sea" as provided in Rule 1, for permitting the yachts to collide.

ARGUMENTS

B contends:

1. That when she established an overlap to leeward the yachts then were governed by Rule 30 (A) and (C) as modified by Rule 29 (7) Proper Course.

2. The clause of Rule 30 which then became applicable continued in force until Overtaking terminated.

3. Overtaking-to-leeward conditions continued up to the time of contact.

4. After the yachts jibed around Mark 2, Mark 3 became "the next mark" within the meaning of Rules 29 (7) and 30 (C), and that there was, therefore, a proper course between Marks 2 and 3.

5. Although *A* had the right gradually to luff *B* to the straight line between Marks 2 and 3, she (*B*) was entitled to complete freedom from interference to windward of such line.

6. After jibing around Mark 2, it would be unfair to compel her deliberately to slacken speed, fall astern of *A* and endeavor to pass on *A's* then leeward (starboard) side.

THE SAILING RULES

7. Rule 30 (B) is not applicable because when she established her overlap B did not "attack," and, therefore, had a right to unmolested, free passage subject to Rules 29 (7) and 30 (C).

8. If, after rounding Mark 2, the situation is one not expressly covered by the Yacht Racing Rules, the following sections of the *U. S. Pilot Rules for Inland Waters* are applicable:

Article 17 (d): When both are running free, with the wind on the same side, the vessel which is to the windward shall keep out of the way of the vessel which is to the leeward.

Article 21: Where, by any of these rules, one of the two vessels is to keep out of the way, the other shall keep her course and speed.

It followed, therefore, that if the foregoing parts of the U. S. Pilot Rules were applicable, A had no right to change her course by further luffing after Mark 2 was rounded and the yachts had squared away for Mark 3.

A contends:

1. The purpose of the last sentence of Rule 30 (C)—"The lee side shall be considered that on which the leading yacht of the two carries her main boom at the time she ceases to be clear ahead"—is twofold:

a. To provide a means of determining which side is the official windward or leeward side when two yachts are sailing with the wind practically dead astern and with booms on opposite sides.

b. To prevent the leading yacht, after an overlap has been established on her leeward side, from jibing merely to luff the overtaking yacht and force her wide of the course to the next mark.

2. Rule 30 (C) does not specify when it shall cease to apply, and common sense requires that it should no longer

be applicable when conditions change and there is no further need to resort to the rule in order to determine which is the windward or leeward side.

3. After rounding Mark 2 both yachts were sailing a new and entirely different course, with new wind conditions that clearly indicated which was the windward yacht.

4. The act of simultaneously jibing around Mark 2 involved a substantial alteration of course by both yachts, and terminated the former status of overtaking.

5. If rounding Mark 2 and commencing a new leg of the course did not terminate overtaking, *B,* by jibing, deliberately and on her own initiative, voluntarily surrendered the freedom from hindrance to which she theretofore had been entitled, and, when *A* jibed also, became the overtaking yacht to windward in law as well as in fact, and that Rule 30 (A) and (B) governed the case thereafter.

6. If, after rounding Mark 2, neither Clause (B) nor Clause (C) of Rule 30 was applicable, Clause (G) governed the situation for the reason that when both yachts jibed around the mark the governing principle then became the position of the yachts with reference to the direction of the wind, and the situation became analogous to the change of windward and leeward status when two yachts ranking under Rule 30 (A) and (B) not only luff head to wind but accidentally fall away on the opposite tack, thereby terminating overtaking and causing Rule 30 (G) or (H) to become applicable.

7. The jibe around Mark 2 involved a substantial change of course equivalent to that of a tack, and Rules 29 (7) and 30 (C) are limited to situations where overtaking continues after a jibe by one or both of the yachts but no substantial alteration of course follows.

8. The English case of *Su Su* v. *Endrick,* Y. R. A.,

THE SAILING RULES

1908, is not in point because in that case only the overtaken-to-leeward yacht jibed, whereas in the instant case both yachts jibed simultaneously.

DISCUSSION

The Yacht Racing Rules must be interpreted as written, and not as one might wish they were worded. Only if what would appear to be a correct interpretation of the rules as worded brings about a result clearly contrary to the principle of fair sailing implied by Rule 1 are we justified in coming to a different conclusion.

There seem to be three somewhat divergent opinions, or viewpoints, as to which clause of Rule 30 governed after the yachts jibed around Mark 2, *viz.*:

I. Overtaking-to-leeward continued, and the yachts still were governed by Rules 29 (7) and 30 (A) and (C).

II. Overtaking continued but an entirely new situation arose, and Rule 30 (A) and (B) governed.

III. An entirely new situation arose, overtaking terminated, and Rule 30 (G) came into effect.

Let us discuss these three viewpoints in the order enumerated.

I. RULES 29 (7), AND 30 (A) AND (C) CONTINUED TO GOVERN

Rule 29 (6)—Overtaking—specifies with utmost clarity four acts or conditions, the doing or fulfilment of any one of which terminates existing overtaking conditions. There is no intimation by implication, or otherwise, that the act of rounding a mark without tacking terminates an existing overtaking status. We must conclude, therefore, that the omission of a fifth act or condition terminating overtaking was deliberate and that the International Conference of 1929 intended to limit the acts or conditions which terminate overtaking to the four enumerated in the definition. To read into the rule a fifth act or condition would be judicial legislation.

When the yachts rounded Mark 1, they ranked under Rule 30 (A). When B endeavored to pass on A's leeward side the yachts ranked under Rule 30 (A) and (C). Overtaking conditions once having been established, they continued until one of the four acts or conditions enumerated in Rule 29 (6) should develop. Up to the time of contact, no one of these acts or conditions had occurred and, therefore, B still ranked as overtaking yacht.

Before B established an overlap to leeward, A had the right to jibe and luff, but after the overlap had been made, although A still had the right to jibe, she no longer had the right to luff (*Nyria* v. *White Heather,* British Y. R. A., 1922, Case 6), because such luffing would constitute "bearing away" out of her proper course for Mark 2 in order to hinder B passing to leeward (*Su Su* v. *Endrick,* British Y. R. A., 1908).

The purpose of Rule 30 (C) when read in conjunction with Rule 29 (7) is not only to prevent a yacht which overtakes and elects to try to pass to leeward from being forced unduly wide of the next mark but also to compensate her for the disadvantage she suffers (1) if she tries to overtake to windward and (2) if she tries the more difficult task of attempting to pass to leeward.

When *A first ceased to be clear ahead* (cf. last sentence of Rule 30 (C)) she was carrying her main boom to port. Until the yachts reached Mark 2 that mark was "the next mark" (Rule 29 (7)). After the yachts jibed around Mark 2 overtaking-to-leeward conditions technically continued because the yachts had neither tacked nor drawn clear as provided in Rule 29 (6). Mark 3, therefore, became "the next mark" within the meaning of Rule 29 (7).

THE SAILING RULES

There still existed a proper course for *A, viz.:* a straight line for Mark 3. Paradoxical as it may seem, *A's* lee side *for the purpose of the overtaking Rule* 30 (C), continued to be her port side, although as a physical fact it then was her windward side. *A* had the right gradually to bear away (luff) to her proper course for Mark 3, but had no right to bear away (luff) beyond that point (*Su Su* v. *Endrick, ubi supra*).

There is in the rules, as worded, nothing to differentiate between a jibe involving a slight alteration of course and a jibe involving a change of course equivalent to or greater than a tack, *i.e.*, substantially 90° or more in the case of small yachts. Were such differentiation read into the rules, the door would be opened wide to argument as to the approximate number of degrees of a circle involved in any particular jibe. Obviously, that is a question of fact often impossible to determine.

Now, how do the adherents of viewpoint I answer *A's* contention that Rule 30 (B) governed the case after the jibe around Mark 2?

Their argument is as follows:

a. Clause (B) applies only "If the overtaking yacht steers a course to pass the overtaken yacht on the side opposite to that on which the latter then carries her main boom. . . ." They contend that the word "then" refers to an instant or period of time during which the overtaking yacht is still clear astern.

b. Obviously to "steer a course to pass the overtaken yacht" either to windward or to leeward, the overtaking yacht must at that time be clear astern. She may elect which course to pursue. Once she establishes an overlap —to leeward in the instant case—she no longer has a free choice of course. *A's* right to alter course thereafter becomes restricted by Rule 29 (7) and Rule 30 (C) and

(K). The question of overlap is material in three ways only:

1. It definitely determines the particular clause of the overtaking rule which thereafter governs the case until the yachts tack or draw clear as provided in Rule 29 (6).

2. It qualifies A's right to luff should she jibe after the overlap is established.

3. It entitles B to room at the mark as inside yacht.

II. RULE 30 (A) AND (B) GOVERNED

The words "proper course" may be found but twice in the Sailing Rules, *viz.*, in Rule 30 (C) and in Rule 29, Definitions (7). They apply only if and when overtaking-to-leeward conditions exist (*Alerte* v. *Freida,* N. A. Y. R. U., Appeal No. 2, December 12, 1932). They are used only to define a course to leeward of which a yacht overtaken to leeward may not bear away to hinder another passing to leeward.

In the British cases (*Nyria* v. *White Heather,* and *Su Su* v. *Endrick* heretofore cited) *only* the leading (overtaken) yacht jibed and then luffed. They are authority, therefore, only for the doctrine that if the overtaken-to-leeward yacht jibes and luffs after the overtaking yacht establishes an overlap, such alteration of course constitutes an illegal bearing away out of her proper course for the next mark in order to hinder the overtaking yacht passing to leeward; provided always that the overtaking yacht does not jibe voluntarily.

The proponents of viewpoint II admit that the two British cases are good yachting law and that if, after an overlap has been established to leeward, the overtaken yacht jibes and luffs to such an extent that the overtaking-to-leeward yacht in order to keep clear is herself forced to jibe, such a forced jibe should not abrogate Clause (C) of the overtaking rule which governed the case at the time the overlap first was established.

In the instant case, however, *B* deliberately, and on her own initiative, voluntarily jibed around Mark 2 and became, in fact, the weather yacht. It seems only fair that *A,* after jibing also, should have some means of defense from being blanketed and passed to windward. Her only defense is luffing. None of the four acts or conditions enumerated in Rule 29 (6) have occurred. Overtaking conditions still exist. The only clause of the overtaking rule applicable is Rule 30 (B).

The situation is one which does not seem to be covered by the Sailing Rules. There was a substantial and voluntary alteration of course by both yachts. To acquiesce in *B's* contentions, Numbers 2, 3, 4, 5, 7, and 8, might result in situations which not only would be contrary to the principles of fair sailing implied by Rule I, but might lead to much confusion in the actual sailing of yacht races. Therefore, when *B* voluntarily and, on her own initiative, deliberately jibed, the best interests of yacht racing as a whole will be better served by ruling that the yacht overtaken to leeward (*A*) became the yacht overtaken to windward, and the yacht overtaking to leeward (*B*) became the yacht overtaking to windward, with the rights and obligations of each yacht governed by Rule 30 (A) and (B) *after* the jibe by both yachts, instead of by Rule 30 (A) and (C) as theretofore.

They believe, however, that a sudden luff by *A,* simultaneously with or immediately after the jibe, and before *B* has an opportunity to trim sheets and square away on her new course would not be fair sailing. In other words, that Rule 30 (B) should not become applicable until both yachts are under proper control on their new course.

THE SAILING RULES

III. A NEW SITUATION AROSE; OVERTAKING TERMINATED; RULE 30 (G) GOVERNED

Those who view the situation from viewpoint III agree with practically all the contentions enumerated in II with one exception, *viz.,* that after the jibe Rule 30 (B) governed the case. They claim that *both* yachts have made a substantial alteration of course with new wind conditions which clearly indicate that B is windward yacht. Common sense, therefore, dictates that Rule 30 (C) can no longer apply. Rule 30 (B) cannot apply because at the time of the jibe B is not clear astern of $A,$ and, therefore, the only rule that can apply is Rule 30 (G). It follows that A may luff in a manner to which B can easily respond, and, as windward yacht, B must keep clear.

Furthermore, it would be most unfair to hold that Rule 30 (B) became applicable. In the ordinary case of overtaking to windward, the overtaking yacht should be careful to sail a course sufficiently to windward of her adversary to be able to respond to a sharp luff. In the instant case, A need only allow B sufficient room to keep clear both of the mark and A. The election as to the distance between the yachts in rounding the mark rests with $A,$ *not* with B. It is conceivable, therefore, that after the jibe around the mark the yachts will be so close to each other that it would be physically impossible for B to keep clear of A in the event of a sharp luff by the latter.

Now let us consider A's protest of B for violation of:
1. Either Rule 30 (A) or 30 (G), and
2. The "ordinary customs of the sea," Rule I.

All hands seem to agree that if overtaking continued up to the time of contact, A's protest for violation of Rule 30 (A) and Rule I should be sustained. If overtaking had ended, then B violated Rule 30 (G) and Rule I.

THE SAILING RULES

Rule 30 (A), the first written, basic rule of yacht racing, reads as follows: "A yacht overtaking another shall keep out of the way of the overtaken yacht."

This sentence is terse and clear. As is the case with each of the other clauses of Rule 30, Clause (K) only excepted, it is mandatory upon the non-right-of-way yacht to keep clear. The fact that the right-of-way yacht herself violates another clause or rule will not excuse the yacht which "must" or "shall" keep out of the way of the other. It is a clear example of the old adage "two wrongs do not make a right." Only if the right-of-way yacht violates Clause (K), making it difficult if not impossible for the other to keep clear, will the other be absolved from blame. When A luffed either gradually or sharply, and whether or not she had the right to luff, it was B's duty to "respond to the luff and protest if she thinks fit." B was at fault in that she did not continue her endeavor to keep clear.

The first but unwritten rule of yacht racing as well as its counterpart in the Rules of the Road at Sea is *Avoid a Collision.*

If we were asked to be so rash as to guess how a "Florida Case" protest would be decided on an appeal to the Executive Committee of the N. A. Y. R. U., we should reply as follows:

That the particular situation that arose in The Florida Case was not foreseen by the 1929 Conference and is not covered by any of the right-of-way rules; that "no rules can be devised capable of meeting every incident . . . of sailing"; that it is a situation in which the broad equity powers of Rule 1 should be availed of in order to avoid arriving at an illogical and absurd result; and that after the yachts had completed rounding Mark 2 and had straightened out on the reach for Mark 3, they were governed by Rule 30 (G)—Converging.

THE SAILING RULES

The last case to be discussed under Clause (C) is that of the *double-jibing* case of *Lurcher* v. *Kaga*.[17] This decision, while valuable as establishing an important precedent under Clause (C), is also a Ruling Case under Clause (K). We will, therefore, postpone its consideration until we come to that clause.

We may now summarize the important decisions governing the rights and obligations of a yacht being overtaken to leeward, as follows:

1. *Before* the overtaking yacht has established an overlap, the overtaken yacht may jibe *and* then luff.[18]

2. *After* the overtaking yacht has established an overlap, the overtaken yacht may jibe but may *not* luff,[19] because such luffing technically would constitute bearing away out of her proper course to hinder the yacht overtaking to leeward.[20]

3. To jibe *twice* in front of an overtaking yacht attempting to pass to leeward, even *before* an overlap has been established, is a violation of Clause (K).[21]

A complement to the foregoing three rules is:

4. If the overtaking yacht luffs before she has drawn clear ahead, and the overtaken yacht is obliged to alter course to avert a collision, the overtaking yacht will be disqualified on protest.[22]

In Diagram 20 we illustrate a situation in which, on a particular tack, overtaking conditions terminate, and when the yachts again come within range of risk of collision, they rank under Clause (G)—Converging.

A rounds the weather mark about two lengths ahead of

[17]*Lurcher* v. *Kaga.* Y. R. A., 1923, Case 7.
[18]*Widgeon* v. *Chittabob.* Y. R. A., 1931, Case 2.
[19]*Nyria* v. *White Heather.* Y. R. A., 1922, Case 6.
[20]*Su Su* v. *Endrick.* Y. R. A., 1908, page 153.
[21]*Lurcher* v. *Kaga.* Y. R. A., 1923, Case 7.
[22]*Thistle* v. *Felma.* Y. R. A., 1927, Case 2.

Diagram 20.

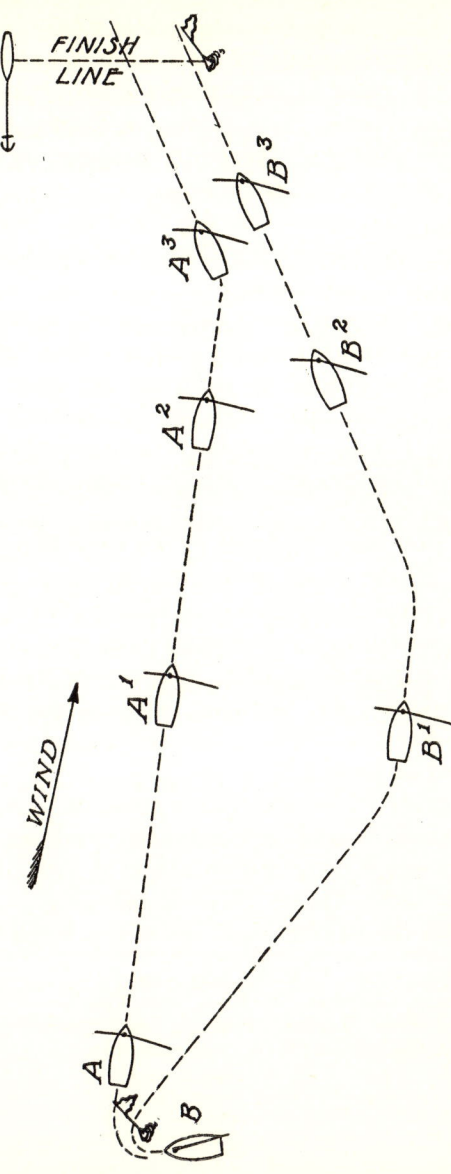

B, and both yachts set spinnakers to port for the run home; the wind being about 1½ points on the port quarter. After rounding the mark, B works to leeward, and at position A^1, B^1, has widened out beyond range of risk of collision. A no longer ranks as overtaken yacht. (Rule 29—Definitions—Section 6, Clause 2.) Therefore, no sailing rules apply.

For a considerable period of time their courses remain parallel, both yachts holding a course somewhat to leeward of the finish line. Approaching the finish, B commences to luff. This she has a perfect right to do. Due to sailing somewhat closer to the wind, she picks up speed, and at position A^2, B^2, is slightly ahead of A, and just laying the leeward end of the line. At this point the yachts again come within range of risk of collision. No longer does A rank as overtaken yacht, however, because when the yachts again came within the Zone, at position A^2, B^2, she was not clear ahead. The yachts now rank under Clause (G)—Converging—wind free on the same side. As windward yacht, A is obliged to keep clear (Rule 30 (G)). If B cannot safely reach across A's bow without a change of course by the latter, A must luff in order to keep clear.[23]

[23] *Prestige* v. *Carolina*. N. Y. Y. C., 1927 Report of Race Committee, page 7.

Chapter X

RULE 30
(CONTINUED)

MEETING, CROSSING AND CONVERGING

These clauses are framed particularly to avoid collision and the yacht which by rule has to keep out of the way must always do so (see Clause (K)).

Before the starting signal is given there are no restrictions upon the manœuvring of the yachts other than the provisions of Rules 30, 31 and 32, and the yacht holding right of way may alter course in any reasonable manner (but a luff so sudden that it cannot be easily responded to would not be considered reasonable).

As soon as the starting signal is given, yachts must sail a course consistent with the intention of crossing the line, but in all other respects the only restrictions on manœuvring are those provided in Rules 30, 31 and 32. After crossing the line the only restrictions upon manœuvring are those provided in Rules 30, 31 and 32.

The Sailing Rules, more especially the Meeting, Crossing and Converging clauses, were designed primarily to prevent collision between large yachts. When two large yachts are about to cross each other on opposite tacks, things happen quickly. They are approaching each other rapidly; especially in a breeze of wind. If a sizable sea is running, the danger of and damage from collision is greatly increased. In a strong breeze and lumpy sea the

THE SAILING RULES

Risk of Collision Zone is greater in extent. The greater the speed, the more a vessel will fore-reach when she tacks. A slight touch in heavy weather will cause incalculably more damage than in light air and smooth water. This is true in all classes, large or small.

It therefore behooves skippers to be doubly cautious when yachts are meeting, crossing or converging.

After the reader has finished this chapter he probably will agree that it may be "boiled down" to two additional basic rules:

>PORT-TACK YACHT KEEPS CLEAR.
>WINDWARD YACHT KEEPS CLEAR.

An examination of many protest decisions arising out of a breach of Rule 30—Right of Way—should convince the reader that the disqualified yacht was to blame because she:

1. Was overtaking yacht, or
2. Was on the port tack, or
3. Was windward yacht, or
4. Either tacked directly ahead of her opponent or altered her course when so close that her adversary could not keep out of her way.

Clause (D)

A yacht which has the wind free shall keep out of the way of one which is close-hauled.

How often we hear one skipper say to another, "I had right of way over you. I was *nearly* close-hauled while you were running 'broad off the wind.' You were more 'free' than I was."

He should have known better. There are no degrees of "free." For the purpose of the Definition (Rule 29, (1),

(b)), a yacht with sheets slightly started is sailing just as free as a yacht running dead before the wind. Even if her sheets are flattened in but she is not sailing "by the wind as close as she can lie with advantage in working to windward"—or, as the saying is, "full and by," she is sailing free.

There is one topic related to Clause (D) which it may be just as well to speak of at this point, although it might perhaps more properly be discussed under Clause (K).

Suppose A is beating up to the windward mark. A competitor has already rounded the mark and is running home. It is her duty under Clause (D) to keep clear of A. She steers a course to give A a clear path. Perhaps through ignorance or some other and less worthy motive, A suddenly and without warning tacks directly in front of her. A has violated Clause (K) and on protest should be disqualified.[1] It should be borne in mind, therefore, that A must never tack suddenly and without warning directly in front of a yacht sailing free. That A is close-hauled makes no difference. It is her duty not to alter her course in such a manner as to mislead or balk the other while in the act of keeping out of her way.

Clause (E)

A yacht which is close-hauled on the port tack shall keep out of the way of one which is close-hauled on the starboard tack.

This clause contains the second basic rule of yacht racing:

PORT-TACK YACHT KEEPS CLEAR

It might perhaps be called the first basic rule because the first recorded American starboard and port tack de-

[1] *Tramontana* v. *Triphon*. Y. R. A., 1904, page 132.

THE SAILING RULES

cision was rendered, without comment, in 1850. Both yachts were disqualified, *Breeze* being ruled out later on account of being found "to weigh more than she was entered at."[2]

The first British official appeal case on this rule involved two schooner yachts in a race held in 1876, about a year after the founding of the Y. R. A.

Olga, close-hauled on the port tack, thought she could cross *Egeria*, close-hauled on the starboard tack. *Egeria* claimed she was obliged to bear away and pass under *Olga's* stern to avoid a collision. At the hearing there was a direct conflict of testimony as to whether *Egeria* was in fact obliged to alter her helm to avoid a collision. *Olga* contended that had *Egeria* held her course there would have been no collision. On appeal to the Council, *Olga* was disqualified. The decision contained these words:

"Any infringement of Rule 19 (that was the number of the port and starboard tack rule in 1876) which may be brought under the notice of the Council will invariably lead to the disqualification of the vessel on the port tack in all cases where the slightest risk of collision may be satisfactorily proved."[3]

As bearing upon the question of where lies the burden of proof, the following quotation from an American decision is important: *"Flying Cloud* (starboard-tack yacht —the Author) contends that had she continued her course a collision would have occurred, and asserts that she went about to avoid this collision. This puts the burden of proof on *Vagrant* (port-tack yacht—the Author) to show that *Flying Cloud* would not have collided with *Vagrant* and that she tacked unnecessarily. . . . *Vagrant*, not hav-

[2]*Breeze* v. *Ultra*. N. Y. Y. C., 1850. *Decisions and Rulings of the Regatta and Race Committees,* 1849–1923, compiled and edited by Gherardi Davis, Esq., page 2.
[3]*Egeria* v. *Olga*. Y. R. A., 1876.

ing proved herself free of fault, that is, that she could have cleared *Flying Cloud,* is therefore disqualified."[4]

In 1931 the Council handed down another decision on Clause (E) which, by way of interpretation, further confirmed the "sacredness" and "inviolability" of the starboard tack close-hauled. The Council said: "If a yacht close-hauled on the port tack is about to meet a yacht on the starboard tack which, in the former's opinion is not sailing close-hauled as defined in Rule 29, (1), (a), the yacht on the port tack shall give way and protest if she so desires, but the burden of proof will lie with her."[5]

In 1901 occurred a case which might just as properly have been discussed in Chapter VII, under Rule 27—Start and Recall—as under Rule 30 (E).

The start was to windward. The wind was nearly at a right angle to the starting line. Just *before* gunfire *A*, close-hauled on the starboard tack, converged with *B*, close-hauled on the port tack. The yachts would have met just back of the middle point of a long starting line. *B* observed that if *A* held her course she would be over the line at gunfire whereas if *B* bore away under *A's* stern *A* in turn could then bear away slightly, "coast" along the proper side of the line until gunfire and then harden up and cross the line properly. *B* held her course. At gunfire *A* was slightly over the line; subsequently was recalled; started anew; and completed the course. Immediately *after* gunfire the yachts collided. *A* protested under Rule 30 (E). *B* protested under Rule 27. *B* contended that because *A* was prematurely over the line she was to be considered a returning yacht and was bound to keep clear of *B*.

"The Sailing Committee decided that *A* having prema-

[4]*Flying Cloud* v. *Vagrant.* N. Y. Y. C., 1924 Report of Race Committee, page 5.
[5]*British Boat Club, Alexandria, Egypt.* Y. R. A., 1931, Case 4.

THE SAILING RULES

turely crossed the starting line was in the wrong." The Council reversed the decision and disqualified B.[6]

This case is interesting for several reasons. In the first place, B should have been disqualified whether or not A was a "returning" yacht, because B committed the cardinal sin in yacht racing, that of deliberately running into another vessel and not making every effort to avoid a crash. Secondly, she violated the first paragraph of the Meeting, Crossing and Converging clauses of Rule 30, which reads: "These clauses are framed *particularly to avoid* collision and the yacht which by rule has to keep out of the way *must always do so.*" (Italics—the Author.) This introduction to the Converging Clauses (D) to (K) *forbids all idea of a collision.* A had shown no "obvious intention" to start anew. Her recall signal had not been displayed when the collision occurred. The yachts ranked under Rule 30 (E). It was B's duty to "keep out of the way." Lastly, B made a grave tactical blunder. There was plenty of room between B and the Committee boat to port. No yacht overtaken by her to leeward was to windward. She should have tacked to starboard under A's lee bow and then have luffed A across the starting line prematurely.

Now let us examine the case of *Rainbow* v. *Yankee,* which had to do with an episode that took place just prior to the start of the race for the Astor Cups off Newport, R. I., on August 16, 1934.

The Committee found the facts at the time of the alleged foul to be as follows: "The wind was ESE, 11 knots; first leg of course was SE x E¼E; starting line was at right angles to the wind about 2200 feet long; tidal current turned S x W at the Lightship at 12:49 P.M.; sea was moderate. Time of start was 12:15 P.M.

"About 45 seconds before the start, *Rainbow* and

[6]*Girleen* v. *Piccolo.* Y. R. A., 1902, page 110.

THE SAILING RULES

Yankee were to leeward of the starting line. *Rainbow* was approaching the line on the starboard tack, trimmed flat, and going to windward on a course to cross the line. *Yankee*, close-hauled on the port tack, but under the necessity of coming on the starboard tack in order to fetch the

Diagram 21.

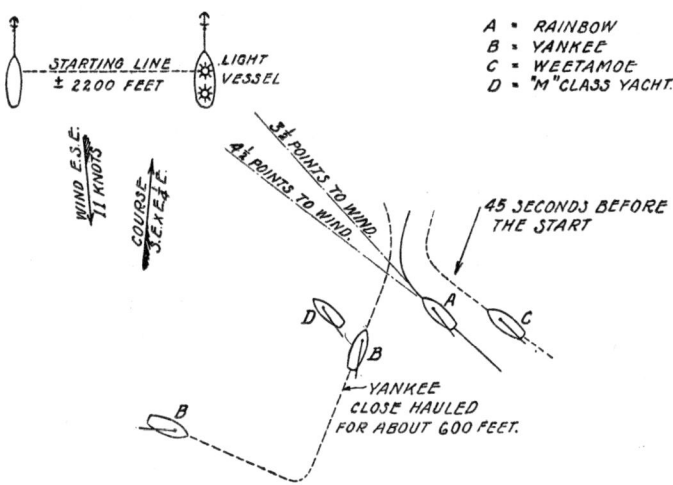

starting line, forced *Rainbow* to luff to avoid a collision."

Both yachts were travelling at a speed of 10 knots. "It seemed that *Yankee* and *Rainbow* would meet bow to bow. Instantly the helms on both yachts were put hard down and both luffed until they were sailing side by side a few feet apart almost in the wind's eye. It was a close call, but not as close a call as the *Weetamoe-Rainbow* situation. Only the promptest action on board *Weetamoe* prevented her from coming aboard us. Visualize her position. She was sailing along peacefully, a few feet astern of us and

THE SAILING RULES

just to windward of our wake, when suddenly she saw us make an unexpected luff, far sharper than the rules allow before the start. She could not bear off under our stern, her normal manœuvre, because she would have hit *Yankee*. She had no alternative but to luff like mad, three men grinding her wheel hard over."[7]

Rainbow protested *Yankee* for violation of Rule 30 (E). *Yankee* claimed that *Rainbow* was sailing about $4\frac{1}{2}$ to $5\frac{1}{2}$ points from the wind, whereas if truly close-hauled as prescribed in Rule 29 (1) (a) she should have been sailing not over $3\frac{1}{2}$ to 4 points from the wind, and therefore that *Rainbow* was free and violated Rule 30 (D). *Rainbow* contended "that in the quick and close work required before a start it is almost impossible to have in mind such considerations as whether your boat could be held a point or a half point higher on the wind, and whether the boats are tacking in 7 or 8 points under existing conditions. These are questions of trial and experiment for which there is then no time nor" (and ?) "to which no thought can then be given. If the sanctity of the starboard tack, before the start, is not to be preserved when two boats are approaching each other at right angles it is time we packed up our belongings and went home before we get sunk. *Yankee* could not tack sooner owing to the presence of an M boat and there was not room for her to tack between the M boat and *Rainbow*."

The Race Committee sustained *Rainbow's* protest saying: "The Committee is of the belief that under the conditions which existed at this time the starboard tack Rule 30 (E) applied and *Yankee* is therefore disqualified.

"In view of the importance of preventing collision between racing yachts which is the primary object of the Racing Rules, especially when many yachts are in close proximity in manœuvring, we think it desirable to state

[7] *On the Wind's Highway,* page 199.

THE SAILING RULES

our opinion that *when any reasonable doubt exists the starboard tack rule must be upheld.*"[8] (Italics—the Author.)

We believe this decision has established a precedent of the utmost importance to racing yachtsmen and also to Race Committees. No comment can surpass that of Mr. Vanderbilt who was at the wheel of *Rainbow*. He says: "It seems to me that it would be difficult to devise a more perfect interpretation of the existing rule."[9]

In the case next to be discussed we shall learn that there comes a time when even a yacht claiming to be close-hauled on the starboard tack may, by altering course, jeopardize her supposedly "sacred and inviolable" rights. Although this case might just as properly be discussed under Clause (K), it may add to our understanding of Clause (E) if we discuss it at this point.

Suppose A is close-hauled on the starboard tack and meets B close-hauled on the port tack, and slightly ahead. A has right of way. It appears doubtful which of the two will cross the other. The yachts approach nearer; B shows no indication of giving way. A's skipper begins to get nervous, although there is still plenty of time to avoid a collision. A luffs, then resumes her course. A's luff causes her to lose enough headway so that when she again bears away her opponent just succeeds in crossing her. A files a protest and is surprised and pained when her protest is "Not Sustained." The reason should be clear.

Although a yacht sailing higher than full and by, *i.e.*, in the wind, is not sailing free (Rule 29 (1) (b)), yet if when A luffed she misled B, she laid herself open to a charge of breaking Rule 30 (K).[10] She should have held to her

[8] *Rainbow* v. *Yankee*. N. Y. Y. C., 1934 Report of Race Committee, page 8.
[9] *On the Wind's Highway*, page 198.
[10] *Istalena* v. *Avatar*. Y. R. A. of L. I. S., 1932 Year Book, page 99.

course until she could no longer safely do so and avoid a collision. Then, and not until then, she should either have borne away under the stern of *Avatar* or have flung about onto the port tack, and filed a protest which surely would have been sustained.

Clause (F)

When both yachts have the wind free on different sides, and neither can claim the rights of a yacht being overtaken, the yacht which has the wind on the port side shall keep out of the way of the other.*

*A yacht is deemed to have the wind on the side opposite to that on which she is carrying her main-boom.

This clause requires no comment other than to call attention to the fact that it applies *only* if neither yacht can claim the rights of an overtaken yacht. To illustrate: If A is running before the wind on the port tack, and B on the starboard tack overtakes A and attempts to pass on $A's$ leeward (starboard) side, the fact that B is on the starboard tack will not relieve her, as overtaking yacht, from the responsibility of keeping clear of A until such time as B draws clear ahead of A and, in turn, herself *ranks* as overtaken yacht.

Endeavour v. Rainbow

Now let us discuss one of the most famous international protest cases of all time, that of *Endeavour* v. *Rainbow* in the Fourth Race for the America's Cup on September 22, 1934. The case is inserted at this point because it would have been decided under Rule 30 (F) had it been heard. It was not heard because Mr. Sopwith did not display code flag "B" "promptly" as required by Rule 45 of the Racing Rules of the New York Yacht Club, the Rules under which the match was being sailed. As a mat-

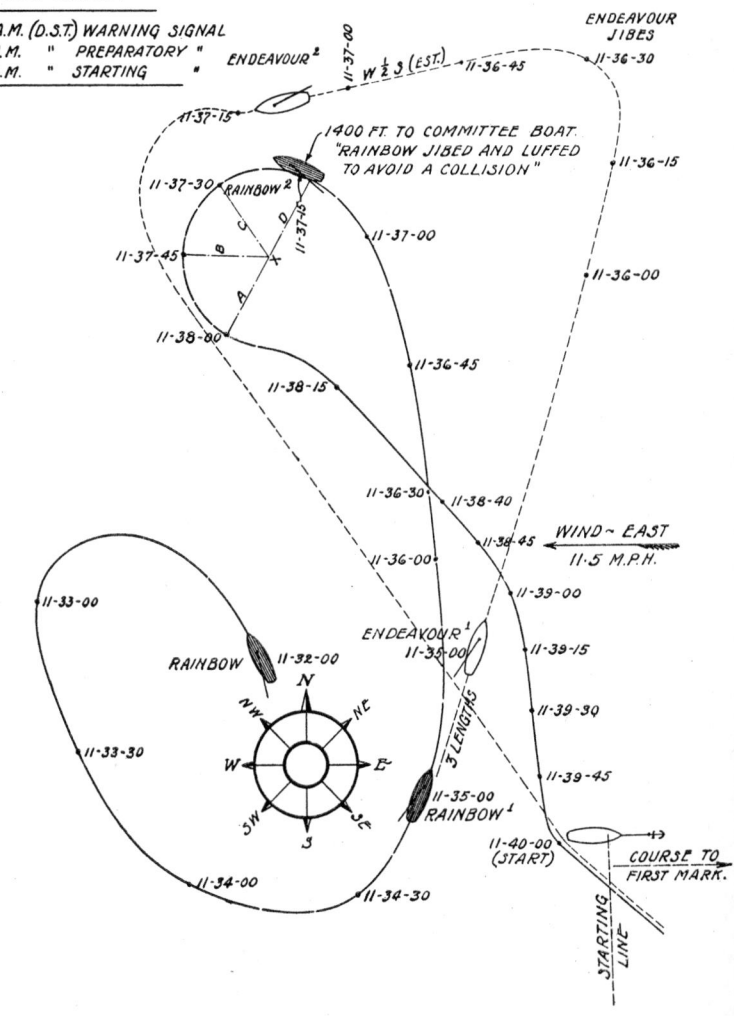

Diagram 22.

THE SAILING RULES

ter of fact Mr. Sopwith did not display his protest flag until about three hours after the episode in question.

Endeavour's protest consisted of two "counts." The first alleged an infraction of Rule 30 (A), (C) and (K), and related to a manœuvre which occurred shortly prior to the start. The second alleged a violation of Rule 30 (A) and (B), and concerned an episode that took place shortly after rounding the first mark. We shall discuss "count" one only. It read as follows:

"I protest against *Rainbow* during the race today under Rule 30, Clauses A, C (3rd paragraph) and K.

"After the preparatory signal both yachts were reaching away from the starting line on starboard tack, *Rainbow* being the overtaking yacht as defined by rule 29, clause 6.

"*Endeavour* jibed to come on the wind but before she could complete the manœuvre *Rainbow* bore away apparently with the intention of also jibing but held away before the wind baulking *Endeavour* and forcing her to bear away to avoid a collision."[11]

Now let us see what really took place.

"On September 22, just prior to the start of the Race in question, this Committee had observed what it considered to be a foul on the part of *Endeavour*. Full notes of the situation had been made as it developed, and set down in the expectation that there would be an immediate protest by *Rainbow*. The fundamental facts as we observed them were as follows:

"Immediately after the Preparatory Signal, at which time the yachts became amenable to the Racing Rules, *Endeavour* was sailing away from the line on the starboard tack on about a N.N.E. course. The wind was from the East, velocity 11.5 miles per hour. *Rainbow* at that time was sailing about the same course as *En-

[11] *Endeavour* v. *Rainbow*. N. Y. Y. C., 1934 Report of Race Committee, page 10.

deavour and following her some three lengths clear astern and to leeward of her wake. For the next minute neither yacht made any material alteration of course, but *Endeavour* increased her lead.

"At about 11:36 A.M. *Endeavour* bore away, jibed and changed her course to the westward, and *Rainbow* bore away to about North. At this moment they were approaching each other at right angles. We observed that *Endeavour* continued on a westerly course for the next minute or so, while *Rainbow* was slowly bearing away, and that while so steering they were approaching each other at an angle, both sailing free, *Rainbow* on the starboard and *Endeavour* on the port tack.

"Thereafter *Rainbow* jibed and luffed very smartly under *Endeavour's* bow, a necessary manœuvre, so it seemed to us, to avoid a collision. Your Committee were of opinion that neither yacht could be regarded as 'overtaking' as they approached one another, since 'no question of overtaking can arise unless the yachts are sailing approximately the same course' (Rule 29 (6)) and this condition had ceased when *Endeavour* had jibed and altered her course over 90 degrees.

"It seemed impossible to your Committee that the taking of evidence at a hearing could cause us to materially alter the views formed as a result of our own very clear observation and now substantiated by photographs of the incident.

"We are reliably informed that the international character of the race alone prevented *Rainbow* from protesting at the start, it having been agreed between Commodore Harold S. Vanderbilt and the America's Cup Committee, prior to the commencement of the races, that as a matter of policy protests should be avoided.

"Your Committee were unanimously of opinion that

THE SAILING RULES

in the event of a hearing held by them under Rule 47 they would have had to disqualify *Endeavour* for having failed to observe Racing Rule 30 (F).

"Your Committee believed that it would serve no useful purpose to hold a hearing which, in its opinion, could only have resulted in the disqualification of *Endeavour*, and furthermore that to institute a proceeding on its own initiative where in the language of the Rule it had 'reasonable grounds to believe' that the challenger had fouled the defender and not the defender the challenger, and the defender had not protested, would be regarded by many as indicating an advocacy of the *Rainbow* on the part of a Committee whose sole duty was to enforce impartially the agreed rules of the Race.

"Edmund Lang, Chairman,
E. Vail Stebbins, Secretary,
Clinton Mackenzie,
Race Committee."[12]

At position 2 "*Rainbow*, to avoid hitting *Endeavour*, jibed and luffed with wheel hard over, changing course 90°. I was steering *Rainbow* and called Jack Parkinson, a member of our afterguard, to my assistance to help me spin the wheel. *Endeavour*, after *Rainbow* jibed, bore away a little to avoid a collision. This was the bearing away referred to at the end of the first count of the protest. *Rainbow's* jibe and subsequent luff was a 'necessary manœuvre, so it seemed to us, to avoid a serious collision.' "[13]

Mr. Sopwith had been racing under the British Y. R. A. Rules for many years and the British Right-of-Way Rules were practically identical with those of the N. Y. Y. C. He must or should have known, therefore, that *Endeavour*,

[12]*Endeavour* v. *Rainbow*. N. Y. Y. C., 1934 Report of Race Committee, pages 13–15.
[13]*On the Wind's Highway*, page 205.

Diagram 23.

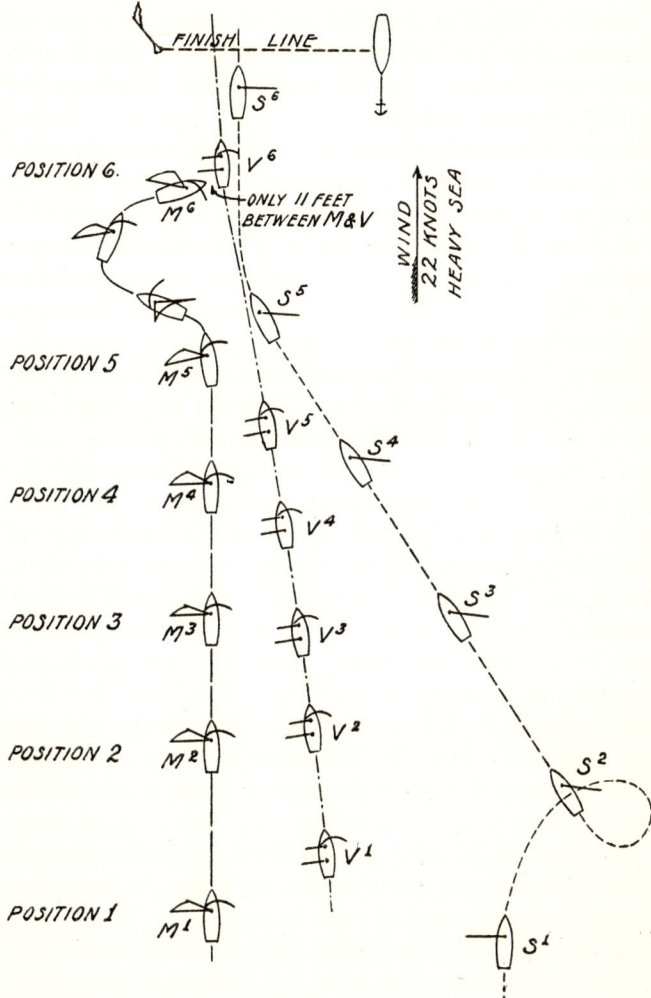

THE SAILING RULES

ranking as overtaken yacht at position 1, could not "at any time jibe and then have the right to an unimpeded course back to the starting line."[14]

We have been questioned so many times in regard to the photograph reproduced on the jacket of this treatise that we now present a diagram to show just what occurred that day, August 4, 1930.

In the photograph on the jacket the yacht in the foreground with spinnaker set to starboard is the schooner *Venturer*. Strange as it may seem she was not involved in the foul in any way. The yacht whose topmast is seen crashing is *Marilee* one of the N. Y. Y. C. 40-foot class, as was *Shawara*.

We quote from the report of the Race Committee: "The velocity of the wind was 22 knots and there was a heavy sea prevailing. On the run from Newport to Mattapoisett, *Marilee* was approaching the finish line off Nye Ledge (only a few hundred yards away) dead before the wind, with her boom to port. *Shawara* was approaching the same finish line with her boom to starboard with the wind over her port quarter, a short distance ahead of and converging with *Marilee*. There were at least five yachts in close proximity at the time as proven by the fact that *Shawara* and three other yachts crossed the finish line within fourteen seconds of each other.

"We find that *Shawara* with the wind on the port side approached so close to *Marilee* with the wind on the starboard side that *Marilee,* in order to avoid the imminent danger of collision, was forced to bear away and in doing so jibed and goose-winged; and the Committee therefore disqualifies *Shawara* for violation of Rule 30 (F)."[15]

[14]*Rainbow* v. *Yankee*. N. Y. Y. C., 1936 Report of Race Committee, page 7; Committee on Racing Appeals, Jan. 22, 1937.
[15]*Marilee* v. *Shawara*. N. Y. Y. C., 1930 Report of Race Committee, page 6.

THE SAILING RULES

At position 5 *Marilee* (*M*), right of way yacht, bore away. She jibed accidentally with everything standing. Her boom went over to starboard but her gaff did not, so that she "goose-winged." Immediately thereafter her boom went back to port, her topmast crashing between the two jibes. It was at that instant that Edwin Levick snapped the now famous photograph. Mr. E. I. Cudahy, *Marilee's* owner, was knocked overboard and badly injured. He was rescued by the crew of another yacht. Note in the reproduction of the official diagram that at position 6 *Venturer* cleared *Marilee*, then out of control, by only eleven feet.

Clause (G)

When both yachts have the wind free on the same side, and neither can claim the rights of a yacht being overtaken, the yacht to windward shall keep out of the way of the yacht to leeward.

This clause contains what is generally called the third "basic rule" of yacht racing:

WINDWARD YACHT KEEPS CLEAR

Formerly it read thus:

"When both have the wind free on the same side, the yacht to windward shall keep out of the way of the yacht to leeward."

There was nothing said as to what, if any, change of respective rights and obligations might arise if overtaking conditions existed. This ambiguity has been clarified by the wording of the present rule. It matters not on what tack either yacht may be; the overtaking yacht must keep clear of the overtaken yacht.

It would seem that under Clause (G) "luffing a yacht

THE SAILING RULES

head to wind would be ground for disqualification for trying to cause a foul."[16]

Clause (H)

When two yachts, both close-hauled on the same tack, are converging by reason of the leeward yacht holding a better wind, and neither can claim the rights of a yacht being overtaken, then the yacht to windward shall keep out of the way.

This clause was adopted by the British Y. R. A. verbatim from the rules of the New York Yacht Club. Credit for the rule, however, should be given to Mr. William Avery Cary, one of the "grand old yachtsmen" in this vicinity and a famous racing skipper in the 1870's and 1880's. Mr. Cary was elected Secretary of the Hull Yacht Club on January 14, 1888. He served in that capacity until that Club was absorbed by the Boston Yacht Club in December, 1898, and continued as Secretary of the latter club until January 25, 1905, a continuous service of seventeen years. When the first edition of this treatise was published in July, 1933, Mr. Cary, although in his eighty-fifth year, was still actively engaged in business and as much interested in yachting as when he was in "active service." It was from his own lips that we obtained the information concerning the origin of the present rule.

The Year Books of the Boston Yacht Club show that in 1900 that Club's rule read:

"CONVERGING CLOSE-HAULED

"(13) When two yachts, both close-hauled on the same tack, are converging by reason of the leeward yacht holding a better wind, and neither can claim the right of a yacht being overtaken, then the yacht to leeward shall keep clear."

[16]B. Heckstall-Smith. *Yacht Racing, A Text Book on the Sport*, 2nd Ed., 1933, page 79.

THE SAILING RULES

The following year it read:

"(13) When two yachts, both close-hauled on the same tack, are converging by reason of the leeward yacht holding a better wind, and neither can claim the right of a yacht being overtaken, then the yacht to windward shall keep clear."

Mr. Cary, from experience, realized the injustice of the rule as formerly worded, and during his term of office as Secretary of the Boston Yacht Club corresponded with Mr. J. V. S. Oddie, Secretary of the New York Yacht Club from 1889 to 1902, concerning the advisability of a change in wording.

Although Mr. Oddie was in hearty accord, the Year Books of the N. Y. Y. C. show that not until 1906 was the change adopted by that Club. That same year it was adopted by the Eastern Yacht Club of Marblehead, Massachusetts. It may be found in the 1906 Year Books of both Clubs—Rule XIII—Right of Way—Section 4.

Clauses (A), (D), (E), (F), and (G), as worded prior to the November, 1929, conference at London, were taken from the Rules of the Road at Sea. The Overtaking provision in (F) and (G) was added at that time.

The Rules of the Road at Sea make no mention of the respective rights and obligations of two vessels converging close-hauled on the same tack. We have been unable to find out how Clause (H), as worded formerly, happened to be included in the Sailing Rules. Certain it is that in its earlier form it was directly contrary to the maxim "Windward Yacht Keeps Clear."

In its present form it is a useful, clear and practical explanatory clause, and follows to a logical conclusion the idea common to all the Right of Way clauses, that the windward yacht shall keep clear in every instance except when she is being overtaken to leeward.

THE SAILING RULES

Diagram 24.

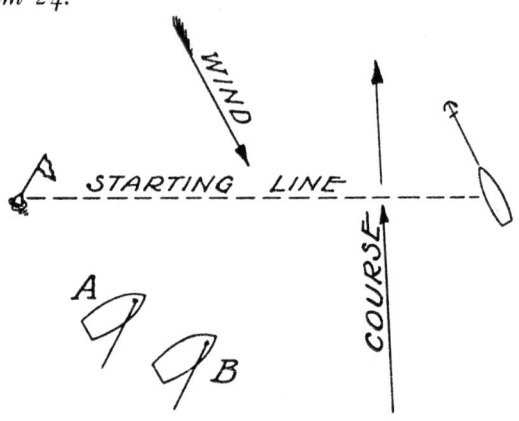

Before the start, no question of proper course can arise and *B,* leeward yacht and holding right of way, may alter course in any reasonable manner. If, during the preliminary manœuvres, *A* became overtaking yacht, she would have to keep clear under Clause (A), and *B* would have the right to luff gradually. (Second paragraph of Meeting, Crossing and Converging). If, prior to the start, neither was overtaking, and they were sailing free, *A* would have to keep clear under Clause (G). Again, if they were close-hauled and converged, *A* would have to keep clear under Clause (H). In fact in any case before the start, unless *B* was overtaking yacht, *B* could sail where she pleased.

Chapters IX and X—Rule 30—Right of Way—Clauses (A) to (H) inclusive, now may be summarized as follows:

1. Overtaking yacht keeps clear.
2. Port-Tack yacht keeps clear.
3. Windward yacht keeps clear.

Chapter XI

RULE 30
(CONTINUED)

ALTERING COURSE

Clause (I)

A yacht may not tack so as to involve probability of collision with another yacht unless she can gather proper way on her new tack before a collision would occur; nor so as to involve probability of collision with another yacht which, owing to her position, cannot keep out of the way. A yacht which tacks so close in front of another as to cause the latter to alter course to avoid a collision before the former has gathered proper way must be disqualified.

At the International Yacht Racing Union Conference in London on October 16–18, 1933, the words "proper way" were substituted for the words "full way" in the two instances in Rule 30 (I) in which the latter words were used.

American yachtsmen felt that although the new phrase was an improvement over its predecessor it still was far from satisfactory. For the sake of uniformity, however, the amendment was adopted by the North American Yacht Racing Union at its Annual General Meeting on November 17, 1933, and by the New York Yacht Club at its Annual Meeting on December 20 following.

At the Annual General Meeting of the N. A. Y. R. U. on November 17, at which we were present, there was a full discussion of Rule 30 (I) as amended. In order to clarify the new phrase as much as possible a resolution was adopted, not as an official interpretation of the phrase by

THE SAILING RULES

the Executive Committee—because that Committee may make an interpretation of a racing rule only upon a formal appeal to the Union from a decision of a Race Committee of a club or the Executive Committee of one of its member Y. R. A's—but as a suggestion that might be helpful to Race Committees in deciding protests occasioned by possible ambiguity in the phrase "proper way." The resolution was as follows:

"Resolved, that it is the sense of this meeting that where the words 'proper way' occur in Rule 30 (I), they should be interpreted as meaning *'filled away, gathered way on her new course and is under full control.'* "

It seemed clear from the discussion that the words "filled away" meant that at least all working sails then in use had filled and had been sheeted home. Query: Is a large genoa jib a working sail?

It must not be forgotten that although the official text of the I. Y. R. U. Rules is the English text, yet the English text must be translated into Danish, Dutch, French, German, Italian, Spanish and perhaps other languages. To find an English phrase that conveyed what practical English and American racing yachtsmen believed to be the intended meaning of the phrase was no small task. To find an English phrase that could be translated into each of many foreign languages with equally satisfactory results probably was an impossibility. For lack of a better term the Conference adopted the neutral and exceedingly indefinite phrase "proper way."

Our British cousins like to do everything "properly," just as the Germans desire (or at least formerly desired) to do all things "according to plan." It transpires that when translated literally into English the French and also the Spanish translations use words which mean "safe" or "settled."

THE SAILING RULES

The English idea of the meaning of the former term "full way" appeared to be that a yacht only had to have her sails trimmed and hard full, and have way on her new tack. In other words a yacht which had settled down on her new tack with all sheets trimmed, and under full control was considered to have full way and full rights on her new course. In America we interpreted the term in pretty much the same fashion although we supposed that "full way" meant "full speed."

It is difficult, if not impossible, accurately and in terms of distance to define just what the words "gather proper way" mean because the time and distance a yacht requires to gather "proper way" depends not only upon varying conditions of wind and sea but also upon the size, type and manœuvrability of the yacht involved. Each case must be determined upon its own particular facts.

At a meeting of the Council of the Y. R. A. on October 20, 1911, a Sub-Committee of Seven was appointed to consider proposals for altering the Sailing Rules. At the Annual General Meeting on February 23, 1912, the recommendations of the Sub-Committee, consisting of a series of explanatory footnotes to the Definitions and Right of Way Rules, were adopted. The footnote to Rule 30 (I) read as follows: *"A yacht which tacks so close to another as not to be able to gather full way before a collision would occur must be disqualified."*

On May 10, 1933, the Council debated the suggested change of "full way" to "proper way." During the debate Sir Charles MacIver said that the Council had always interpreted the term "full way" as follows:

"A yacht must not tack so as to involve probability of collision with another yacht, and if a yacht made a tack so that she did involve any probability of collision, she would be liable to disqualification, and if there was any doubt about it, the onus was upon the yacht making the tack. That was the principle from which the Y. R. A. should not depart." The records of the meeting, Y. R. A., 1934, page 166, state that "The Council concurred."

Clause (I) covers three different situations and may be rephrased nearly verbatim, as follows:

A yacht may not tack so as to involve *probability* of collision with another yacht:

1. Unless she can gather *proper way* on her new tack before a collision would occur.

2. When the latter, *owing to her position*, cannot keep out of the way.

3. When such tack is made *so close in front of another* as to cause the latter to alter course to avoid a collision before the tacking yacht has gathered *proper way* on her new tack.

In a fair breeze a dinghy will gather proper way in ten to fifteen seconds. On the other hand the great Class "J" sloops *Enterprise, Yankee, Rainbow, Ranger,* and *Endeavour* I and II require a distance of about a quarter of a mile.

Now let us discuss the three subdivisions in their enumerated order.

I

GATHER PROPER WAY ON NEW TACK

When, after tacking and filling away, does a yacht acquire rights on her new course, and when, only after she has acquired "proper way," does she become entitled to such rights?

The Race Committee found that *A*, close-hauled on the port tack, crossed *B*, close-hauled on the starboard tack. After crossing *B*, *A* tacked to starboard and both yachts sailed approximately parallel courses. When *A* filled away

Diagram 25.

CURRENT: SLACK
SEA: ROUGH

NIKE = A
INDRA = B

NO OVERLAP AT POSITION 2.
ADMITTED OVERLAP AT POSITION 3.

RACE COMMITTEE DIAGRAM
INDRA VS NIKE.

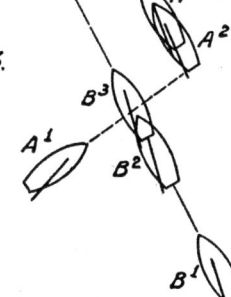

on the starboard tack she was about half a boat's length to windward of *B* and "clear ahead" of her, but as *B* was moving faster than *A*, *B* had established an overlap by the time *A* had gathered proper way. From this point both boats sailed the same or nearly the same course toward the next mark, neither yacht drawing clear ahead nor widening out abeam beyond risk of collision. As they approached the mark *A* realized that both boats had overstood and, while pulling away from *B*, eased sheets and bore off for the mark. *A's* boom hit *B's* forward deck and forestay.

B contended that since *A* had not "gathered proper way" on the starboard tack until *after B* had established an overlap, no question of overtaking could arise, and that *A*, as the windward yacht, must keep clear.

The Race Committee also found as facts that *A's* bearing away from the course upon which she originally placed herself when she tacked to starboard was not for the purpose of hindering *B* from passing to leeward, and that in the event that she ranked as overtaken yacht, *A's* course after easing sheets actually was her proper course to the next mark.

The Race Committee ruled that *B* was not an overtaking yacht; that the yachts were governed by Rule 30 (G) or (H), *not* Rule 30 (A) and (C), and disqualified *A* for not keeping clear.

On appeal the Executive Committee of the Union said:

"The sole question for our determination is whether *Nike,* having been 'clear ahead' of *Indra* when *Nike* filled away on the starboard tack, lost her rights as the overtaken boat because by the time she had 'gathered proper way' on that tack *Indra* had established an overlap and *Nike* was then no longer 'clear ahead.' Obviously, *Nike,* having been 'clear ahead' when she filled away on the starboard tack, was the overtaken boat at that instant (Rule

THE SAILING RULES

29, Section 6) and was, therefore, entitled to the rights of an overtaken boat unless, as *Indra* contends, she was entitled to no rights on her new tack until she had 'gathered proper way' thereon. It is *Indra's* contention that Section (1) of Rule 30, although limited by its language to specific instances, should be construed to cover every instance in which a boat comes on a new tack. In this conclusion we cannot agree. Section (1) of Rule 30 applies by its express terms to only three situations—(a) 'A yacht may not tack so as to involve probability of collision with another yacht unless she can gather proper way on her new tack before a collision would occur.' Obviously, this condition did not exist in the present case. (b) 'A yacht may not tack so as to involve probability of collision with another yacht which, owing to her position, cannot keep out of the way.' Obviously, this condition did not exist in the present case, nor is the question of 'proper way' involved in this provision. (c) 'A yacht which tacks so close in front of another as to cause the latter to alter course to avoid a collision before the former has gathered proper way must be disqualified.' While this last provision is obviously a limitation upon the overtaking rule in the specific situation mentioned therein, that situation did not exist in the present case.

"In our opinion Section (1) of Rule 30 clearly does not lay down the general principle that a yacht in all instances must have 'gathered proper way' on her new tack before becoming entitled to her rights thereon. In so far as 'proper way' is concerned, that Section merely provides that in two specific cases, and in two cases only, a yacht must have 'gathered proper way' in order to be entitled to her new rights. If it had been the intent of the Rule to cover every instance it is inconceivable that it should have been drawn to cover but two specific and limited instances.

THE SAILING RULES

We believe that the specific statement that in two limited situations a yacht must have 'gathered proper way' to be entitled to her rights on a new tack leads irresistibly to the conclusion that in all other situations that is not necessary. We hold then that a yacht becomes entitled to her rights on a new tack when she has filled away thereon, except only as those rights are specifically limited by Section (1) of Rule 30, and that in this case *Nike* was the overtaken yacht and *Indra* as the overtaking yacht, had to keep clear so long as *Nike* did not bear away below her proper course to prevent *Indra* passing her to leeward. The decision of the Race Committee is reversed and *Indra* is disqualified under Rule 30 (A)."[1]

A case in which the facts were practically identical was that of *Yankee* v. *Rainbow* in a race of the New York Yacht Club held on July 21, 1936. The Race Committee found that *Yankee*, (*A*), windward yacht, whose overall length was 125.47 feet, was 73 feet ahead of *Rainbow*, (*B*), at the time *Yankee* filled on the port tack. *Rainbow*, (*B*), luffed *Yankee*, (*A*), claiming that she had the right to do so as a converging leeward yacht. *Yankee*, (*A*), protested *Rainbow*, (*B*), for such luffs claiming that *Rainbow*, (*B*), as overtaking yacht, was required to keep clear under the provisions of Rule 30 (A) and (C). The Committee disqualified *Yankee*, (*A*), the windward yacht. On appeal to the Committee on Racing Appeals, that Committee reversed the decision of the Race Committee and disqualified *Rainbow*, (*B*).

A few months later the Committee on Racing Appeals reconsidered and reversed its previous decision "solely on the ground that this Committee did not correctly interpret a finding of fact made by the Race Committee in connection therewith, in that this Committee interpreted a finding

[1] *Indra* v. *Nike*. N. A. Y. R. U., Appeal No. 6, February 10, 1937.

THE SAILING RULES

of the Race Committee that *Yankee* after filling away on the port tack was 73 feet ahead of *Rainbow* as meaning that *Yankee* was 73 feet clear ahead of *Rainbow* at that time," whereas "the correct interpretation of that finding was that the bow of *Yankee* was at that time 73 feet ahead of the bow of *Rainbow* and that the yachts then were overlapped so that under that finding of the Race Committee, which is not subject to review by us, an overlap existed at the time *Yankee* filled away and both yachts commenced to sail the same or nearly the same course, this Committee reverses its decision heretofore made on *Yankee's* appeal and sustains the decision of the Race Committee."[2]

In *Indra* v. *Nike, Nike,* (*A*), filled on her new tack *before Indra,* (*B*), the leeward yacht, established an overlap. That fact cause Rule 30 (A) and (C) to apply. In *Yankee* v. *Rainbow, Yankee,* (*A*), windward yacht, did not fill away on her new tack until *after Rainbow,* (*B*), had established an overlap to leeward. That fact distinguished the case from *Indra* v. *Nike,* and caused Rule 30 (G) to be applicable. Under that rule the leeward yacht had the right to luff. Under Rule 30 (A) and (C) the leeward yacht not only had no right to luff but was obliged to keep clear of the windward yacht so long as the latter did not bear away below her proper course for the next mark.

Although the American cases *Indra* v. *Nike,* and *Yankee* v. *Rainbow* are the most recent and outstanding decisions bearing upon the interpretation of our so-called subdivision No. 1 on page 130, we believe that discussion of two leading British cases, illustrated in Diagrams 26 and 27 respectively, may be of interest.

[2]*Yankee* v. *Rainbow.* N. Y. Y. C., 1936 Report of Race Committee, page 4; Committee on Racing Appeals, January 22, 1937. For reconsideration and reversal of the appeal decision see *N. Y. Times,* Sunday, April 4, 1937.

THE SAILING RULES

Diagram 26.

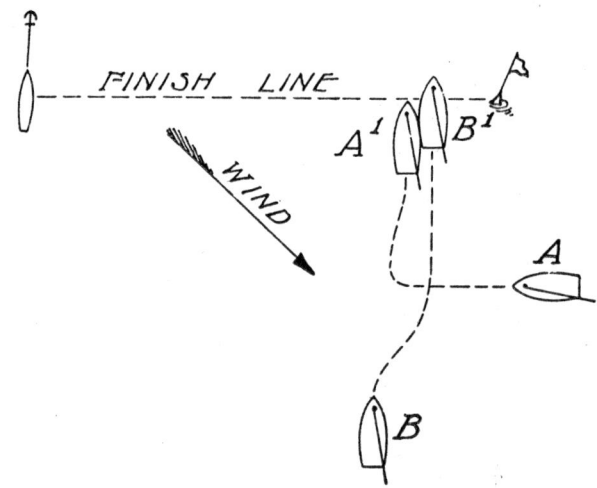

B, on the port tack, being unable to cross ahead of *A*, bears away under *A's* stern. Before *A* has crossed safely beyond *B's* path or "water"—the term commonly used—*A* tacks, and losing headway as she comes about finds, as is so often the case, that *B's* momentum has carried her into an overlap to leeward. As *A* gathers headway on her new tack she falls slightly to leeward and fouls *B*. On protest, *A* must be disqualified. She tacked in *B's* "water."[3]

A yacht cannot claim right of way under Rule 30 (E) unless and until the conditions specified in Clause (I) have been fulfilled; *i. e.*, until she not only has filled but has *gathered proper way* on her new tack. To illustrate:

[3] *No. 11 Dinghy* v. *No. 13 Dinghy.* Y. R. A., 1927, Case 11. *Beryl* v. *Zmoya.* Y. R. A., 1932, Case. 2. *Fintra* v. *Coral.* Y. R. A., 1932, Case 4.

THE SAILING RULES

Diagram 27.

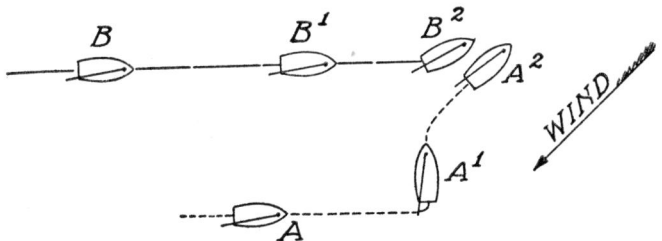

At position *A, B, A* was so close to *B* that although when *A* tacked to starboard she had filled, she could not gather proper way before she met *B*. On protest, *A* was disqualified under Rule 30 (I).[4]

The decision in each case hinges solely on the facts. It is merely a question of the size of the yachts and the distance they are apart. Had *A sufficient* room in which to tack? Was she sufficiently ahead and to leeward of *B*, so that when she tacked to starboard she not only could fill, but could gather proper way before she met *B?* *A* was protested for tacking when she had not sufficient room to tack—for tacking when she was too close. The burden of proof that she *did* have room to tack and gather proper way before she met *B* rested upon *A*, the yacht accused of violating the rule. The entire responsibility is upon the yacht which made the alteration of course complained of.

According to Diagram 27, when *A* tacked to starboard she was only about two boat-lengths ahead, and the same distance to leeward of *B*. Obviously she could not gather even reasonably proper way before she met *B*. On the facts the decision clearly was justified.

[4] *Mustang* v. *Frothblower.* Y. R. A., 1933, Case 8.

THE SAILING RULES

2

OWING TO HER POSITION CANNOT KEEP CLEAR

Diagram 28.

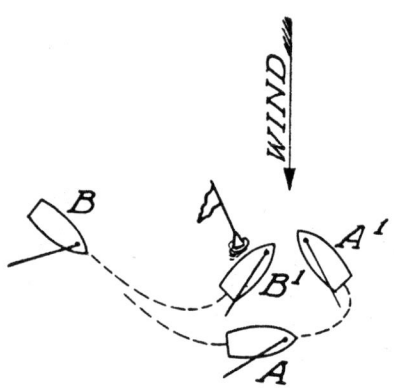

A, clear ahead of B, reaches the mark and instead of hauling on the wind and rounding it properly, continues on her course, and then makes such a wide and unseamanlike turn that B, clear astern, is able to head up and make a proper turn. At this point although A is well ahead, she may not tack because B^1, owing to her position between A^1 and the mark, can neither bear away under her stern, nor tack without fouling the mark.

This clause means that a yacht may not tack in front of another so as to involve probability of collision, when the other, owing to her position, cannot keep clear.[5]

[5]*Ibis* v. *Resolute.* N. Y. Y. C., 1927 Report of Race Committee, page 5.

THE SAILING RULES

3

TACKING TOO CLOSE IN FRONT OF ANOTHER YACHT

This situation frequently arises in a beat to windward. B, on the port tack, is about to meet A, on the starboard tack. B, although slightly ahead, realizes she cannot cross ahead of A. She believes, however, that she is just far enough ahead to enable her to tack to starboard on A's lee bow and secure what Dr. Manfred Curry terms the "Safe leeward position."

To be successful this manœuvre requires judgment and skill of the highest order. The speed of both yachts must be estimated to a hair. B must tack to leeward and slightly ahead of A, at the exact time and place, so that when she has gathered proper way on the starboard tack her bow will be at least abreast of that of A—a few feet ahead would be preferable—and at the same time B must be berthed sufficiently to leeward so that A is not obliged to alter course in the slightest degree. If B has successfully executed this manœuvre, it will be a matter of only a few moments when her backwind will cause A to drop astern into B's wake.

If, on the other hand, B miscalculates either speed or distance she will fail and her skipper will wish he had given his ship a rapt full and driven her under A's stern with accelerated speed. But worst of all will it be if B holds on just a wee bit too long. When she tacks, her forereaching takes her slightly more to windward than is anticipated. As she swings she loses headway and before she gathers proper way, A, who has been travelling at undiminished speed, is obliged to luff to avoid a collision. Result! Withdrawal or disqualification for B.

The moral is:

DON'T TACK TOO CLOSE

THE SAILING RULES

Clause (K)

When by any of the above clauses one yacht has to keep out of the way of another, the latter (subject to clause (B)) shall not alter course so as to prevent her doing so. Although the right-of-way yacht is not bound to hold her course, she must not so alter it as to mislead or baulk the other, in the act of keeping out of the way.

A yacht may be disqualified on a protest arising out of a breach of any of these clauses whether a collision result or not.

Clause (K) is in a sense the keystone which completes and locks together the arch composed of the ten Right of Way clauses. Many are prone to think of it merely as the clause which says that the yacht holding right of way must not mislead nor balk the other. In reality it is of far greater compass. Perhaps that is why it is the final clause of Rule 30.

If the reader will carefully analyze the other nine clauses, he cannot fail to be impressed by the fact that with the exception of Clause (B), the luffing clause, the other eight clauses prescribe what course the yacht *not* having right of way under each clause, shall pursue.

Clause (K) at its very beginning proclaims an admonition—nay, a command—to the yacht holding right of way under Clauses (A) to (I) inclusive. It says in effect: "When you have right of way—when the other fellow must keep clear of you—don't alter your course in such a manner as will prevent him from keeping clear of you. Above all, don't mislead nor frustrate him while he is in the act of keeping clear."

Now this does not mean that the yacht holding right of

THE SAILING RULES

way may not alter course at all. She *may* alter it *provided* so doing will not (1) prevent the non-right-of-way yacht from keeping clear, nor (2) mislead or baulk her while *in the act* of keeping clear.

The reader will note a slight but very important change in the typographical set-up of Clause (K) as printed in the Year Books of the N. A. Y. R. U., N. Y. Y. C., and Y. R. A. of L. I. S., beginning with 1933, when compared with their Year Books for 1932, 1931, and 1930.

From 1912 to and including 1929, Clause (K) in the British Y. R. A. Year Books was printed as follows:

"Altering Course.

"(k) When by any of the above clauses one yacht has to keep out of the way of another, the latter (subject to Clause (b)) shall not alter course so as to prevent her doing so."

At the bottom of the page on which Clause (k) was printed was the following footnote:

"Altering Course.

"Clause (k).

"Although the right-of-way yacht is not bound to hold her course, she must not so alter it as to mislead or baulk the other, in the act of keeping out of the way.

"Neglect of this clause may disqualify on protest whether a collision result or not."

As was stated in Chapter III, with comparatively few exceptions or changes the former British Sailing Rules, plus most of the 1912 and 1913 footnotes were adopted by the 1929 Conference, the basis upon which the new rules were agreed upon and enacted being the British rules in the 1929 British Y. R. A. Year Book.

The policy adopted by the Conference was to abolish footnotes, and where the principle of a footnote was agreed to by the Conference, to incorporate such footnote

THE SAILING RULES

as an integral part of the rule to which it theretofore had applied. Obviously, incorporating a footnote verbatim into a rule to which it had theretofore been but a footnote did not alter the meaning of the rule and footnote as they theretofore had existed.

In the case of the Y. R. A. footnote to Clause (k), it should be noted that while the first sentence of the footnote was inserted unchanged in the clause to which it had been appended, the second sentence, which up to that time had referred solely to Clause (k), was entirely rewritten and specifically made applicable to all clauses of Rule 30.

For some unexplained reason the first sentence of the footnote, although correctly worded, was printed not as a second sentence of Clause (K) but as a separate paragraph and extending entirely across the page in the same manner as the last paragraph of Rule 30. Evidently, whoever was in charge of the final printing and typographical set-up of the rules, and it must be remembered that the rules as finally printed never were in the hands of the American delegates, mistakenly assumed that both sentences of the footnote to Clause (k) stood upon the same footing, and failed to observe that the two sentences had been treated in an entirely different manner, the second sentence having been entirely rewritten and extended to cover not merely Clause (K) but all the preceding clauses of Rule 30, while the first sentence was not touched in any manner except to incorporate it as an integral part of Clause (K).

This erroneous typographical set-up in the American and also in the British 1930, 1931, and 1932 Year Books made it arguable on this side of the Atlantic at least, that the four-line, page-wide paragraph immediately following the narrower five-line paragraph comprising Clause (K) as then printed, stood upon the same footing as the last

THE SAILING RULES

paragraph of Rule 30 which applied specifically to all the lettered clauses of the rule. By Rule 29—Definitions—Section 2, a luff whether sudden or gradual is an alteration of course. Standing alone, the five-line sentence which apparently constituted Clause (K) in its entirety in 1930, 1931, and 1932, seemed to command the right-of-way yacht not to alter course so as to prevent the other from keeping clear. It was thought that the effect of this sentence might compel a yacht holding right of way after the start, to maintain the course she was sailing when first the yachts came within Range of Risk of Collision, and that a leeward yacht converging with or sailing parallel to another yacht within Range of Risk of Collision, and where no question of Overtaking was involved, might not have the right *gradually* to luff the weather yacht.

The American viewpoint was and is that such right is desirable, and should be permitted unless prohibited by the Rules.

There are two schools of construing the rules. The first would permit all manœuvres not specifically prohibited by the wording or by a fair and reasonable interpretation of the entire context. The second and narrower viewpoint would permit only such manœuvres as are specifically enumerated. Obviously, the second method of construction is too narrow in scope. If strictly adhered to and with Clause (K) consisting of the single sentence of five lines only, it seemed to follow that only an overtaken yacht (under the express provisions of Clause (B)) could luff a competitor.

The former American Right of Way rule corresponding to present Clause (K) was Section 5—Altering Course—and read as follows:

"When of two yachts one is obliged to keep clear, the other (subject to the provisions of Section 6, Clause (a)),

THE SAILING RULES

shall not so alter her course as to involve risk of fouling."

Section 6, Clause (a) was present Rule 30, Clause (B). The American interpretation of Section 5 was that it merely forbade the right-of-way yacht from making a sudden alteration of course which made it difficult, if not impossible for her opponent to keep out of her way.

Prior to the 1929 Conference, and as to yachtsmen racing under the jurisdiction of the British Y. R. A., the right of the leeward of two converging yachts, or of the leeward of two yachts sailing abreast, to luff her windward opponent was controlled by the British proper course footnote to their Meeting, Crossing, and Converging Clauses (d), (f), (g) and (h) of Rule 30. It followed that when two yachts were converging, or had commenced a tack abreast or overlapped, and on that tack neither had been clear astern of the other, the leeward yacht was not permitted to luff her opponent above the former's "own proper course for the next mark."[6] This footnote was abolished by the Conference.

In the spring of 1933 the question of whether or not a leeward, converging yacht had the right gradually to luff her weather opponent came to the attention of the N. A. Y. R. U., the N. Y. Y. C., and the Y. R. A. of L. I. S. For the first time since the 1929 London Conference the erroneous typographical set-up of Clause (K) was noticed. As a result the N. A. Y. R. U., N. Y. Y. C., and Y. R. A. of L. I. S. took cognizance of the situation and directed that in their respective 1933 Year Books Clause (K) should read and be typographically arranged as hereinbefore printed.

As now printed it cannot be said that the purpose of Clause (K) or its proper interpretation is to hold that it forbids a yacht which holds right of way under Clauses

[6]*Fortuna* v. *Circus Girl.* Y. R. A., 1924, Case 7.

(G) or (H) from altering her course by luffing in a reasonable manner which may be easily responded to by the yacht which is required by those clauses to keep clear. When Clause (K), in its 1933 form, is read as a whole, it is clear that under its provisions:

(1) The yacht having right of way is not bound to hold her course (this right is specifically granted by the second sentence of the rule), and

(2) The only restriction on her right to alter course is that she must not do so in such a manner as to "mislead or baulk the other, in the act of keeping out of the way."

Although a sudden luff into the weather yacht, by the leeward yacht holding right of way under Clauses (G) or (H), would be a contravention of the rule, Clause (K) does not forbid a luff by the leeward yacht which may easily be responded to. In short, as adopted by the London Conference and as now printed, Clause (K) was never intended to alter or override the rules laid down in the preceding clauses of Rule 30 but was intended solely to protect yacht *A*, which is required by the other clauses to keep clear of yacht *B*, from being misled or baulked in so doing by a sudden alteration of course by yacht *B*, which makes it difficult, if not impossible, for yacht *A* to keep clear.

"It is for the Race Committee, in each case, to determine whether the actions of any yacht, otherwise holding right of way, were such as to baulk or mislead a *reasonably experienced* competitor."[7] (Italics—the Author.)

The tenets of Clause (K) of Rule 30 and of Rule 1 are identical in spirit, and the skipper who contravenes either Rule should be disqualified for conduct unbecoming a seaman and a sportsman.

[7] *Star Dust II* v. *Queen Mary*. N. A. Y. R. U., Appeal No. 9, September 5, 1939.

THE SAILING RULES

In discussing Clause (D) it was stated that it is a violation of Clause (K) to tack suddenly, and without warning, in front of a yacht running free and clearly endeavoring to keep out of the way.[8]

Now let us discuss the celebrated case of *Lurcher* v. *Kaga,* involving jibing *twice* in front of an overtaking yacht attempting to pass to leeward.[9] This case was submitted to the Council on an appeal from the decision of the Sailing Committee of the Dar-Es-Salaam Yacht Club, Tanganyika Territory, East Africa.

Diagram 29.

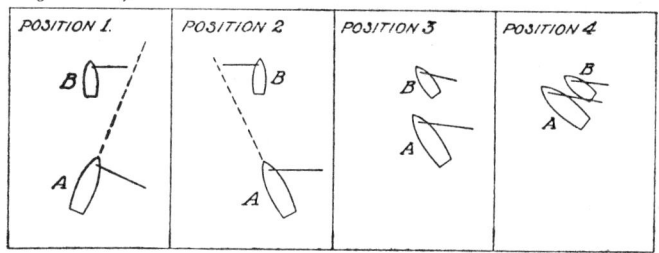

"Both yachts, on the port tack, are running before the wind. *A, Lurcher,* is rapidly overhauling *B, Kaga,* a much smaller yacht.

"*Position 1.* A attempts to make her overlap on *B's* lee (starboard) side.

"*Position 2.* B jibes over onto the starboard tack, and *A* alters her course to make her overlap on *B's* port side.

"*Position 3.* B jibes a second time, straightens her course, holds on for a few lengths, and then luffs *A*. At the time of *B's* second jibe, *A* was on *B's* port quarter, if not already overlapping.

"*Position 4.* A responds to *B's* luff, but being unable to haul in her main boom in time, that spar fouled *B*.

[8]*Tramontana* v. *Triphon.* Y. R. A., 1904, page 132.
[9]*Lurcher* v. *Kaga.* Y. R. A., 1923, Case 7.

THE SAILING RULES

"*B* protested *A* for violating Rule 30 (A) and *A*, in turn, protested *B* for violating Rule 30, Clauses (C) and (K)."

The Council disqualified *B* under Rule 30 (K). It is clear, therefore, that jibing *twice* in front of an overtaking yacht endeavoring to pass to leeward, even *before* an overlap is established, is a violation of Rule 30 (K).

Bear in mind that it is not necessary that a collision result from violation of any clause of Rule 30. Disqualification may be decreed "whether a collision result or not."

THE PRESENCE OF MARKS DOES NOT AFFECT RULE 30[10]

There have been many protests due to occurrences when rounding marks which, when analyzed, are found to involve not Rule 31 but some clause of Rule 30. In the main they resolve themselves into questions under Clause (E), port and starboard tack, and Clause (I)—Don't tack too close.

Take this case which occurred at night:

Diagram 30.

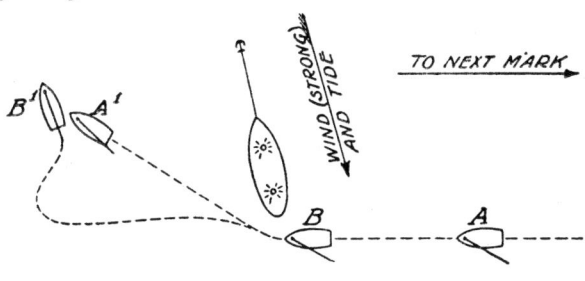

The wind was strong and a heavy sea was running. *B*,

[10] *Rosalind* v. *Lassie*. Y. R. A., 1933, Case 11.

THE SAILING RULES

Gracie, passed close under the stern of the Lightship about twenty seconds ahead of *A, L'Amoureuse.* *B* luffed slightly and then, in order to make sure of weathering the mark when she tacked, was given a good full and made a wide sweep. On reaching the stern of the Lightship, *A* hauled in her sheets until she was close-hauled on the starboard tack.

Immediately upon tacking, *B* saw *A* heading directly for her, still on the starboard tack. To avoid a collision, *B* put her helm hard down and endeavored to tack to starboard. As she had not yet gathered much way on the port tack she came up slowly and the yachts collided as shown in the diagram. *B* protested *A* under Rule 31 and contended that her (*B's*) own act of luffing after clearing the stern of the Lightship constituted an alteration of helm "for the purpose and in the act of" rounding the mark, and that she was justified in making as wide a sweep as she deemed necessary. The Sailing Committee decided that the collision "was caused by *B* staying about from starboard to port tack without taking care that she had room to weather *A,* and that she must be held primarily responsible."

On appeal to the Council, the decision of the Sailing Committee was upheld. The Council said:

"The collision between *B* and *A* was caused by *B* throwing around onto the port tack when she could not clear *A,* and so bringing about the collision.

"No blame whatever attaches to *A,* which was close-hauled on the starboard tack and held the right of way."[11]

This case was not a question of rounding marks, but solely one of port and starboard tack.

Tacking immediately upon rounding a mark is often a dangerous manœuvre.

[11] *Gracie* v. *L'Amoureuse.* Y. R. A., 1908, page 137.

For example:

Diagram 31.

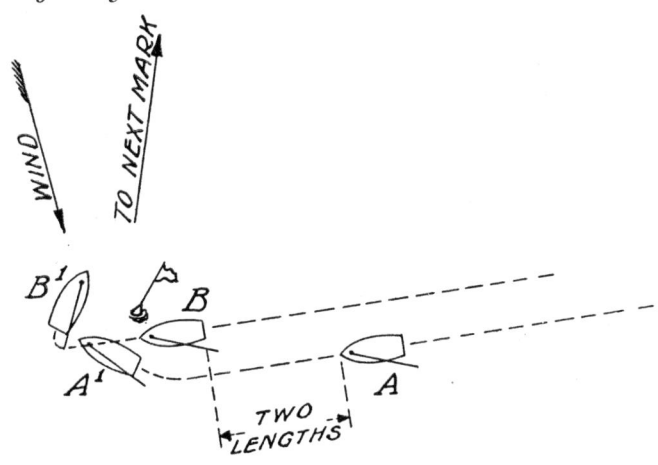

"B, on a broad reach, is leading A by about 2 lengths—36 feet—when she obtains an overlap on the mark. She luffs up to round the mark and when in a position to clear it, she comes about onto the port tack. A, following astern, takes the mark rather wide and also luffs but seeing B dead ahead bears away to save a serious collision. A's shrouds catch B's boom-end, thereby causing her to lose way and drift onto the mark, striking amidships."

The Sailing Committee disqualified A. On appeal, the Council reversed the decision and disqualified B.[12]

The reason for the Council's decision seems clear. If B, leading yacht, had merely altered her course to pass the mark, A would have continued to *rank* as overtaking yacht and would have been obliged to keep clear. But as soon as B *tacked* she broke Rule 30 (I) because she tacked so close in front of A that she (B) was unable to

[12] *Satanita Too* v. *Mallard II*. Y. R. A., 1932, Case 7.

THE SAILING RULES

gather sufficient way on her port tack to enable her to cross *A's* bow without interfering with the latter as *A* hauled on the wind.

The reader should note that in the second line of Rule 31 (quoted at the commencement of Chapter XII) occur the words "without tacking." These words often escape notice. They are very important because they mean that if the leading yacht tacks when rounding a mark, Rule 30, and *not* Rule 31, applies. Rule 31 applies only when yachts are passing marks or obstructions *without tacking and are overlapped*.

Take another example:

Diagram 32.

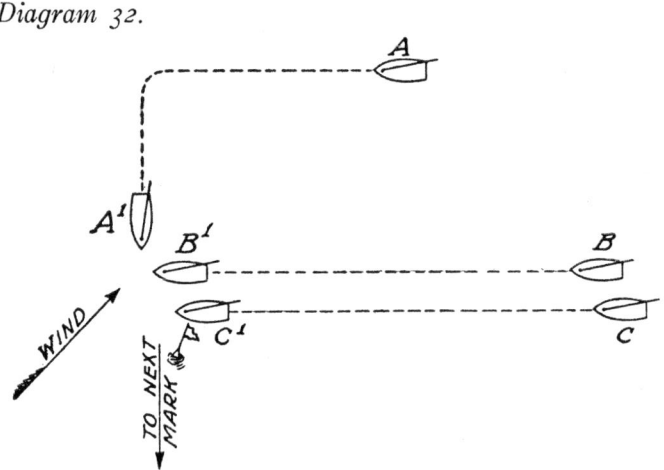

Here again no question of rounding a mark is involved. As is the case in Diagrams 30 and 31, it is merely one of port and starboard tack under Rule 30 (E).

Take away the mark and then ask, "What are the respective rights of the several yachts?" In nearly every

THE SAILING RULES

instance it will be found that it is merely a question of port and starboard tack. It is helpful to remember that the "Overtaking," "Port and Starboard," and "Don't tack too close" rules, are not altered by the presence of marks, and that in approaching a mark on the port tack when other yachts are approaching on the starboard tack, and also when he is intending to tack immediately upon rounding, and another yacht is following close astern, it behooves a skipper to "watch his step."

Now let us revert for a moment to the very first paragraph of Rule 30 reading as follows:

When one yacht is approaching another yacht, so as to involve risk of collision, one of them SHALL KEEP CLEAR *as follows.* (Caps.—the Author.)

Just what do the words "SHALL KEEP CLEAR" mean? The clearest interpretation that has come to our notice is by Captain R. T. Dixon, a well-known English racing helmsman and a member of the Council of the Y. R. A. Mr. Dixon says:

"In the absence of any special definition of 'keeping clear' I think this must be taken to mean that the yacht having to keep clear must not steer a course which causes another yacht to alter course to avoid a collision, or even which will cause the other undue anxiety as to the possibility of collision, but the yacht may otherwise sail any course she pleases, even to the extent of taking the other yacht's wind.

"In other words, she may not obstruct the other in the sense this word is used in the rules, but she may 'hinder' her. Clause (C) entirely alters this in the case of overtaking.

"If the overtaking yacht bears away and would, in consequence, have the right of way under Clause (H)," (were Rule 30 (C) not involved) "the other must not only not

THE SAILING RULES

bear away so that the overtaking yacht would have to alter course to avoid a collision, but she must not even hinder her passing to leeward.

"Incidentally, this gives the overtaking yacht some compensation for the serious disadvantage under which she suffers under Clause (B) if she tries to pass to windward; this seems only fair and reasonable.

"The word 'hinder' in Clause (C) to my mind . . . must be taken to include also any action which . . . will cause delay or inconvenience to another."[13]

[13] *Yachting World,* March 20, 1936, page 243.

Chapter XII

RULE 31

GIVING ROOM AT MARKS OR OBSTRUCTIONS TO SEA ROOM

If an overlap exists between two yachts when both of them, without tacking, are about to pass an obstruction to sea room, or a mark on the required side, the outside yacht must give room to the yacht in danger of fouling such mark or obstruction, whether she be the windward or leeward yacht, provided the yachts are overlapping on actually reaching such mark or obstruction. An overtaking yacht shall not be justified in attempting to establish an overlap, and thus force a passage between the leading yacht and the mark or obstruction, after the latter has reached it or altered her course for the purpose and in the act of rounding it. A craft under way (including another yacht racing), of which the yacht concerned has to keep out of the way, ranks as an obstruction for the purpose of this or the following rule.

Rule 31 makes exception to Rule 30 only so far as to require the outer yacht, although otherwise holding right of way under the latter rule, to allow the inner yacht room if her overlap has been made in proper time. In all other respects Rule 30 remains in full force.

As an example, a leading yacht may tack round a mark or obstruction only when she can do so and clear the yacht astern, just as she would be required to do if she made

THE SAILING RULES

her tack in open sea without any mark or obstruction being there.

In all protests under this rule the onus of proof that the overlap has been made in proper time rests with the yacht that previously had been astern.

Prior to the adoption by the British Y. R. A. of the twelve footnotes to Rule 30 in 1912, and of the footnote to Rule 31 in 1913, there were more protests in England based on rounding marks than under any other rule. We must ever bear in mind that Rule 30, Clauses (A), (B), and (C), Overtaking, Clause (E), Port and Starboard Tack, Clause (I), Don't Tack Too Close, and Clause (K), Keep Your Course, is *not* altered by the presence of marks.[1]

PURPOSE OF THE RULE

The purpose of the Rule is to protect the inner of two overlapping yachts from injury by collision with an obstruction to sea room or a mark of the course about to be passed on the required side without tacking, and which the inner yacht is in danger of fouling unless she can alter course.

The inner yacht is in a "jam." To clear the obstruction or mark she must alter course. This she cannot do without fouling the outer yacht which otherwise holding right of way under Rule 30, can prevent such alteration of course on the part of the inner yacht. In such a contingency, if the overlap has been made in proper time, the inner yacht is entitled to ample room to keep clear of both. The Rule is not intended nor is it necessary for it to apply to a situation adequately covered by Rule 30.

---

[1]*Gladys* v. *Mosquito,* Rule 30 (E); *Larkspur* v. *Rosalind,* Rule 30 (K). Y. R. A., 1914, Cases 1 and 2.

THE SAILING RULES

REQUISITES NECESSARY TO INVOKE THE RULE

The requisites generally recognized as necessary to invoke the rule are:
1. Overlap made in proper time;
2. Without tacking, both yachts about to pass
    (a) an obstruction to sea room, or
    (b) a mark on the required side; and
3. Danger of fouling such obstruction or mark on the part of the inner yacht unless she can alter course.

It is submitted that in view of the second paragraph of the rule there should be added a fourth requisite, viz.:

4. The outer yacht must hold *some* right of way over the inner yacht.

We believe that too little importance has been attached to the short but clearly worded SECOND paragraph of the rule.

Do not the words "although otherwise holding right of way under the latter rule," Rule 30, mean that the outer yacht must hold sufficient right of way over the inner yacht to prevent the latter from altering course to clear the obstruction or mark?

In other words, that the outer yacht must hold what we may term either positive or negative right of way over the inner yacht under Rule 30 but that, due to the fact that the inner yacht has made her overlap in proper time, the outer yacht is obliged temporarily to surrender or yield such right of way and permit the inner yacht to alter course to clear the obstruction or mark. The inner yacht cannot be "hemmed in" with no chance of escape or be forced to pass the mark on the wrong side while her opponent leaves it on the required side, any more than a yacht overtaking to windward can be luffed onto the shore by her right-of-

THE SAILING RULES

way competitor. If the outer yacht has not *some* right of way over the inner yacht, she has no rights which she can "allow" or "give" to the inner yacht. If the inner yacht holds full and complete right of way under Rule 30, it will be unnecessary for her to avail herself of the means of escape afforded by Rule 31.

Now what do we mean by the terms "positive" right of way and "negative" right of way?

If B overtakes A to windward, (Rule 30 (B)), B is practically without rights. A may luff head to wind if she pleases. She has practically complete freedom of action. B not only is overtaking but also is windward yacht. A has *positive* rights of way over B.

So, too, where A and B converge, (Rule 30 (G) or (H)), A being leeward yacht. In this situation A has a *positive* right of way over B in that she may luff in a manner to which B can easily respond. But B must respond and *must* keep clear. A may not luff B sharply, however. It may be said, therefore, that B has a *negative* right of way over A, viz.: the right *not* to be luffed sharply.

Likewise, if B overtakes A to leeward, A has the *positive* right not to be interfered with by B so long as A ranks as overtaken yacht, and yet B has a *negative* right of way over A, viz.: the right not to be forced to leeward of A's proper course for the next mark if the yachts are sailing free or to leeward of A's full and by course if the yachts are close-hauled.

DURATION OF PERIOD OF APPLICATION OF THE RULE

Rule 31 is one of the two "excepting" or "overriding" rules—Rule 32 is the other—to Right of Way Rule 30. During the time that the conditions requisite to cause Rule 31 to become operative are in existence and the inner yacht is in danger of fouling the obstruction or mark, Rule 30

THE SAILING RULES

is superseded and temporarily suspended by Rule 31 and the outer yacht "must give room" to the inner yacht to keep clear. When the obstruction or mark has been passed and the emergency has terminated, Rule 30 again comes into effect.[2]

DEFINITION OF OBSTRUCTION TO SEA ROOM

The modern definition of an obstruction to sea room may be inferred from the wording of the first part of the first sentence of Rule 32 which reads:

"If two yachts are standing close-hauled on the same tack toward the shore, or an obstruction to sea room which requires the leeward yacht to alter course to clear it, . . ."

"To alter course to clear it," are the important words. May we not, therefore, define an obstruction to sea room as follows:

Anything a yacht cannot clear without an alteration of course.

"The *size* of the object is not the index to whether the object is an obstruction. If it is really necessary to alter course to clear the object then it becomes an obstruction."[3]

"The use of this word (obstruction) in the Sailing Rules is confined to a physical obstruction which necessitates an alteration of course to avoid collision, and this seems to me the ordinary meaning of the word."[4]

Mr. Dixon continues:

"The word 'hinder' in Clause (C) of Rule 30 to my mind has a much wider meaning, and must be taken to include also any action which, in the case of yacht racing, when taken by one yacht will cause delay or inconvenience to another.

"For instance, a vessel at anchor is only an obstruction

[2] *Yachting World,* September 15, 1933, page 225.
[3] B. Heckstall-Smith. *Yachting World,* May 19, 1933, page 386.
[4] Capt. R. T. Dixon. *Yachting World,* March 20, 1936, page 243.

THE SAILING RULES

if she causes a yacht to alter course to avoid a collision. If the yacht can sail her course without alteration of helm the vessel does not count as an obstruction, although if the vessel is close to windward the yacht may be becalmed and lose all way. The vessel might very fairly be called a hindrance, but she could not be claimed as an obstruction."

Now although an object as small as a spar buoy may be a physical obstruction, is it such an obstruction to sea room within the meaning of Rule 31 as to oblige a right-of-way yacht to permit her overlapping opponent to pass on the same side of it as does the former? Of course, if the buoy marks a shoal, Rule 31 will apply as the inner yacht is entitled to pass on the channel side even though there may be deep water between the buoy and the shoal. "The contention of the yacht complained of that there was actually sufficient depth of water inside the buoy is not convincing, as the rules of safe navigation require the leaving of the buoy to port."[5] But suppose the overlapped yachts are approaching a government mid-channel buoy; that the yachts are governed by Rule 30 (G); that the buoy is dead in the path of the windward yacht; and that the leeward yacht will clear it without changing course in the slightest degree. There is clear water on both sides of the buoy and a momentary and very slight alteration of course by the windward yacht will permit her to clear it. The only case we have found that bears on this topic is *Arcadian* v. *Margitta*.

A and *B*, overlapped, were reaching broad on the starboard tack, and governed by Rule 30 (G). In their course lay a government mid-channel buoy about twelve feet in diameter. *B*, windward yacht, claimed the right to pass to leeward of it. She bore away to leeward and forced *A* to follow suit in order to avoid a collision. *A* protested

[5]*Flying Cloud* v. *Advance*. N. Y. Y. C., 1926 Report of Race Committe, page 8.

THE SAILING RULES

under Rule 30 (G). The Sailing Committee held that "under the circumstances the . . . buoy did not rank as an 'obstruction to sea room' in the meaning of Rule 31, and that B should have passed this buoy to windward or otherwise have kept clear of A. . . . The windward boat must show there was a real danger of fouling the obstruction. The obstruction in question was a buoy under twelve feet in diameter, and in the Committee's opinion B was in no danger of fouling this buoy until after she had illegally borne away and forced A to follow suit in order to try and avoid a collision. They read Rule 31 to mean that before the windward yacht can hail for room, she must be in such a position that without a decided alteration of course she cannot avoid fouling the obstruction. In this case it is considered that without any appreciable alteration of helm, B could have passed to windward of the buoy. B is disqualified under Rule 30, Clause G."

The Council of the Y. R. A., without comment, upheld the decision.[6]

The vital point decided by this case would seem to be that where an obstruction can be avoided by a very slight alteration of course danger of fouling is not a factor. In the instant case B never was in the slightest danger of fouling and could not claim right of way over A under Rule 31 and force her to leeward of the buoy. As the Committee said, it was only *after* she had illegally borne away that danger of fouling became a factor. While this is not an absolutely clear cut decision to the effect that unless an obstruction requires an appreciable alteration of course it is not an obstruction to sea room within the meaning of Rule 31, yet the wording of the third from the last sentence of the decision is significant.

[6] *Arcadian* v. *Margitta.* Y. R. A., 1920, Case 2.

THE SAILING RULES

SITUATIONS CONTEMPLATED BY THE RULE

Four situations would seem to be contemplated by the Rule:

1. A fixed obstruction such as a shore, shoal, wreck, vessel or structure at anchor or aground, pier, fish weir, traps and other similar objects;
2. Craft under way, including another yacht racing;
3. Marks of the course other than marks of the line of start or finish;
4. Marks of the starting line, (a) before, (b) after the making of the starting signal.

SITUATION NO. 1
FIXED OBSTRUCTIONS

The first part of the first sentence of paragraph one reads as follows:

"If an overlap exists between two yachts when both of them, without tacking, are about to pass an obstruction, . . ."

This would seem to imply that the obstruction must rank as such to both yachts simultaneously. The middle part of the sentence, however, speaks of *"the yacht"* in danger of fouling such . . . obstruction." (Italics—the Author.) The outer yacht is not hemmed in; she may alter course at will. Obviously, only the inner yacht can be "in danger of fouling" the obstruction. The wording of the first sentence of the rule clearly indicates, therefore, that only the inner yacht need be in danger of fouling the obstruction.

SITUATION NO. 2

CRAFT UNDER WAY, INCLUDING ANOTHER YACHT RACING

The third and last sentence of paragraph one states that a craft under way, including another yacht racing, of which

THE SAILING RULES

the yacht concerned has to keep out of the way, ranks as an obstruction for the purpose of Rules 31 and 32.

Do the words "the yacht concerned" apply to *both* the overlapped yachts or do they apply *only* to the inner yacht?

At first glance it would seem that the rule intended that the "other yacht racing" should hold what we have termed positive rights of way over *both* the inner and also the outer yacht. It is significant, however, that in one place only does the word "both" occur, whereas in at least two instances the rule speaks of "the yacht." Furthermore, when one considers the purpose of Rule 31, it seems clear that the words "the yacht concerned" in the last sentence of the first paragraph can refer only to the inner yacht. The inner yacht is in danger of fouling the "other yacht racing" unless the outer yacht, the yacht which by the particular clause of Rule 30 then applicable has sufficient right of way over the inner yacht to prevent the latter from altering course, herself alters course and "gives" the inner yacht "room" to keep clear not only of the "other yacht racing" but also of the outer yacht herself. The outer yacht may alter course at will. Only the inner yacht is in danger of fouling the other yacht racing unless she is permitted to alter course. This particular situation will be discussed at length when we take up the case of *Moana* v. *Victory*. We shall learn from that case that the words "the yacht concerned" in the third and last sentence of the first paragraph of the rule refer only to the inner yacht, the yacht in danger of fouling the "other yacht racing."

The vital point to be remembered is that when her overlap has been made in proper time to entitle her to overlapping rights the inner yacht, whether she be windward or leeward, right-of-way or non-right-of-way yacht under Rule 30, may not be hemmed in with no means of escape.

THE SAILING RULES

It would seem, therefore, that we *mentally* could read into the first paragraph of Rule 31 the following:

1. First sentence: After the words "an obstruction to sea room," the thought "to the inner yacht";
2. Third sentence: After the words "of which the yacht concerned," either the thought "the inner yacht," or, if one prefers, the thought "the yacht in danger of fouling the other yacht racing."

SITUATION NO. 3

MARKS OF THE COURSE OTHER THAN MARKS OF THE
LINES OF START OR FINISH

Now let us leave the first sentence for a moment and analyze the second sentence of the rule. It relates *exclusively to Overtaking*. The entire sentence prescribes what the overtaking yacht must *not* do. It specifies two conditions or rather situations, after which she may neither establish nor *even attempt* to establish an overlap. The first is *after* the leading yacht *"has reached"* the mark or obstruction. The second is *after* the leading yacht *"has altered her course for the purpose and"* is *"in the act of rounding it";* in other words, when the alteration of helm is part of the act of rounding.[7]

The often overlooked second paragraph of the rule establishes as a condition precedent to the acquisition of inside rights of way by an overtaking yacht, that *"her overlap has been made in proper time."* In other words, the inside overlap must have been established *before* either of the aforesaid situations came into being.

There is nothing illegal in "forcing a passage" or "cutting in" at turning marks or even in attempting such tac-

[7] B. Heckstall-Smith and E. Du Boulay. *The Complete Yachtsman*, 1928 Ed., page 185.

THE SAILING RULES

tics, unless (1) a collision results or (2) in the reasonable belief that there *will* be a collision unless she alters course, the leading yacht *does* in fact alter course. Danger of collision always should be avoided. A good motto for the stern yacht to remember might be:

"If in doubt, the overtaking boat is 'out.'"

OVERLAP MADE IN PROPER TIME

Has the overtaking overlap been made in proper time? This is probably one of the most difficult questions to answer in yacht racing.

"It is not possible to define the exact moment when—

1. A mark or obstruction is reached, or
2. The yacht's course is altered for the purpose and in the act of rounding it,

... so as to satisfy seamen sailing yachts of all sizes on the sea, in all weathers, and taking marks, in strong tides, heavy seas, of all sizes like lightships or buoys."[8]

As the leading yacht nears the mark or obstruction she has the right to determine *in what manner* she will pass or round it. She holds right of way and has the right to alter course either away from or toward the mark in order to pass or round it in the manner and at the distance which will benefit her the most. So long as she passes or rounds the mark or obstruction in a reasonably seamanlike manner and without tacking, she has the right *not* to be interfered with by the yacht clear astern.

When a yacht alters her course to jibe around a mark she loses headway. In such a situation the yacht astern may not take advantage of the lessened way of the leading yacht to secure or even to attempt to secure an overlap and claim buoy room under Rule 31. The overtaking

[8] B. Heckstall-Smith. *Yacht Racing,* 2d Ed., 1933, page 123.

yacht "must *not* hang on to her stuff longer than the leading vessel to try to get an overlap. That is a hard saying, but it is rotten seamanship to play the trick of hanging on to gear to try to get an overlap. You must treat your opponent with respect; he is as good a seaman as yourself, and when he gets his stuff inboard you must do the same at the same place. . . . Sailing Committees should show not the slightest sympathy with the man who cuts in at a mark or is suspected of being guilty of 'forcing a passage.' "[9]

The larger the yacht, the longer the time required to take in light sails and/or trim sheets. Varying conditions of wind and sea, tidal conditions, the size, type and manœuvrability of the yachts all point to the inescapable conclusion that no hard and fast rule as to time and/or distance can be established in determining whether an overlap has been made in proper time. Each case must be decided upon its own particular facts in the light of the general principles discussed in this chapter.

In doubtful cases the stern yacht must remember that Rule 30 (A), Overtaking, is staring her in the face, and that by the last paragraph of Rule 31 "the burden of proof that the overlap has been made in proper time rests with the yacht that previously had been astern."[10]

Let us revert for a moment to the former American rule corresponding to present Rule 31.

It was Rule XII—Right of Way—Section 8, and read as follows:

"*If an overlap exists between two yachts when both of them, without tacking, are about to pass a mark on a required side, then the outside yacht must give the inside yacht room to pass clear of the mark.*

"*A yacht shall not, however, be justified in attempting to establish an overlap and thus force a passage between*

[9] B. Heckstall-Smith. *Yacht Racing,* 2d Ed., 1933, page 124.
[10] *Saga* v. *Finetta.* Y. R A, 1938, Case 9.

another yacht and the mark after the latter yacht has altered her helm for the purpose of rounding."

Note the similarity in wording of the first paragraph of the former rule and the first sentence of the present rule. Also the similarity between the second paragraph of the former rule and the second sentence of the present rule.

The interpretation of the former rule by an American authority should be of assistance in determining the meaning of the present rule.

So far as we are aware the only American commentators on the former rule have been Messrs. H. de B. Parsons, Joseph M. Macdonough and Frederic O. Spedden, who for some years constituted the Regatta Committee of the New York Yacht Club. We have never heard any criticism of their comments on former Rule XII—Right of Way—Section 8.

This is what they said about the establishment of an overlap prior to rounding a mark:

"If an overlap exists before the outside yacht reaches the mark, that is before she has to alter her helm, in any manner, to clear or round the mark, then the outside yacht must give the inside yacht sufficient room for safety. In the same way the inside yacht cannot claim room unless she establishes the overlap before the outside yacht reaches the mark, that is *before* the latter is about to alter her helm for the purpose of clearing or rounding the mark. As the inside yacht knows (they mean 'as the stern yacht knows'—the Author), without being actually told, that the other is about to alter her course to round the mark, ignorance of the fact that this change of course will slacken speed, is no excuse for an inside yacht (they mean 'a stern yacht'—the Author) to rush up and claim room. The rule contemplates a **fair** establishment of an overlap, while sailing the same or nearly the same course on the same tack, at some reasonable distance *before* the mark is reached.

THE SAILING RULES

"The second paragraph forbids a yacht trying 'to force a passage' by establishing an overlap at the last instant, when the leading yacht is about to alter her course for the purpose of rounding or is about to pass a mark."[11]

The second paragraph of Rule 31 is identical in wording with the former British footnote to their former and present Rule 31.

"CUTTING IN" AT MARKS

We are indebted to the British Y. R. A. Year Books for very full records and clear diagrams of many interesting and instructive appeal cases on this topic. In America we are apt not to be strict enough in protecting the rights of the leading yacht when rounding marks. Her skipper should feel free to take plenty of room and not be apprehensive that the yacht just astern will "cut in" between him and the mark. The leading yacht should be protected in rounding the mark in a seamanlike manner.

For example: Suppose *A* is running before the wind on the starboard tack; the mark to be left to starboard; the next leg a beat to windward. A good seaman does not steer straight for the mark. On the contrary, as he gets fairly close he steers a course which, if projected in a straight line, will leave quite a bit of water between his starboard side and the mark. When nearly down to the mark he gradually hauls on the wind so that when his mid-ship section passes the leeward side of the mark he is close-hauled, giving the mark the least clearance consistent with safety. He knows the skipper of the yacht just clear astern is a fine seaman and that he will round the mark so as to squeeze out the last available inch of windward position. Surely the leading yacht should be protected in

[11]*Handbook on American Yacht Racing Rules*, 2d Ed., 1923, pages 96–97.

Diagram 33.

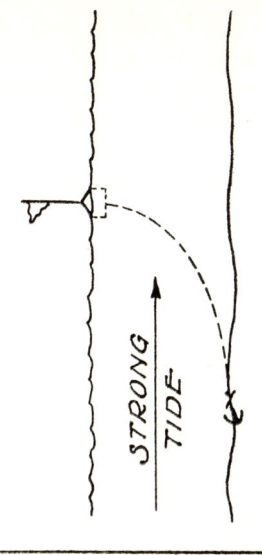

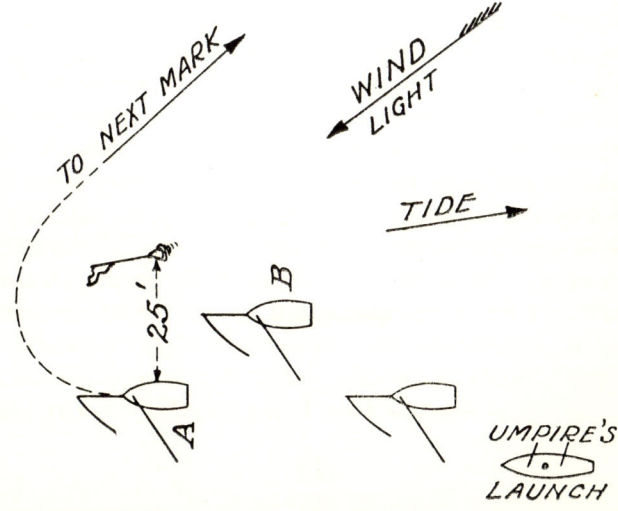

THE SAILING RULES

rounding the mark in the same manner as will her opponent.

"This is proper seamanship on *A's* part. . . . The only safe game for *B,* the boat behind, . . . is to play 'follow my leader' when the two vessels get near the mark. If she does not play it, but selects tactics of a 'cutting in' nature, she will be inviting her opponent to hoist a protest flag, and will thereby bring the onus of the case upon herself."[12]

Our British cousins are meticulous in protecting the rounding rights of the leading yacht. (Note Diagram 33.)

In this case the wind was very light and the yachts, fourteen feet overall with eight foot bowsprit, were "bucking" a strong tide which caused the mooring rode of the mark to make an acute angle with the surface of the water. (See Diagram.) To allow for the tide, *A* not only allowed about twenty-five feet between her starboard side and the mark, but continued on for about the same distance beyond the mark. *B,* seeing what she considered a "large opening," "cut in" between *A* and the mark. As *A* rounded up, the yachts collided. On protest, *B* was disqualified.[13]

In another case *B's* defence was that *A* "left an *absurd* amount of room in rounding the mark." The Race Committee found "that no overlap existed when *A* reached the mark; and that *B* assumed risk of collision." On appeal, the Council upheld the decision of the Race Committee, and disqualified *B*.[14]

The stern yacht should be doubly on her guard against "cutting in" when it is a case of jibing. It is easy for the stern yacht to force an overlap to leeward when the leading yacht begins to bear away to jibe around a mark. It

[12] B. Heckstall-Smith. *Yachting World,* January 15, 1937, page 58.
[13] *Harmony* v. *Sealark.* Y. R. A., 1930, Case 1.
[14] *Alouette* v. *Una.* Y. R. A., 1928, Case 6.

THE SAILING RULES

is a manœuvre which requires ample time and space if done properly. The speed of the leading yacht is reduced much more than in hauling on the wind around a mark, and while her way is deadened by hauling in her sheets and bearing away, the leading yacht is comparatively helpless.

Here is another excellent example under, and interpretation of Rule 31.

Diagram 34.

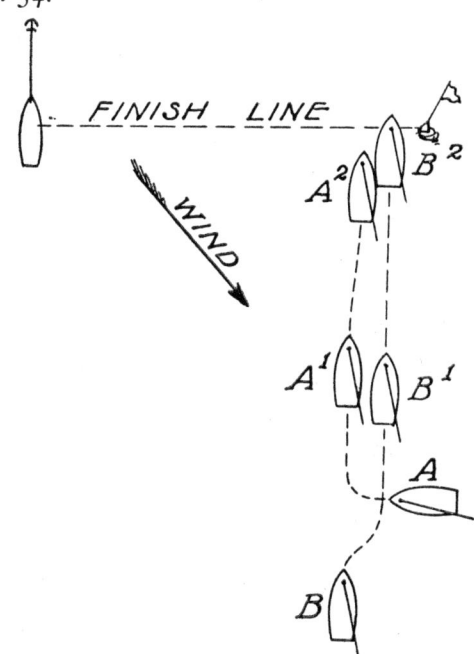

When *A* lost headway in coming about onto the port tack, *B's* momentum carried her so far ahead that before *A* gathered speed on her new tack, *B* had established an

THE SAILING RULES

overlap to leeward. Such being the case, A was obliged to give room to B to weather the mark at the leeward end of the finish line—which B could do without tacking. The yachts touched. A was diqualified.[15]

We have endeavored to formulate our personal ideas as follows:

From the time A, leading yacht, and sailed by a reasonably skilful skipper and crew:

1. Starts to take in her light sails preparatory to jibing around a mark, or
2. If no light sails are set, begins to trim sheets preparatory to hauling around the mark, or
3. Begins to alter course to round the mark in a reasonably seamanlike manner,

then in any one of such three situations B, still being clear astern, may not thereafter establish or attempt to establish an overlap and claim buoy room.

"The rules do not compel A to 'hug' the mark. Unless A makes such a 'shocking bad' rounding that nothing could justify it, B must be disqualified if she 'cuts in' and 'cuts out' A.

"Bad steersmen make bad roundings and will do so till doomsday, so surely good helmsmen will find a loophole to cleverly and quite safely nip in and cut the duffers out at the mark boat. That is all part of the game and fair and proper. But when experienced helmsmen are racing there is not much chance of cutting out the overtaken boat at the mark. A will say 'I merely took my mark in the manner I thought best, neither too close nor too wide.' B will say 'You left me plenty of room and I took advantage of it.' One man's word is as good as the other's. The Sailing

[15]*Rosalind* v. *Newt.* Y. R. A., 1931, Case 5. *Circe* v. *Fantasy.* Y. R. A., 1932, Case 1.

THE SAILING RULES

Committee will disqualify the overtaking boat for forcing a passage and this decision is not at all likely to be upset."[16]

SITUATION NO. 4
MARKS OF THE STARTING LINE

Situation No. 4, Marks of the Starting Line, must be subdivided into two parts, (a) before, and (b) after the making of the starting signal. This topic was discussed in Chapter VI wherein we commented on Rule 34—MARKS OF THE COURSE. We stated in that chapter that the second sentence of that rule defined marks of the starting line to be marks of the course during the preparatory period but that there was no side on which they were required to be passed until *after* the making of the starting signal. Read in conjunction with the second sentence, the fourth and last sentence of Rule 34 seemed clearly to indicate that although during the preparatory period marks other than marks of the starting line ranked as obstructions, yet the marks of the starting line, ranking as marks of the course, did not. It follows, therefore, that Situation No. 4, in so far as Rule 31 is concerned, does not come into being until *after* the starting signal has been made.

(b) AFTER THE MAKING OF THE STARTING SIGNAL
"BARGING"

Just what do we mean by the word "barging"? It is an attempt to secure the weather berth at the start by manœuvring well to windward and then running down with eased sheets with the object, *a few seconds before reaching the starting line,* of drawing parallel with a leeward, converging, right-of-way yacht which either is close-hauled or is starting in a normal manner, and then claiming that

[16]B. Heckstall-Smith. *Yachting World*, December 8, 1933, page 475.

THE SAILING RULES

because an overlap as defined by Rule 29 (4) had been established *before* either yacht actually reached the starting line mark *after* gunfire, the overlap "had been made in proper time."

As a rule, marks of the start and of the finish may be said to be "passed" as distinguished from the intermediate or turning marks of the course which generally are "rounded." "As used in Rule 31, the phrase 'to pass' does not mean 'to round.' It must be interpreted to mean 'to sail by.' "[17]

In our discussion of Situation No. 3—rounding turning marks of the course—we saw that "forcing a passage" and "cutting in" at such marks was quite effectively stopped by the second sentence of the rule. Citations from yachting writers of note both British and American confirmed our opinion. Almost always Overtaking, not Converging, is the issue in such cases.

Unfortunately, however, barging at the start would seem to be technically legal by virtue of the wording of the last clause of the first sentence of the rule, *"provided the yachts are overlapping on actually reaching such mark . . .,"* unless such tactics are barred by some other provision of the rule. It is contended that paragraph two gives Race Committees authority effectively to prohibit barging at the start. It is argued that this paragraph prescribes a condition precedent upon which the transfer of right of way to the inner yacht is predicated, namely *"overlap made in proper time";* and that in each particular case the Committee may determine in terms of distance or of time or of both, how far or how long *before* the mark or obstruction is reached the overlap should have been established. In other words, that although Rule 31 is an exception to Right of Way Rule 30, it is not a general exception but

[17] *Dinghy No. 33* v. *Dinghy No. 16.* N. A. Y. R. U., Appeal No. 7, December 14, 1936.

THE SAILING RULES

merely an exception that comes into being only upon the happening of the specific condition precedent therein specified, and as may be determined by the Committee upon the facts of each particular case.

It is an axiom of law that no single paragraph, sentence, clause or phrase of a document may be interpreted by itself alone. It must be construed in the light of the wording of the entire instrument. To give any part of Rule 31 a meaning and interpretation separate and distinct from its relation to the remainder of the rule would be incorrect. It must be read in conjunction with the other provisions of the rule.

Now were it not for the words *"provided the yachts are overlapping on actually reaching such mark . . ."* it would be simple to uphold the contention that the words *"in proper time"* in paragraph two could be defined by Race Committees in terms of distance or of time before the mark was reached. Such a construction definitely would stop barging. Unfortunately, however, each of the aforesaid phrases must be construed with reference to the other. There is, therefore, just as much, if not more, force to the argument that an overlap established *ever so soon before* a starting line mark is reached has been made in proper time as there is to the argument that a last instant overlap has *not* been made in proper time. We must, therefore, conclude with regret that the words "on actually reaching" mean just what they imply, and that in passing, "sailing by," a mark of the starting line an overlap established at the last instant is legal from the point of view of the literal meaning of these ten words quoted.

Now what evidence have we of the intent of the framers of the rule in so far as it pertains to barging at the start?

As we pointed out in Chapter VI, the no-required-side-to-starting-line-marks-until-after-gunfire provision in Rule

34 was inserted by the 1929 Conference at the urgent suggestion of Mr. Johan Anker of Norway who felt that it would prevent barging at the start. One of the American delegates wrote that "The clear intention of the Conference at that time was to prevent this practice." Major B. Heckstall-Smith says that such tactics are unfair sailing and utterly contrary to Rule 1, from which we would seem to be justified in inferring that he would disqualify a barger under Rule 1 and not under Rule 31. Apparently he, too, does not think that Rule 31 prevents barging at the start.

What stronger evidence could we have that not only Mr. Anker but indeed the Conference as a whole believed that Rule 31 as drafted did not prevent barging at the start? Why should the Conference have endeavored to prohibit that practice by revising Rule 34 if such tactics already had been prohibited by Rule 31? Unfortunately all that the Conference succeeded in accomplishing was to prevent barging *before* the making of the starting signal. *After* gunfire the situation remained unchanged.

It also seems clear that all who hold that the proper interpretation of the rule permits last-second barging deprecate such a construction. The writer, for one, most certainly disapproves of such tactics.

We have, therefore, an instance where the actual wording of the rule permits a practice which the framers of the rule intended to prohibit. Apparently the rule says one thing. It was intended to say the opposite. In other words, the rule as it stands is ambiguous.

Now it is a further axiom of law that in construing a statute which contains an ambiguity a court will interpret the law in accordance with the intention of the legislature if that intent is known and is reasonably clear.

The reason for both the stringent provisions in the second sentence against "forcing a passage" and "cutting in"

THE SAILING RULES

at turning marks, and the almost unanimous sentiment of yachtsmen against barging at the start is that in both instances the offending, non-right-of-way yacht is endeavoring to obtain an unfair advantage on the forthcoming leg of the course. Such tactics not only constitute unfair sailing but in almost every instance they contravene either the Overtaking or the Converging Rule.

By far the greater number of skippers endeavor to start at the windward end or at the starboard tack end of the line, and because in the excitement of the moment many helmsmen forget that under Rule 29, Definitions, Section 4, there can be no legal overlap and consequently no overlapping rights, unless both yachts are sailing approximately the same course—that is to say, to all intents and purposes parallel courses—they call for buoy room when they are not entitled to it, and are surprised and "pained" when they are protested and disqualified for fouling leeward, right-of-way yachts or forcing them to alter course to avoid a collision.[18] They forget that the leeward yacht holds right of way, and that the windward yacht *"shall keep clear."* The word "shall" is *mandatory*.

"The Council of the British Y. R. A. strongly discourages attempts to get the weather berth at the start by manœuvring high to windward of the line and running down free or before the wind with the object of drawing parallel and securing the weather berth a few seconds before gunfire from yachts which have made their start more normally to leeward. They are sailing utterly contrary to Y. R. A. Rule I, because they are trying to snatch the weather berth by the unfair means of running down before the wind with free sheets to secure the weather berth from other boats which are either close-hauled or starting in a normal manner.

[18]*Georgia* v. *Grey Dawn.* N. Y. Y. C., 1923. *Decisions and Rulings*, 1849-1923, page 56.

THE SAILING RULES

"If it is practical for the weather boat, which is contemplating establishing an overlap as the two yachts draw near to the mark, to bear up (the American term is 'bear away'—the Author) and go under the stern of the leeward boat, she must do so."[19]

The foregoing remarks were made by Major B. Heckstall-Smith in commenting upon two decisions of the Y. R. A., in which the weather boat was disqualified in each instance.[20]

It is our hope that in the near future a protest based on a clear cut instance of last moment barging at the start will be appealed to our yachting tribunal of last resort and that the Executive Committee of the N. A. Y. R. U. will interpret the rule on the basis of legislative intent rather than in accordance with the strict and literal meaning of the words "on actually reaching such mark or obstruction" in the last clause of the first sentence of the rule.

If such a decision fails to interpret Rule 31 so as to prevent barging, then all racing yachtsmen should demand a revision of the rule.

SQUEEZING THE INSIDE YACHT

Squeezing or failing to give room early enough is just as unfair a practice as is "barging." Here is a case in point.

Seven 18-foot, centerboard, jib and mainsail yachts, overlapped, were reaching broad on the starboard tack for a mark to be left to starboard. There was a good breeze. All yachts ranked under Rule 30 (G). B was the windward (inside) yacht, A was the yacht next to leeward. Both yachts were heading slightly above the mark. Thirty yards from the mark B called for room. A did not re-

[19] B. Heckstall-Smith. *Yachting World,* November 20, 1936, page 474.
[20] *Royal Albert Yacht Club, Z_{28}* v. Z_6 and Z_{12}; Z_{19} v. Z_{12}. Y. R. A., 1937, Case 2.

THE SAILING RULES

spond. *B* bore away in order to pass the mark on the required side, and fouled *A*. The Sailing Committee disqualified *A*. The Council upheld the decision, and said: "*B* had reached the mark within the meaning of Rule 31. When it is obvious that the outside boat has to give room there is no object in the outside boat squeezing the inside boat to practically the last moment, and this practice should be discouraged."[21]

In other words, the outside yacht may not delay too long her alteration of course. She must begin to "give room" at a point sufficiently distant from the mark to enable the inside yacht to clear it safely.

We come now to the three three-yacht cases of *Humming Bird* v. *Dolphin* (1890); *Nancy* v. *Redshank,* and *Wraith* v. *Redshank* (1925); and *Moana* v. *Victory* (1928). Discussion of the first two will be deferred until the next chapter for the reason that *Moana* v. *Victory,* although it discusses Rule 32, involves Rule 31 only, while *Humming Bird* v. *Dolphin* and *Nancy* v. *Redshank,* and *Wraith* v. *Redshank* involve, simultaneously and interlinked, the interpretation of Rule 31 and Rule 30 (A), (B), (C), (G), and (K).

Moana v. *Victory* is outstanding not only in principle but also on account of the thorough manner in which it was considered and minutely reported by the Council. It will be given in full.[22]

In the diagram, *A* is *Moana*; *B, Victory,* and *C, Prize.* The race was held in Australia, January 29, 1927.

Facts: The three yachts were beating to windward, *C* laying the mark which had to be left to port. Had *A* kept her course, she would have just cleared the stern of *C*. Had *B* held her course she would have collided with *C*.

[21]*Pyxie* v. *Sylvia.* Y. R. A., 1925, Case 1.
[22]*Moana* v. *Victory.* Y. R. A., 1928, Case 14.

THE SAILING RULES

Diagram 35.

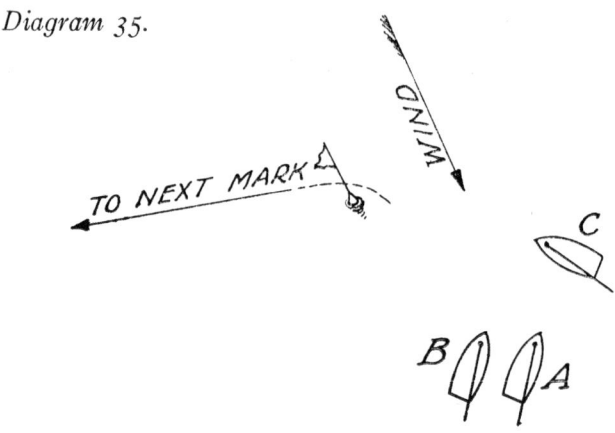

B could have luffed and avoided C and then have come back on her course on the port tack. B bore down on A who was compelled to alter course and bear away about two or three points. B could have tacked without interfering with A and causing her to be placed under a disadvantage as regards C.

B contended that C ranked as an obstruction and that B could call upon A for room to pass under the stern of C as an overlap existed between A and B.

The Sailing Committee held:

B being windward boat had to keep clear; that she had ample room in which to manœuvre between herself and the mark without interfering with other yachts in the race; and that C, a moving yacht in the race, did not rank as an obstruction to sea room. Therefore Rule 31 did not apply. B was disqualified.

In 1927, the last clause of the first sentence of Rule 31 read:

> "provided the yachts are not clear of each other on actually reaching such mark or obstruction."

THE SAILING RULES

In Rule 31 now in force, this clause reads:

"provided the yachts are overlapping on actually reaching such mark or obstruction."

In 1927, the pertinent clause in Rule 32, viz., line four of the first sentence of the Rule, read:

"which the leeward yacht cannot clear without tacking."

In Rule 32, now in force, this clause reads:

"which requires the leeward yacht to alter course to clear it."

Continuing *Moana* v. *Victory:*

The appeal came before the Council on December 7, 1927. It was considered with great care and a Sub-Committee was specially appointed to investigate and report back to the Council.

At a later meeting of that body, the Council reversed the decision of the Race Committee and disqualified *A.*

The Council said:

"Rules 31 and 32 only operate when the precise conditions specified therein are fully established. In regard to Rule 31, the essential conditions are:

1. Without tacking,
2. Overlap (made in proper time),
3. Danger of fouling the obstruction.

"1. *Without Tacking:* May be accepted as meaning that the yacht nearest to the obstruction would not have to tack if she could ignore the outside yacht.

"2. *Overlap:* For the purpose of this rule must mean that the inside yacht is so placed that she cannot transfer

THE SAILING RULES

herself from the inside berth to the outside berth without fouling.

"3. *Danger of Fouling:* Should be held to be present when a yacht is closely approaching a position in which an immediate alteration of course will be necessary if a foul is to be avoided.

"In regard to Rule 32, the essential conditions are:
1. Close-hauled on the same tack.
2. Cannot clear without tacking.
3. Cannot tack for want of room.
4. Special reservation in regard to Mark of the course.

"Numbers 1, 3 and 4 seem to require no special explanation.

"2. 'Cannot clear without tacking' should be interpreted as meaning:

'has no other reasonable means of clearing the obstruction except to tack.'

"The incidence of the two Rules differs in the following respects:

"Rule 31 can be invoked to claim room whether or not there are alternatives, provided the danger of fouling—as defined—exists.

"Rule 32 can only be invoked provided no reasonable alternative is available. The Council thus find that C did rank as an Obstruction under Rule 31, and that by that Rule A was obliged to give room to B to pass under the stern of C. The Council therefore reverse the decision of the Committee and dismiss A's protest and find B should not be disqualified."

It will be noticed that the respective 1927 and present-day Clauses of Rules 31 and 32, quoted immediately following the decision of the Sailing Committee, differ slightly in wording. While the change in the 1927 Rule 32 is fundamental in that it broadens the right of the leeward yacht to hail the other about, the change in Rule 31 is inconsequential. In our opinion the decision of the Council in *Moana* v. *Victory* would have been the same under the present-day rules.

It seems strange that nowhere in the decision did the Council allude to the last sentence of the first paragraph of Rule 31, then, as now, reading: "A craft underway (including another yacht racing), of which the yacht concerned has to keep out of the way, ranks as an obstruction for the purpose of this and the following rule." By this sentence, C clearly was an obstruction. She had right of way over the other two yachts, and was "another yacht racing."

The vital point in the decision seems to be this: Does the fact that the inside yacht (B) had *alternative* means of escape from the position in which she found herself, alter the strict interpretation of the wording of Rule 31? The Council replied, "No."

This strict and literal interpretation will result in justice being done in probably every situation save one. The rare exception would seem to be this:

A and B, overlapped, are close-hauled on the same tack. X is an anchored vessel 50–150 feet in length with clear water all around. A can just lay the mark and clear X's stern without altering her course. Both A and B are "about to pass an obstruction" and B is rapidly approaching a position in which an immediate and appreciable alteration of course will be necessary to avoid a collision with X. B hails for room to pass under the stern of X. A, knowing that if she bears away in order to give B room,

THE SAILING RULES

Diagram 36.

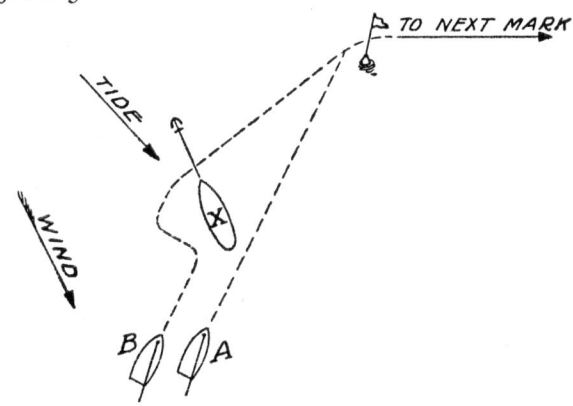

she (*A*) cannot weather the mark without tacking, and remembering that by the last sentence of the first paragraph of Rule 32 she would have no right then to hail *B* about, refuses to bear away. *B*, therefore, tacks, passes to windward of *X*, and protests *A* under Rules 31 and 32.

In *Moana* v. *Victory* the Council laid down the essential conditions requisite to invoke Rule 31 and/or Rule 32.

In the case illustrated in Diagram 36, *A* can pass astern of *X* without altering her course. It follows that *B* has no ground of protest under Rule 32. If *X* were a moving vessel, whether or not she was another yacht racing, it is clear that *B* could call for room to pass astern. It is also true that were *X* a shoal or a point of land with a safe passage to leeward only, or a mark of the course which had to be passed on a required side, or if both yachts were sailing free,[23] so that after passing under the stern of *X*, *A* still could lay the mark without tacking, then *B* could

[23]*Lackagh* v. *Laragh.* } Y. R. A., 1929, Case 1.
   Glynn v. *Lackagh.*

THE SAILING RULES

claim room because the three essential conditions requisite to invoke Rule 31 were established.

Does the fact that there is clear water all around X alter the case?

In *Moana* v. *Victory* no great loss of ground was caused to the leeward yacht. It was not a case, as in Diagram 36, where by bearing away to leeward to give B room, also to pass astern of the obstruction, she (A) would be obliged to tack in order to weather a mark a short distance ahead. In the English case even had C not been in the way of either A or B, B could have prevented A from tacking until she (B) chose to permit her to do so. The Council's decision on the facts in that case was sound.

Following the decision of the Council we should be obliged to rule in the case illustrated in Diagram 36, that B could claim room to pass astern of X, even though it would have the result, a few moments later, that A would have to check her speed until she was clear astern of B, then take a short hitch on the starboard tack until she could fetch the mark; again come onto the port tack, and *follow B* around the mark.

The Council lays down the premise that if the three conditions requisite to invoke Rule 31 are existent, then *irrespective* of the fact that B has an *alternative* means of escape, she is entitled to invoke the Rule.

It seems reasonable to assume that had the Council, prior to 1927, made any exception to Rule 31 on facts identical with or similar to those of the hypothetical case illustrated in Diagram 36, they would have referred to it in *Moana* v. *Victory*. No case has been found wherein either the Council or any American authority has made *any* exception to Rule 31.

In the supposititious case in Diagram 36, there is no required side on which X must be passed. There is clear water all around the obstruction. To compel B to pass to windward of it will not put her out of the race. It will merely cause her slightly to overstand the mark. B is not hemmed in with only one means of escape. To compel A to bear away will, in all probability, result in B being first around the mark. Even so, is it not the course of wisdom to refuse to abrogate the rule?

While the spirit of justice, fair play, and good sportsmanship ever should be borne in mind, it is of no less importance that the literal interpretation of the rules be adhered to except in a case where grave and outstanding injustice would result. In the case illustrated in Diagram 36, A is simply "out of luck" but that is hardly a sufficient reason to abrogate the rule. Such a practice inevitably would lead to all kinds of complications, and Race Committees would be plagued by pleas of "mitigating circumstances" and "special facts."

LUFFING AND FORE-REACHING PAST A MARK

Visualize, if you will, A and B close-hauled on the starboard tack approaching a mark to be left to port. B has overtaken A to leeward and has established an overlap "in proper time." A is the outer, windward, yacht holding right of way under Rule 30 (A) and (C). A can fetch the mark comfortably. B can clear it on the required side only by luffing and fore-reaching. She cannot luff and keep clear both of the mark and of A unless A luffs also. Has B the right to alter course in a manner that neither misleads nor balks A, and if so to what extent may she luff and fore-reach past the mark?

We have seen that Rule 31 is in the nature of an excepting clause to Right of Way Rule 30, in that during the existence of certain conditions specifically enumerated in

THE SAILING RULES

Rule 31, the respective rights and obligations of the yachts under Rule 30 are temporarily superseded and suspended until the inner yacht is no longer in danger of fouling the mark or obstruction.

Although the words "luff" or "luffing" are not to be found in the rule, the title of the rule itself "Giving Room at Marks . . .," and the use of the words "without tacking" and "allow the inner yacht room" are significant. They imply a possible and forced alteration of course by the outer yacht even if she holds right of way under Rule 30. They mean that if the outer yacht elects to pass the mark on the required side she may be obliged to luff or to bear away if such alteration of course is necessary to permit the inner yacht to pass the mark on the required side also.

In the instant case all the requisites to cause Rule 31 to operate have been established. Were the yachts sailing free so that B could luff and clear the mark with her sails full, A most certainly would be obliged to luff also, her rights as overtaken-to-leeward yacht to the contrary notwithstanding. Does the fact that it is necessary for B to luff and fore-reach for one or more boat-lengths alter the situation?

Most problems arising under Rule 31 have already been adjudicated. We have found no decision, however, which deals squarely with the question under discussion. The *only* reference we found which discussed luffing past a mark was an article entitled *"Character of a Mark"* written by the Regatta Committee of the New York Yacht Club and printed in the 1891 Report of the Committee.[24] The article was not a part of any protest decision but was in the nature of a ruling or statement by the Regatta Committee in order to make clear the 1891 yacht racing law

[24]*Decisions and Rulings.* N. Y. Y. C., 1849–1923, pages 9–14.

THE SAILING RULES

involved in approaching and turning marks. It resulted from the *Volunteer-Gracie* foul which occurred on August 7, 1891.

In 1891, N. Y. Y. C. Rule XVII—Right of Way—Section 14—*Passing and Rounding Marks*—first sentence, read as follows:

"If an overlap exists between two yachts when both of them, without tacking, are about to pass a mark on the required side, then the outside yacht must give the inside yacht room to pass clear of the mark."

Neither in the 1891 rule nor in its present day equivalent, Rule 31, is the word "luffing" to be found.

On page ten of "Decisions and Rulings" the Committee said:

"An obstruction in a course is an object which has *sea room* on one side only. . . . A mark is not an obstruction, for it can be passed on either hand. Indeed it is somewhat in the nature of a *point,* with position but without magnitude. And to reduce its character to an idiom—*A mark is not a lee shore.* . . . Therefore 'passing or rounding' is considered as a manœuvre lacking the element of danger. For this reason Section 14 calls on an outside yacht to give an inside yacht room to 'pass clear' with a *luff* but without tacking; . . . She is entitled to a luff and in this should be accommodated whether she calls for room or not."

Obviously the Committee's remarks that "an obstruction in a course is an object which has *sea room* on one side only" and that "a mark is not an obstruction for it can be passed on either hand" would not be good yacht racing law under the present rules and decisions.

We do not believe that the question under discussion can be determined satisfactorily on a purely technical basis. The answer lies in the meaning of the phrase "about to pass . . . a mark on the required side."

THE SAILING RULES

Three possible interpretations of the phrase are:
1. May pass a mark in a normal manner with all sails filled.
2. May luff and fore-reach past a mark so long as the main boom does not pass the center line of the yacht and she remains under reasonably full control.
3. May pass a mark *in any manner* even stern first if the wind suddenly flattens, so long as the eye of the wind is not passed.

There can be no question as to the correctness of interpretation number 1; nor as to the illegality of interpretation number 3. How about number 2?

"A yacht is luffing when she so alters her course as to sail a course more nearly into the wind." (Rule 29—Definitions—Sec. 2), and continues to be luffing up to the point where she is heading directly into the wind. After her bow has passed that point and the wind is on the side of her mainsail opposite to that on which it was when she began to luff, she is said to have tacked. There is in the Sailing Rules neither an official definition of "tacking," nor of when the act of tacking begins. Major B. Heckstall-Smith says that "after passing the eye of the wind she would have begun the act of tacking."[25]

But suppose putting down the helm, coming up into the eye of the wind, falling away and filling on the other tack is a continuous manœuvre. When may it be said that the act of tacking began? We have been unable to find any decision on that point.

To revert to the topic under discussion. One thing seems certain. If luffing and fore-reaching past a mark by an inner yacht under reasonably full control is permissible,

[25] B. Heckstall-Smith. *Yacht Racing*, 2d Ed., 1933, page 75.

THE SAILING RULES

the manœuvre must be carried out in a manner that neither misleads nor balks the outer yacht.

From a practical standpoint to permit such luffing and fore-reaching might tend to give an inside, leeward yacht an unfair advantage at windward marks. Furthermore, it might be a source of danger at crowded starts.

"The words 'without tacking' which appear in Rule 31 apply only to a case where the inside boat cannot lay the mark."[26] Cannot a yacht be said to be "laying" the mark even if she is obliged to luff and fore-reach in order to pass it on the required side? We must bear in mind that Rule 31 does not even impliedly prohibit luffing and fore-reaching past a mark by an inner, non-right-of-way yacht.

OVERTAKING ALONG A SHORE OR SHOAL

We now come to two situations which frequently occur in landlocked or partially landlocked waters. The first is where both yachts are sailing along a weather shore. In the second, they are sailing along a lee shore. In both cases the stern, overtaking, yacht wishes to pass. In the first instance she essays to pass to windward, viz., between the overtaken yacht and the windward shore or shoal. In the second instance she wishes to pass to leeward, viz., between the overtaken yacht and the lee shore or shoal.

WEATHER SHORE—FORCING WINDWARD PASSAGE NOT ALLOWED

It may generally be taken that in sailing along a weather shore the whole of the shore is an obstruction.[27]

---

[26]*Dinghy No. 33* v. *Dinghy N. 16.* N. A. Y. R. U., Appeal No. 7, December 14, 1936.
[27]B. Heckstall-Smith. *Yacht Racing*, 2d Ed., 1933, page 132.

THE SAILING RULES

Diagram 37.

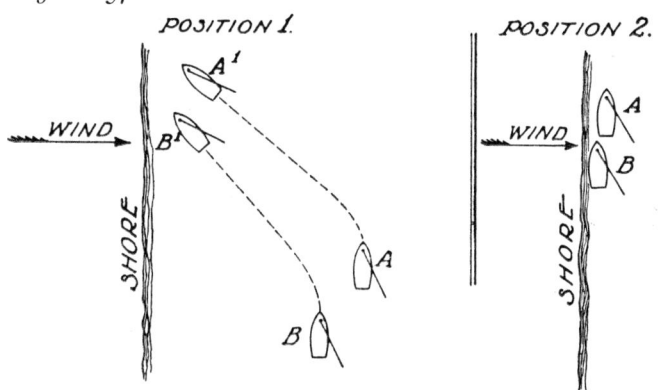

In position 1, *A,* overtaken yacht, may luff *B* close into the shore until it is no longer prudent to approach nearer. If when the yachts have approached the shore as close as *B* deems prudent, *B* has established an overlap, then *A* must give *B* room to pass between herself and the shore or shoal. *A* cannot luff *B* onto the shore.

If, however, as in position 2, *A* already is sailing as close to the weather shore as is reasonably safe, *B* cannot thereafter establish an overlap and force a passage between *A* and the shore. *A* can claim she reached the obstruction *before B* established an overlap and that *B* went to windward at her own risk.[28]

Now this does not mean that if *B* is of shoaler draft than *A* she may not take advantage of that fact to pass between *A* and the shore. *B* may do so even though *A* runs aground in her attempt to checkmate her opponent. In the case next cited the Sailing Committee disqualified *B* saying: "*B* was taking an unfair advantage of her shallow draft by attempting to force a passage between *A* and the

[28]*Sankuntala* v. *Polynia.* Y. R. A., 1901, page 140.

THE SAILING RULES

mud." On appeal to the Council the decision of the Sailing Committee was reversed and *"B's* appeal succeeds."[29]

Somewhat similar to *Sankuntala* v. *Polynia,* although it was in reality a case of port and starboard tack under Rule 30 (E), is the case depicted in Diagram 38.

Diagram 38.

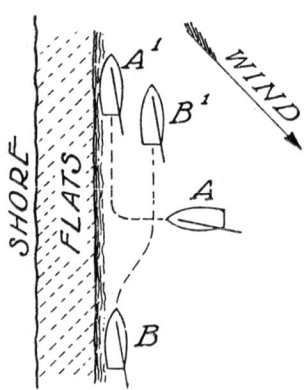

B bore away to pass under *A's* stern, *A* holding her course. When barely across *B, A* hit the shoal and immediately tacked. Although no collision occurred, *B* protested *A* for tacking without hailing. The Council decided "that a hail was unnecessary although it would have been desirable." It did say, however: "under Rule 30 (E) it was *B's* duty to keep clear of *A and to bear in mind* that *A* would be obliged to tack on reaching the flats."[30]

LEE-SHORE PASSAGE

For some years after the case next cited, it was supposed that in sailing along a lee shore the rule was just

[29]*Watersprite* v. *Susan.* Y. R. A., 1938, Case 10.
[30]*Jeanette* v. *Beryl.* Y. R. A., 1926, Case 5.

THE SAILING RULES

the opposite to that laid down in *Sankuntala* v. *Polynia,* and that the overtaking yacht could *force* a leeward passage although she did not establish her overlap until *after* the leading yacht had actually reached the shoal or obstruction. As authority for this doctrine was cited the case illustrated in Diagram 39.

Diagram 39.

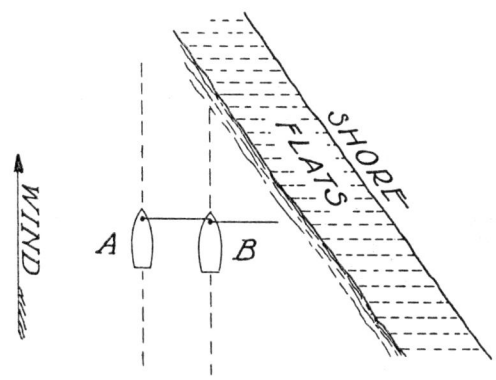

"The yachts were running up the river Thames on the port tack. *A* was leading, and *B* was overtaking her to leeward. *B* ran up under *A's* lee, and when they gradually came into the shallows along the edge of the sand, *B* had established an overlap. Presently *B* hailed for 'water,' but *A* did not respond to her hail and held her course, and a foul occurred as shown in the diagram.

"*A* contended that she had a right to hold her course on the pretext that the shore was an 'obstruction' within the meaning of the rule, and *B* had forced a passage between her and it, because *A* had *reached* the obstruction *before B* obtained her overlap.

"*B* contended that *A* was bound to give her room when

THE SAILING RULES

she hailed for 'water,' and that as *A* did not give her room she had no alternative but to foul her."

The Council decided that *B* was in the right, and disqualified *A*.[31]

Authorities of high standing have been understood to interpret the case of *Eelin* v. *Astrild* as laying down the proposition that when sailing along a lee shore, and as close in as is reasonably safe, an overtaking yacht is entitled to *force* a leeward passage under *all* conditions.

It should be noted that in *Eelin* v. *Astrild,* as contrasted with the facts in *Sankuntala* v. *Polynia, B,* the overtaking yacht, had established an overlap *before* the overtaken yacht actually reached shoal water. In *Eelin* v. *Astrild,* the overtaken yacht was disqualified; in *Sankuntala* v. *Polynia,* the overtaking yacht incurred that penalty.

The two decisions are wholly in accord. Together they decide that if the leading yacht actually reaches the shore or obstruction *before* an overlap has been established, she may hold her course—whether it be along a weather shore or along a lee shore. To contend that *Eelin* v. *Astrild* is authority for the doctrine that in all such cases an overtaking yacht may force a leeward passage—irrespective of whether an overlap has or has not been established before the leading yacht has actually reached the lee shore—does not seem to be justified by the facts in that case which state clearly that when the yachts "gradually came into the shallows along the edge of the sand, *Eelin* had established an overlap."

Moreover, such a deduction would seem to be an unwarranted enlargement of the rights granted to an overtaking-to-leeward yacht by Rule 30 (C).

How, then, may an overtaking yacht pass a competitor sailing along a lee shore as close in as is reasonably safe?

[31] *Eelin* v. *Astrild.* Y. R. A., 1900, page 112.

THE SAILING RULES

Twenty-five years after *Eelin* v. *Astrild* came a decision which seems to answer the question in so far as yachtsmen racing under the jurisdiction of the British Y. R. A. are concerned.

Diagram 40.

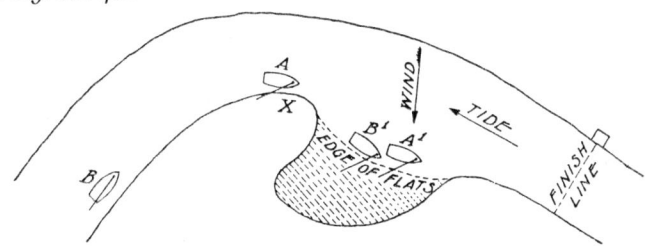

"*A* reached past the point of land *X*, about five boat lengths ahead of *B*, and on rounding that promontory bore away to leeward and sailed along the edge of the flats in order to avoid the head tide. *B* tried to force a passage through *A's* lee and fouled her. *A* protested under Rule 30 (A), and *B* protested under Rule 30 (C). The Sailing Committee disqualified *B*, saying:

"For years it has been the custom on this river to refuse the lee passage to an overtaking yacht when the leading boat was already running or reaching along a lee shore to cheat a foul tide, provided the leading boat was keeping in as close to the lee shore as was reasonably safe, and that the leading boat had not previously refused the weather passage by luffing the overtaking yacht; and it is an understood thing that having refused the lee passage the leading boat may not luff the overtaking yacht."

The Council, without comment, upheld the decision of the Sailing Committee.[32]

The decision of the Sailing Committee in *Sapphire* v.

[32]*Sapphire* v. *Ruby*. Y. R. A., 1924, Case 10.

THE SAILING RULES

Ruby as confirmed by the Council, in no way conflicts either with *Sankuntala* v. *Polynia* or with *Eelin* v. *Astrild*.

From it may be deduced the following two rules regarding overtaking while sailing along a lee shore or obstruction and as close in as is reasonably safe:

1. If the leading yacht luffs the overtaking yacht to prevent her passing to windward, she may not refuse the latter a leeward passage thereafter.
2. If the leading yacht refuses the overtaking yacht a leeward passage, she may not luff to hinder the overtaking yacht if, later, the latter attempts to pass to windward.

Only where yachts pass along a channel or a shore can a situation like that in *Sapphire* v. *Ruby* arise. Such cases are infrequent. Still less frequent are recorded appeal decisions based on such unusual facts. Until overruled or modified by the Council, *Sapphire* v. *Ruby* would appear to be binding upon yachtsmen racing under the jurisdiction of the British Y. R. A.

It is extremely doubtful if this decision would be followed in this country, and for the following reasons:

As leading yacht, A is clothed with certain inalienable, tactical rights whereby she may hinder the passage of her opponent. A has already reached the obstruction, in this case the edge of the flats, while still clear ahead of B. For the avowed purpose of "cheating a foul tide" she may and does sail as close in as she deems prudent, and B may not force a passage between A and the shore. (See *Sankuntala* v. *Polynia, supra*.) If B attempts to pass to weather, A may luff (Rule 30 (B)).

Now let us assume that B is unsuccessful in her attempt to pass A to windward, and after the luffing match has carried both yachts a short distance off shore, B falls astern, bears away to leeward and shapes a course to overtake *A* to leeward. May *A* again bear away and endeavor to reach the lee shore?

The answer would seem to hinge on the question of what is *A's* proper course to the next mark judged by and from the point reached by her when the luffing match ended. If that point is sufficiently off shore that it may be held that to return to the lee shore would cause *A* to sail a course unreasonably to leeward of the next mark, *A* would have no right to deny *B* a leeward passage. If *A* persists in bearing away toward the shore, and *B* protests under Rule 30 (C), *A* would have to prove that her return to a course close in along the shore was for a reason "other than the desire to hinder the competitor overtaking to leeward."

The third paragraph of Rule 31 is explanatory of the second, and confirms the statement made toward the end of Chapter XI, that the presence of marks does not affect Rule 31. To repeat: take away the mark and then decide the rights and obligations of each yacht.

Let us reiterate what was said in the *Aileen* v. *Canvasback* decision discussed in Chapter IX, viz.: that the word "tack" in the first and fourth lines of the third paragraph of Rule 31 "does not include 'gybing.' "[33]

Again let skippers remember always to bear in mind that "In all protests under this rule (31) the onus of proof that the overlap has been made in time rests with the yacht that previously had been astern."

Concluding our discussion of Rule 31 let us offer the second "Bit of Advice":

GIVE AMPLE ROOM AT MARKS.

[33]B. Heckstall-Smith. *Yachting World*, June 12, 1931, page 564.

Chapter XIII

OBSTRUCTION TO SEA ROOM—OVERTAKING —THREE YACHTS INVOLVED

Rule 30, (A), (B), (C), (G), and (K), and Rule 31

The Sailing Rules make mention of the rights and obligations of *two* yachts only. In general it is not difficult to interpret the rules in a case involving two yachts. Let a third yacht be in the picture, however, and the problem becomes more complicated. Of the several hundred protest cases examined during the preparation of this book, only two were found in which more than two yachts were in a mix-up involving, simultaneously, one or more clauses of Rule 30 (A), (B), (C), (G), and (K), and Rule 31.

In Digrams 41, 42 and 43 the three yachts will be lettered the same for the corresponding position in each case, viz.:

L is the most leeward yacht;
M is the middle yacht; and
W is the most windward yacht.

For many years prior to the 1929 Conference, yachtsmen racing under the jurisdiction of the International Yacht Racing Union of which the Y. R. A. of Great Britain was and still is a member, were governed by the proper course footnotes to the Sailing Rules of the Union. The footnote to the Y. R. A. Meeting, Crossing and Converging rules, adopted by the Y. R. A. at its Annual General Meeting on February 23, 1912, and adopted by the 1919 International Conference at London, sanctioned the

THE SAILING RULES

disqualification of a right-of-way yacht, *after* the start, "if she obstructs the other by steering a course unreasonably wide of her own proper course for the next mark, taking wind and tide into consideration." As we have seen in Chapter VIII, this footnote was deleted from the Rules which were adopted in November, 1929, and the only "proper course" provision now retained in the Rules is that set forth in Rule 29 (7) in conjunction with Rule 30 (C).

The two British cases, *Humming Bird* v. *Dolphin* (1890), and *Nancy* v. *Redshank* (1925), were decided under the former proper course footnote to the Meeting, Crossing and Converging rules. We shall discuss them under the former rules and also under the present rules. Case III, the supposititious case, will be discussed under the *present rules only.*

Where three yachts are sailing in the same general direction or as the rules say, "are sailing approximately the same course," it is of vital importance to their helmsmen to be able to determine which of the two outside yachts constitutes the obstruction as defined in the last sentence of the first paragraph of Rule 31 reading as follows:

"A craft under way (including another yacht racing), of which the yacht concerned has to keep out of the way, ranks as an obstruction for the purpose of this or the following rule."

We have seen in Chapter XII that the words "the yacht concerned" refer only to the inside yacht, *i.e.*, the yacht in danger of fouling the "other yacht racing."

Now Rule 31 is specific in designating which of the two outside yachts constitutes the obstruction. *The obstruction is that outside yacht which the two overlapped yachts "are about to pass."* To cause Rule 31 to operate, the middle yacht and one of the outside yachts must be overlapped

THE SAILING RULES

before either of them overlaps the third yacht—the other outside yacht. Obviously, neither of the two overlapped yachts can be the obstruction which *both* of them "are about to pass." (See *infra* in our discussion of *Humming Bird* v. *Dolphin,* and *Nancy* v. *Redshank*; also *Dinghy No. 33* v. *Dinghy No. 16*.[1]) It follows, therefore, by elimination, that the yacht which ranks as the obstruction *must* be the third yacht on which neither of the two overlapped yachts has as yet established an overlap. Furthermore—and this is vital—the third yacht must be one of which the middle yacht, the inside yacht of the other two yachts already overlapped, *i.e.,* "the yacht in danger of fouling such . . . obstruction," "has to keep out of the way."

Now let us discuss our three three-yacht cases.

CASE I

Humming Bird v. *Dolphin*[2]

SOLENT YACHT CLUB

$W = $ Nancy Bell
$L = $ Dolphin
$M = $ Humming Bird
$D = $ Troublesome

Diagram 41.

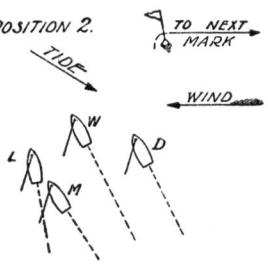

[1] *Dinghy No. 33* v. *Dinghy No. 16.* N. A. Y. R. U., Appeal No. 7, December 14, 1936.
[2] *Humming Bird* v. *Dolphin.* Y. R. A., 1890.

THE SAILING RULES

At the start both L and D were clear astern of W, and M was clear astern of both L and D. As the yachts neared the buoy, L and D overtook W; all yachts "reaching broad to avoid being set the wrong side of the buoy by the tide. L was luffed in the hope of drawing across W's bow, but failed and dropped back again to the position shown in Position 2, where she was overtaken and fouled by M; the latter then luffed into W, who in turn luffed into D."

For some time prior to the foul, and while M still was a length or two astern of W and D, L had been sailing under W's lee about a boat's length distant. L did not luff. M protested L for not giving her room safely to pass to leeward of W.

On appeal to the Council the decision was: "M was to blame for the collisions, L did not contribute thereto."

CASE I

DISCUSSION UNDER FORMER PROPER COURSE RULES

In 1890, Y. R. A. Rule 21—OVERTAKING YACHTS—LUFFING AND BEARING AWAY—was, for the purpose of this discussion, the same as Y. R. A. 1925, Rule 30 (A), (B), and (C), in that the yacht overtaking to windward had to keep clear of the overtaken yacht which might luff as she pleased, and the yacht overtaken to leeward might not bear away out of her course to hinder the overtaking yacht. Nor could the overtaking-to-leeward yacht luff until she had drawn clear ahead.

It may be helpful to quote Y. R. A. Rule 20, Obstructions to Sea Room, as worded in 1890.

Rule 20—Obstructions to Sea Room

"When passing a pier, shoal, rock, vessel, or other obstruction to sea room, should yachts not be clear of

THE SAILING RULES

each other, the outside yacht or yachts must give room to the yacht in danger of fouling such obstruction, whether she be the weather or the leeward yacht; provided always that an overlap has been established before an obstruction is actually reached."

It will be noted that in 1890, Rule 30, the words were: "When passing"; while in 1925 and at the present time they were and are: "About to pass."

Humming Bird v. *Dolphin—Comments by Mr. Dixon Kemp*[3]

"In the foregoing case W would be regarded as an obstruction under Rule 20; and under that rule the question would have to be considered whether L had the right to luff and shut out M, or whether she was bound to bear away and give room. L, it was alleged, had been sailing for some time under the lee of W, and whilst M was a length or two off—astern of W and D. L had therefore arrived at the 'obstruction' (W) before M made the overlap which resulted in the foul, and it is clear she could not, under such circumstances, claim room under the provisions of Rule 20 so far as causing L to bear away is concerned. It also seems clear that L would have the right to luff and shut out M before the latter made an overlap. In short, a yacht sailing in between two other yachts which are in positions resembling those occupied by W and L does so at her own risk, and if L had kept away to give room she would have had a grievance against M."

It will be remembered that the facts were as follows:

1. L and D overtook W; L overtaking W to leeward about a boat's length distant, and D overtaking W to windward. On account of the strong, lee-

[3]Dixon Kemp. *A Manual of Yacht and Boat Sailing*, 8th Ed., London, 1895, page 215.

THE SAILING RULES

bow tide *W* did not exercise her right to luff *D* as she pleased.

As overtaken-to-leeward yacht, *W* held right of way over *L*.

2. *M* overtook both *W* and *L*; overtaking *L* to windward and *W* to leeward. Therefore *M* had to keep clear of both yachts.
3. Although overtaken to windward by *M*, *L* did not exercise her right to luff as she pleased.
4. *M* persisted in her attempt to force a passage between *L* and *W*, struck *L*, caromed off that yacht's weather quarter, and collided with *W*.
5. *M* protested *L* for not giving her room to pass between *L* and *W*.
6. No mention was made of a protest of *M* by *W*.

The decision turned on the point that *L* had overtaken and overlapped *W* to leeward *before M* overlapped *L*, and therefore *M* could not force a passage to weather of *L*. (*Sankuntala* v. *Polynia, supra.*)

CASE I

DISCUSSION UNDER PRESENT RULES

Three protests are filed:

1. *M* v. *L*: Violation of Rule 31.
2. *L* v. *M*: (Assumed) Violation of Rule 30 (A).
3. *W* v. *M*: (Assumed) Violation of Rule 30 (C).

Protest No. 1 should be dismissed because Rule 31 never was applicable as to *M* and *L*. Protest No. 2 should be sustained because *M* deliberately sailed into a pocket, or rather a deadly vise between two yachts already overlapped, and as to both of which she had to keep out of the way. Protest No. 3 should be sustained because Rule 31 never was applicable between *W* and *M*. Had *M* overlapped either of the two outside yachts *before* they themselves became overlapped, there would have been a different story.

CASE II

Nancy v. *Redshank; Wraith* v. *Redshank*[4]

$W = Wraith$
$L \ = Redshank$
$M = Nancy$

Position 6 occurred immediately after position 5, *W* being hit on the quarter by *L,* forced on by the impact of *M* on (*L's*) quarter.

Both *M* and *W* protested *L.*

DISCUSSION UNDER FORMER PROPER COURSE RULES

If *M* was at fault in fouling *L, W's* protest of *L* must be dismissed. If *M* was not at fault both protests must be sustained.

The case will be quoted in full, letters being substituted for the names of the yachts.

"ROYAL CORINTHIAN YACHT CLUB

"Nancy v. Redshank

"This was a case of appeal by *M* against a decision of the Club disqualifying her in a race on August 3, 1925, at Burnham-on-Crouch. A collision took place between *L* and *M,* and a third boat, *W,* was also in the collision. *W* also protested against *L.*

[4]*Nancy* v. *Redshank; Wraith* v. *Redshank.* Y. R. A., 1926, Case 6.

THE SAILING RULES

Diagram 42.

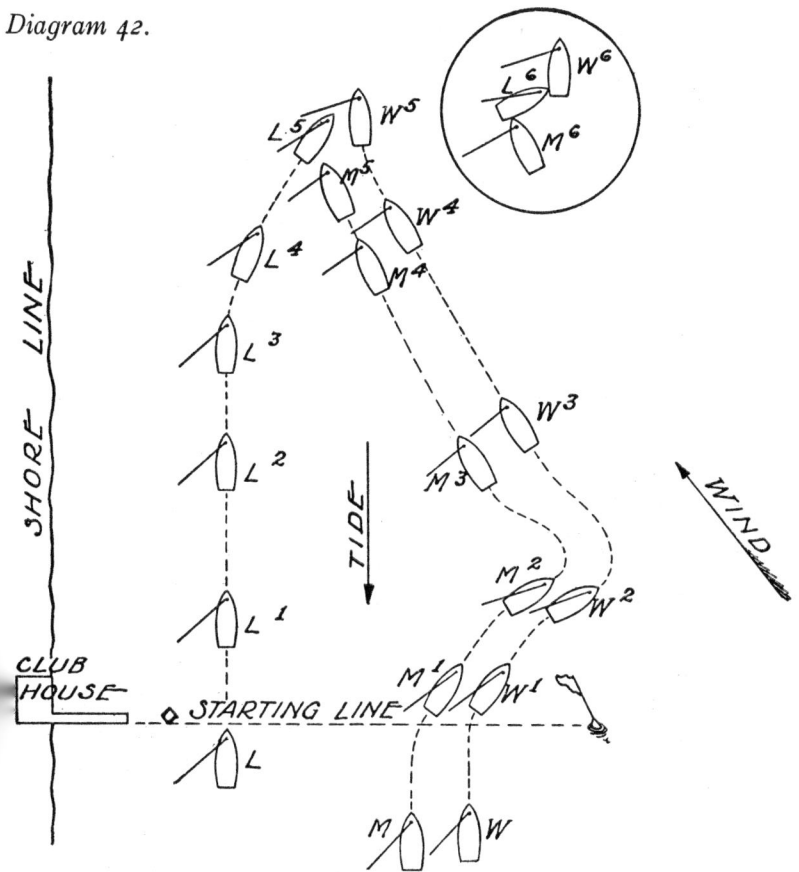

"The Committee found as a fact that *L* at the time of the foul was the overtaken boat, and was entitled to luff *M*, but not *W*.

"They found that *M* should have responded to *L's* luff as she was the overtaking boat, and her helmsman should have checked his boat so as to be able to clear *W* in so doing.

"Committee's Decision.

"The Committee considered the evidence, which they found to be very conflicting, but they were satisfied that according to the official timing, L was clear ahead of M at the start and that M continued to be the overtaking boat until the collision occurred and therefore M's protest was not sustained and she must be disqualified.

"As regards W's protest, the Committee decided that L was wrongfully compelled by M to foul W and therefore L was not disqualified.

"Council's Decision.

"The Council, on the facts stated by the Committee, reverse the Committee's decision. M was only obliged to respond to L's luff as long as she could do so without fouling W (which not being an overtaking boat in relation to either L or M) was an obstruction to sea room. The appeal is upheld and L disqualified."

In 1925, when this foul occurred, Y. R. A. Rule 31 was identical in wording with the first paragraph of Rule 31 at the present time.

The mention by the Council of the words "obstruction to sea room" in Case II, and by Mr. Dixon Kemp in his comments on Case I thirty-five years previously, furnishes the solution to Case II under the former proper course rules.

According to Diagram 42, it would appear that at the start all three yachts were sailing parallel courses, on a broad reach, directly for the next mark; L clear ahead of M and W; W to windward of M, overlapped, and practically abreast. The tide was adverse—bow on.

The Sailing Committee found as a fact:

That at the start, and up to the time of the collisions, M was overtaking yacht in relation to L; but did not say what clause of Rule 30 governed M and W at the start.

THE SAILING RULES

The Committee *ruled:*

1. That L was entitled to luff M;
2. That L had no right to luff W.
3. That M had no right to luff W; and
4. In responding to $L's$ luff, M should have checked her speed in order not to interfere with W.

Rulings 1, 2, and 3 were confirmed by the Council's decision; Ruling 4 was reversed.

Although by Diagram 42, there seems to be a perceptible angle between the courses of L and M at positions 4 and 5, the Committee must have found as a fact, although it was not mentioned in the report of the case, that at those positions the two yachts were sailing approximately the same course, and therefore overlapped as defined by 1925 Y. R. A. footnote to Rule 30, Right of Way, Overlapping and Clear. Plainly, W and M were overlapped. Therefore all three yachts were overlapped.

L had had the right to luff M, but at no time had she been entitled to luff W. It must be assumed, therefore, that W was sailing her proper course under the footnote to Clause (G), before L began to luff. $W's$ rights of way against M, and $M's$ rights of way against W were in the nature of a stalemate; for the reason that while it was $W's$ duty to keep clear of M under Clause (G), it was no less $M's$ duty, although she was leeward yacht, not to luff W to windward of her proper course. W was not overtaking either L or M.

It is hard to understand how Mr. Kemp in commenting upon *Humming Bird* v. *Dolphin,* and the Council in *Nancy* v. *Redshank,* were justified in calling W an obstruction to sea room. In *Humming Bird* v. *Dolphin* M and L were *not* overlapped *before* either of them overlapped W. In *Nancy* v. *Redshank* M and W *were* overlapped *before* either of them overlapped L. The only justification for the Council's statement to that effect in *Nancy* v. *Redshank* would seem to be based upon the 1912 British footnote to the *Meeting, Crossing and Converging* rules. It must have been found as a fact that although W ranked as non-right-of-way yacht under Rule 30 (G) in relation to M, yet she was sailing her proper course and could not be luffed above that course by M on account of the prohibition contained in that footnote. Because of that fact, therefore, and to that extent at least, she was "another yacht racing" of which M had "to keep out of the way." In our opinion L should have been termed the obstruction because she was the "other yacht racing" which M and W, overlapped, were "about to pass."

We will, however, continue our discussion of Case II upon the Council's premise that W, "not being an overtaking boat in relation to either L or M was an obstruction sea room."

At position 4, L and M were overlapped; there was an obstruction (W) to windward of M; L was outside yacht. The three yachts were overlapped. It was $L's$ duty not only to refrain from doing anything which would cause M to foul the obstruction, but also to give her room to keep clear of it. To accomplish this result, L should have ceased to luff when further luffing would have forced M to foul W in $M's$ endeavor to keep clear of L. It follows, therefore, that M was obliged to respond to $L's$ luff only so long as she could do so without fouling W.

When L continued to luff, M had two courses of action. She could respond to the luff, foul W, and be protested, with the chance of being disqualified, or she could hold her course and collide with L. She chose the latter alternative, with the result that the impact of her stem on $L's$ weather quarter caused the latter's bow to swing to

THE SAILING RULES

starboard and collide with *W's* port quarter. Truly a beautiful (?) mix-up.

It would seem that the Council's decision turned on the question whether *W* was or was not an obstruction to sea room within the meaning of Rule 31, in so far as *M* was concerned. If the answer was "Yes," then, as inside yacht, overlapped by *L, M* was entitled to room. The answer was "Yes"—therefore both protests were sustained.

The alternative which *M* elected would have been dangerous in the case of any but the smallest yachts and light airs. One of the cardinal principles of yacht racing is, or at least should be, "Never cause a foul." By that is meant a collision. In a case such as *Nancy* v. *Redshank* where a collision became inevitable, it would have been far better for *M*, when at the last moment she found herself wedged in between *L* and *W*, to have luffed and caused all three yachts, travelling abreast and at nearly the same speed, to have contacted broadside to broadside. This would have lessened the chance of damage to property and possible injury to persons. The decisions of any protests arising therefrom should have resulted in the disqualification of *L* and the exoneration of *M*.

Now let us discuss, for a moment, the *Standard Dictionary* definitions of the words "when passing" as used in 1890 in Rule 20; and "about to pass" as used in Rule 31 in 1925 and at the present time.

The word "passing" means "going by or away." The verb "to pass" means "to go by; over; around; beyond; through, etc.; traverse the extent of." In a recent American decision based upon a protest under Rule 31, the Executive Committee said:

"As used in Rule 31, the phrase 'to pass' does not mean 'to round.' It must be interpreted to mean 'to sail by.' "[5]

[5]*Dinghy No. 33* v. *Dinghy No. 16.* N. A. Y. R. U., Appeal No. 7, December 14, 1936.

THE SAILING RULES

Strictly speaking, M was not "going by" or "about to go by" the obstruction (W) because the obstruction was moving approximately at the same speed and in the same direction of course as was M, and yet if it can be said that M was "about to pass" or "about to traverse the extent of" the obstruction, then W was an obstruction to sea room within the meaning of Rule 31. She was another yacht racing, of which both M and L had to keep out of the way by virtue of the proper course rules.

In his comments on *Humming Bird* v. *Dolphin,* and in the decision of *Nancy* v. *Redshank,* both Mr. Dixon Kemp and the Council termed yacht W an obstruction. To be sure, both authorities broadened the *Standard Dictionary* definition of the words in force at the time of each decision, but can it be said that they were not justified?

Nowhere in the Sailing Rules, except in the last sentence of the first paragraph of Rule 31—as to another yacht racing—was or is there a definition of what constitutes an obstruction to sea room, or when an object, either moving or stationary, becomes such an obstruction. True, the *Standard Dictionary* definition of the words "passing" and "about to pass" implies "going by" a point or an object, whether the point or object be moving or stationary.

We already have seen that reputable authorities of unquestioned standing hold that in sailing along a weather shore the whole of the shore is an obstruction. In passing along a weather shore, at each and every instant a yacht is "passing" or is "about to pass" some particular point on the shore. The shore may be so long in extent that it may take a considerable period of time to pass along it. In such case she surely may be said to be "traversing the extent of" the obstruction.

It would seem correct, therefore, to say that under the

THE SAILING RULES

British proper course rules in force in 1925, the decision in *Nancy* v. *Redshank* was a necessary, logical and inescapable application of the doctrine enunciated by the Council in *Humming Bird* v. *Dolphin* (1890), by Mr. Dixon Kemp in 1895, by the Council in *Sankuntala* v. *Polynia* (1900), and by Major B. Heckstall-Smith in *Yacht Racing, A Text Book on the Sport*, 2d Ed., page 132.

L was disqualified because under the former proper course rules then in force, neither M nor L had the right to luff W to windward of her proper course. Therefore M was entitled to treat W as an obstruction, and M, therefore, could claim room from L under Rule 31.

CASE II

DISCUSSION UNDER PRESENT RULES

In this case the foul occurred in the open sea. We will briefly repeat the facts. At the start, L is clear ahead of both M and W; L and M rank under Rule 30 (B); L and W are beyond range of risk of collision; M and W are overlapped and rank under Rule 30 (G). At position 3 L and W having come within range of risk of collision rank under Rule 30 (G). At position 4 all three yachts are overlapped. At position 5 L luffs sharply; M, being hemmed in by W who luffs only gradually, is unable to respond quickly enough, rams L's starboard quarter, and the impact causes L to ram W's port quarter as shown at position 6.

We will assume that five protests are filed, viz.:
1. M v. W for violation of Rule 31;
2. W v. L for violation of Rule 30 (K);
3. L v. M for violation of Rule 30 (B);
4. M v. L for violation of Rule 31; and
5. M v. W for violation of Rule 30 (G).

THE SAILING RULES

Protest No. 1

M's protest against W for violation of Rule 31 should be sustained. At position 4 M and W, overlapped, are "about to pass" L, another yacht racing, out of whose way M must keep clear. L has a positive right of way over M under Rule 30 (B). She also has a positive right of way over W under Rule 30 (G). W, however, has only a negative right of way over M under that rule, viz., the right not to be luffed sharply. When M overlaps L, Rule 31 supersedes Rule 30 (G) as between M and W. By virtue of the last sentence of the first paragraph of Rule 31, L ranks as an obstruction which M is in danger of fouling unless permitted to keep clear by W. W is outside yacht and must give M room to keep clear of the obstruction L. W alone is to blame for the two collisions.

Suppose, for example, that L were a deep draft yacht sailing in a narrow channel; that at position 5 the channel turned sharply to the right and that she had to make a sharp luff in order not to run aground; and that in order to keep clear of L, M was obliged also to luff sharply. Can there be any doubt that W would have to respond in like manner?

Of course, if at the last moment M could have borne away under L's stern and thus have avoided the crash she should have done so. She should then have protested W under Rule 31.

Protest No. 2

W's protest of L for violation of Rule 30 (K) should be dismissed. W should have kept clear of M, thereby permitting the latter yacht to keep clear of L. W's neglect to give room to M under Rule 31 caused M to ram L. L had the right to luff M sharply. No question of balking is involved.

THE SAILING RULES

Protest No. 3

L's protest of *M* for violation of Rule 30 (B) should be dismissed. *M* and *W* were overlapped before *M* overlapped *L*. Therefore, *L* being the yacht which the two yachts already overlapped "are about to pass" must, by our process of elimination discussed earlier in this Chapter, be the obstruction. Rule 31 is applicable only as between *M* and *W*. It is not applicable as between *M* and *L*. *L's* right to luff *M* sharply under Rule 30 (B) is not impaired. When *L* luffs *M* sharply, *W* loses her negative right not to be luffed sharply in turn by *M*. *W* must give *M* room to keep clear of *L*. *M* is not to blame for the collision between herself and *L* because she was prevented from keeping clear of *L* by *W*, the outside of the two yachts already overlapped.

As we remarked previously, in discussing the case under the former British proper course footnote, it would have been far better seamanship had *M* luffed into *W* and thus have caused the three yachts to contact broadside to broadside.

Protest No. 4

M's protest of *L* for violation of Rule 31 should be dismissed. *W* is not the obstruction to *M*. Rule 31 is not applicable as between *M*. and *L*.

Protest No. 5

M's protest of *W* for violation of Rule 30 (G) should be dismissed. When *M*, already overlapped on *W*, overlaps *L*, another yacht racing and ranking as an obstruction to *M*, Rule 30 (G), which up to that moment had governed *M* and *W*, is temporarily superseded by Rule 31.

Diagram 43.

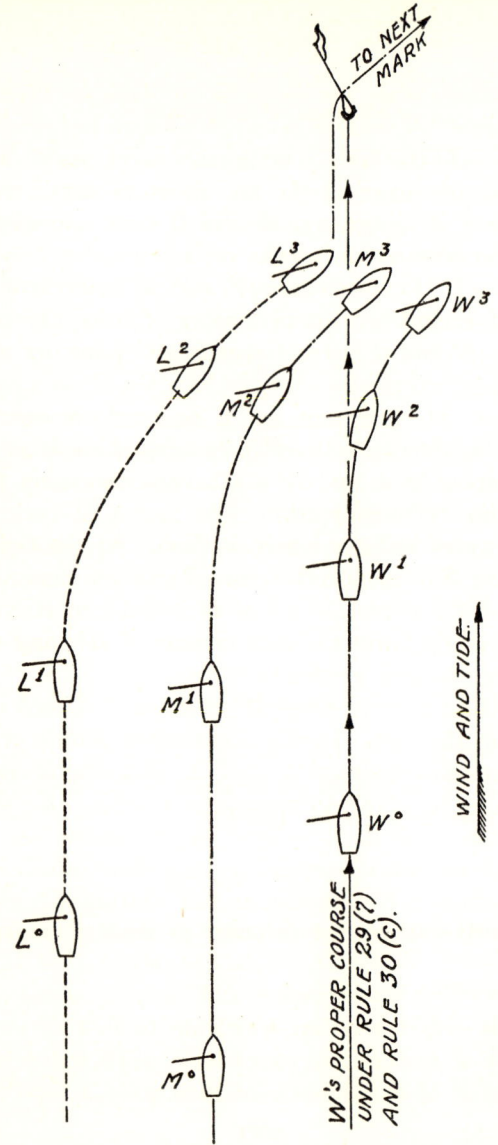

THE SAILING RULES

CASE III

SUPPOSITITIOUS CASE

In this case the facts intentionally were made different from those in either of the two previous actual cases.

In Case I, Diagram 41, W and L were overlapped *before* M established an overlap on L.

In Case II, Diagram 42, W and M were overlapped *before* M established an overlap on L. At the start of the race W and L were beyond the range of risk of collision.

In Case III, Diagram 43, L and M are overlapped *before* M establishes an overlap to leeward on W.

At position O, L and W are beyond the range of risk of collision. M comes from clear astern of both yachts and endeavors to pass between them. At position 1, L and W are still outside the risk of collision zone; M has overlapped L; M and W are within range of risk of collision; L and M still are clear astern of W; and then L commences to luff gradually.

At position 2, M overlaps W to leeward; L and W now are within the zone, having approached within it somewhere between positions 1 and 2, and, therefore, rank under Rule 30 (G)—Converging. L now luffs sharply; M responds; and W is obliged to luff above her proper course for the mark in order to keep clear of M.

At position 3, L continues to luff sharply, M responds, and W luffs still further in order to avoid a collision.

Five protests are filed as follows:

1. M v. L for violation of Rule 31;
2. W v. L for violation of Rule 30 (K);
3. W v. M for violation of Rule 30 (C);

THE SAILING RULES

4. *L* v. *M* for violation of Rule 30 (B); and
5. *M* v. *W* for violation of Rule 31.

Bearing in mind the last paragraph of Rule 30 which reads:

> *"A yacht may be disqualified on a protest arising out of a breach of any of these clauses whether a collision result or not."*

how should each of the five protests be decided?

Protest No. 1.

M's protest of *L* for violation of Rule 31 should be sustained. While *M* is still clear astern of *L* and *W* there is always an uncertainty which of the two outside yachts will eventually rank as the obstruction. (Rule 31, first paragraph, last sentence.) *M* must keep clear of both. It so happens that *M* overlaps *L* before *M* overlaps *W*. At position 1, *L* has the right to luff *M* sharply (Rule 30 (B)) and force her to windward of *W*. She neglects this opportunity and thereby permits *M* to overlap *W* to leeward. Thus the three yachts are overlapped. Under Rule 30 (C) *W* holds right of way over *M* and is entitled to sail her proper course for the mark. *L* holds right of way over the other two yachts but with greater luffing rights over *M* than over *W*. When *L* permits *M* to overlap *W* to leeward, *W* becomes an obstruction to *M* under Rule 31; that rule temporarily supersedes Rule 30 (B) as between *L* and *M*, and *M* as inside yacht can invoke Rule 31 against *L*. *L's* right to luff *M* sharply under Rule 30 (B) temporarily terminates as does also her right to luff *W* gradually under Rule 30 (G).

THE SAILING RULES

Protest No. 2

W's protest of *L* for violation of Rule 30 (K) should be dismissed. No question of balking is involved. Although *L* had right of way over *W* under Rule 30 (G), that right was temporarily suspended when *M* overlapped *W* to leeward and brought Rule 31 into operation.

Protest No. 3

W's protest of *M* under Rule 30 (C) also should be dismissed. Under Rule 31, paragraph one, last sentence, *W* ranks as an obstruction to *M* the moment *M* and *W* are overlapped because of the fact that by Rule 30 (C) *W* holds right of way over *M*. Although *L* holds right of way over both *M* and *W*, *M* established her overlap on *L* *before* *L* negligently permitted *M* to overlap *W* to leeward. Therefore under the wording of the last sentence of paragraph one of Rule 31, *W* becomes the obstruction for the purpose of the rule, and *M* can claim room from *L* because, although *W* is not an obstruction to *L*, *W* *is* an obstruction to *M*, and *L* and *M* are overlapped *before* *M* reaches (overlaps) *W*. *L's* continued luffing, whether sharp or gradual, after all three yachts were overlapped and Rule 31 temporarily superseded Rule 30 (B) as between *L* and *M*, was illegal. *M* properly responded to the luff, however, in order to avoid a collision, and cannot be held to have contravened Rule 30 (C). *L* alone is to blame for all the violations of the rules.

Protest No. 4

L's protest of *M* for breaching Rule 30 (B) should be dismissed for the same reasons that protest No. 1 was

THE SAILING RULES

sustained. When *L* does not luff *M* sharply and, after *L* and *M* are overlapped, permits *M* to overlap *W* to leeward, Rule 31 then becomes operative as between *L* and *M*, *L's* rights under Rule 30 (B) temporarily are suspended by Rule 31, and she is obliged to give *M* room to keep clear of *W*.

Protest No. 5

M's protest of *W* for violation of Rule 31 should be dismissed. *M's* only right of way over *W* is negative, *i.e.*, the right *not* to be forced to leeward of *W's* proper course for the mark. *M's* right of action under Rule 31 is against *L*, the outside of the two yachts already overlapped—alone. Furthermore, *W did* keep clear of *M*.

SUMMARY

Let us summarize the vital points of yacht racing law under the present rules involved in the situations discussed in this chapter.

First, it is risking almost certain disqualification for a yacht clear astern to endeavor to overtake *between* two yachts *already within* their own risk of collision zone *and* overlapped and over neither of which she has right of way.

Second, if the yacht clear astern can establish an overlap inside of one of the yachts clear ahead *before* the latter has established her own overlap on the third yacht, then the third yacht, the other of the two outside yachts, becomes the obstruction, and the inside yacht is entitled to be given room by the yacht on which she first established an overlap.

Third, the third yacht must be a yacht of which the middle yacht "has to keep out of the way."

THE SAILING RULES

SUMMARY OF PROTEST DECISIONS IN CHAPTER XIII UNDER PRESENT RULES

CASE NO.	PROTEST NO.	TITLE OF PROTEST	VIOLATION ALLEGED RULE NO.	DECISION
I	1	M vs. L	20 (1890); 31 (1940)	Dismissed
	2	L vs. M	30 (A) (assumed)	Sustained
	3	W vs. M	30 (C) (assumed)	Sustained
II	1	M vs. W	31	Sustained
	2	W vs. L	30 (K) (assumed)	Dismissed
	3	L vs. M	30 (B) (assumed)	Dismissed
	4	M vs. L	31 (assumed)	Dismissed
	5	M vs. W	30 (G) (assumed)	Dismissed
III	1	M vs. L	31 (assumed)	Sustained
	2	W vs. L	30 (K) (assumed)	Dismissed
	3	W vs. M	30 (C) (assumed)	Dismissed
	4	L vs. M	30 (B) (assumed)	Dismissed
	5	M vs. W	31 (assumed)	Dismissed

Chapter XIV

RULE 32

CLOSE-HAULED, APPROACHING AN OBSTRUCTION TO SEA ROOM OR A MARK

If two yachts are standing close-hauled on the same tack towards the shore, or an obstruction to sea room which requires the leeward yacht to alter her course to clear it, and if she is not able to tack without coming into collision with the yacht to windward; the latter shall, on being hailed by the person in charge of the leeward yacht, at once allow her room to tack. A yacht so claiming room shall be bound to tack immediately her hail is responded to. If the leeward yacht elects to clear the obstruction by bearing away she shall allow the windward yacht room to do the same if she so desires. But if the obstruction is a mark of the course the leeward yacht has not the right to so hail the other about if that other can herself pass the mark without tacking.

Although it is only in this rule that a hail is mentioned, other situations may arise in which under Rule 1 a hail should be given before making an alteration of course which may not be foreseen by the other yacht.

The three requisites to invoke the rule are:

1. Both yachts *close-hauled* on the same tack;
2. Both yachts *approaching* the shore or obstruction;

THE SAILING RULES

3. *Alteration of course by leeward yacht* in order to clear the obstruction by
   (a) tacking, in which case she cannot avoid a collision with the windward yacht, or
   (b) bearing away to leeward of the obstruction.

The fourth essential part of the rule is a reservation pertaining to a mark of the course. It is the last sentence of the first paragraph, and is to the effect that if the windward yacht is able to weather the mark without tacking but the leeward yacht cannot, the latter may not hail the former about.

Rule 32 differs from Rule 31 in that to invoke Rule 31 an overlap is a prerequisite while to invoke Rule 32 it is not.

Rule 32 provides protection for a yacht close-hauled, approaching a shore or an obstruction which necessitates an alteration of course to clear it. The intention is that although a yacht must not call for room too soon, she must not be carried to a point that involves actual danger of grounding or fouling. "The danger point is indefinite, and the relief provided is a hail for room, with the qualification that the yacht hailing shall tack at the same time as the yacht hailed."[1]

This quotation does not exactly convey the correct interpretation of the first sentence of the rule. The yacht hailed is not obliged to tack, her only duty is to "at once *allow*" the other "room to tack."[2] *Jade* v. *Bluebell* is one of the few decisions in which the Council delivered a full and comprehensive opinion.

B, (*Jade*), was so far to leeward of A, (*Bluebell*),

---

[1] *Elmina* v. *Queen*. N. Y. Y. C., 1906. *Decisions and Rulings, 1849–1923*, page 30; Dixon Kemp. *A Manual of Yacht and Boat Sailing*, 8th Ed., page 222.

[2] *Jade v. Bluebell.* Y. R. A., 1936, Case 3.

that when she hailed for water and *A* did not respond by tacking immediately, *B* was able to tack to port and go under *A's* stern.

Some parts of the Council's decision are most instructive. We quote:

"(1) The claim by *B* that Rule 32 dictates that *A* should have 'gone about' is incorrect. Rule 32 provides she should at once allow *B* 'room to tack,' which does not necessarily entail going about.

"(3) *A's* complaint that Rule 32 gives her no indication what she should do in case of doubt is not justified. Rule 32 could not be plainer, she must give room to *B*, she is absolutely compelled to do so whether there is any doubt or not. If room does not already exist she must give room at once.

"(4) . . . It may not be necessary to *come about,* although it is absolutely necessary to see that the leeward boat has room to do so.

"(5) The Committee's observation 'that it is essential that leeward boats should not hail other craft about if it is possible for them to tack without coming into collision' is a misapprehension of the meaning of Rule 32.

"It is a very safe and seamanlike thing for a leeward yacht to hail, and if she has the smallest doubt as to whether she can tack without coming into collision with the weather yacht, she would be very wrong not to hail. Rule 32 emphasises that in this situation a hail must be given, and under Rule I other situations may arise where a hail should be given.

"A hail, in fact, is to be encouraged. It is not necessarily a call for the other vessel 'to go about' but it is a demand for *sea room* for which competitors must be on the lookout."

Even if the windward yacht sees her opponent is in

THE SAILING RULES

danger of running aground she is under no obligation to tack until hailed. Furthermore, she is entitled to reasonable notice of the leeward yacht's intention to tack. The hail must be given in time to permit the windward yacht to give the hailing yacht room to tack. "It is the duty of the weather yacht to give room, namely, to keep out of the way or tack as the case may require directly she is hailed; but there is no obligation upon her to do so earlier. The lee boat should give her hail in time to allow the other to give her room to tack. Decision of Sailing Committee reversed. Appeal of *A* (windward yacht) succeeds and *B* is disqualified under Rule 30 (I)."[3]

In *Red Jacket* v. *Blue Bell* the yachts close-hauled on the port tack were abreast of each other and only a few feet apart when *B,* the leeward yacht, hailed and without giving *A* a chance to respond jammed down her tiller causing her port bow to contact *B's* starboard quarter as the boats swung to windward and nearly parallel.

It is of the essence of Rule 32 that if the leeward yacht hails for water or for other legitimate cause, and the windward yacht tacks in response to the hail, the leeward yacht must tack at as near the same instant as possible. The leeward yacht may not hold on even for a short distance after the windward yacht has started to tack because this might give the leeward yacht an unfair advantage.[4]

In *Blue Bird* v. *Fay,* the boats were 14′ dinghies. *B,* leeward yacht, "carried on for an appreciable distance (at least two boat lengths) after *A* had responded (by tacking) thereby contravening Rule 32 and is thereby disqualified." The Council, without comment, upheld the decision of the Sailing Committee.[4]

The burden of proof should be on the weather yacht to prove that the leeward yacht was not justified in hailing

[3]*Red Jacket* v. *Blue Bell.* Y. R. A., 1938, Case 6.
[4]*Blue Bird* v. *Fay.* Y. R. A., 1939, Case 1.

THE SAILING RULES

for room because the leeward yacht is the judge of her own peril.[5] The hailing yacht, however, is subject to disqualification if she hails prematurely or without proper cause because "a yacht must be held responsible for her hail."[6]

"The rule must be interpreted by the ordinary customs dictated by prudence, and such careful navigation as yacht racing admits of."[7]

Even if there is quite a stretch of deep water between a government buoy and the shoal so that B, the leeward yacht, can pass on the wrong side of the buoy without danger of grounding, she is entitled, nevertheless, to be allowed to pass on the channel side of the buoy. If the weather yacht does not respond to the hail and allow B room to tack she, (A), will be disqualified.[8]

The contention has been advanced that, even if the windward yacht is of opinion that the leeward yacht's hail is unwarranted or illegal, it is her duty always to tack immediately and protest if she sees fit. The following case is often cited in support of that contention.

The incident occurred a few seconds before the start of a race. The starting line was the prolongation of a line between two objects on shore. The start was to windward. Both yachts were approaching the shore close-hauled on the starboard tack, overlapped, A to windward of B. B called for water. A did not respond. The bottom was sand, free from rocks or banks. After hailing, B bore away slightly and reached toward the shore. At gunfire

[5]Dixon Kemp. *An Exposition of the Yacht Racing Rules*, London, 1898, page 92.
[6]*Character of a Mark*. N. Y. Y. C. *Decisions and Rulings*, 1849–1923, page 12.
[7]Dixon Kemp. *A Manual of Yacht and Boat Sailing*, 8th Ed., page 222.
[8]*Flying Cloud* v. *Advance*. N. Y. Y. C., 1926 Report of Race Committee, page 7.

both yachts hauled on the wind, tacked to port and immediately thereafter crossed the starting line. Both skippers were very familiar with the course having raced over it many times. The question before the Sailing Committee was "must the weather yacht 'stay' when hailed for water, although she knows there is water, having seen a sister ship approach the shore much closer a few minutes earlier?"

The Committee answered the question in the negative because they dismissed *B's* protest under Rule 32 "on the ground that *B* called for water when she had no need to. This was borne out by the fact that after hailing she sailed about forty yards (equal to 7 L.W.L. lengths) toward the shore before coming about, and she could have gone farther in without touching the ground."

The Council, without comment, disqualified both yachts.[9] Apparently they disqualified *B* for hailing without cause, and disqualified *A* for not tacking immediately in response to the hail although *A's* disqualification would seem difficult to reconcile with paragraph (1) of the Council's remarks in *Jade* v. *Bluebell, supra,* decided two years later.

There should be kept in mind the distinction—seemingly valid—between hailing another yacht about based upon a clear mistake of law as to the interpretation of a rule, and a hailing about legally made upon a mistaken assumption of facts in respect to hidden, underwater dangers.

In the latter case the danger of precisely marking underwater obstructions and the desirability of avoiding risk of serious mishap, probably justifies the requirement that the right-of-way yacht shall respond immediately to the hail and allow the leeward yacht room to tack, although such immediate response may seriously prejudice her position in respect to other yachts in the race.

[9] *Coomara* v. *Pixie.* Y. R. A., 1934, Case 3.

THE SAILING RULES

The Council's disqualification of *A*, the weather yacht, in *Coomara* v. *Pixie*, would seem to indicate that the Council believed *B's* hail to belong to the second category, and that it would be unwise to make an exception merely because *A's* skipper *knew* that *B* could carry on as she did.

On the other hand where no question of fact as to submerged dangers exists and a yacht hails another about in a situation where the rule governing the case does not permit a hail, to require immediate response on pain of disqualification would seem to be legally unconscionable as well as inequitable from the standpoint of fair sailing. It would seem unjust in such a case to impose upon the yacht hailed any duty other than to avoid actual collision. A protest case based upon such a situation and appealed to competent and final authority would be a welcome addition to yacht racing jurisprudence.

There are many interesting cases involving Rule 32.

Diagram 44.

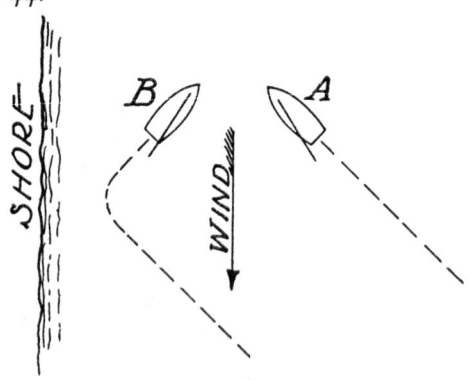

B had been approaching the shore. She tacked to port and stood offshore. Meeting *A*, *B* hailed for room. *A* did not tack, and *B* protested. Her protest was not sustained.

THE SAILING RULES

She was not *approaching* the shore at the time she hailed *A* about. She should either have tacked to starboard, luffed into the wind, or borne away under *A's* stern.[10]

Another case on exactly the same facts as those in Diagram 44 is that of *Princess* v. *Elena,* which occurred in Vineyard Sound, Massachusetts, in 1912 in a race held by the New York Yacht Club.[11]

In each case it was merely a question of port and starboard tack.

Diagram 45.

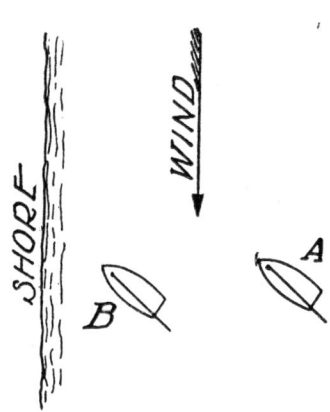

In this case *B* is *approaching* the shore and may, therefore, hail *A* about.[12] If, however, *A* is far enough to windward so that *B* can tack and safely pass astern of *A*, *B* may not hail *A* about.[13]

If, however, at the time *B* hails, there is reasonable

[10]*Halcyone* v. *Bedouin.* Y. R. A., 1879.
[11]*Princess* v. *Elena.* N. Y. Y. C., 1912. *Decisions and Rulings,* 1849-1923, page 44.
[12]*Flying Cloud* v. *Advance.* N. Y. Y. C., 1926. Report of Race Committee, page 7.
[13]*Emerald* v. *Nona.* Y. R. A., 1924, Case 1.

THE SAILING RULES

doubt of her ability to tack and then go under *A's* stern, the latter will be disqualified on protest even if *B does* succeed in clearing *A*.[14]

Two centreboard yachts close-hauled on the starboard tack were sailing nearly parallel to a lee shore. *B,* ahead and to leeward, was in a position to hail *A* about if and when the shore or an obstruction should be reached. It was nearly high water. The finish line was at right angles to the shore. Just short of the finish line was a jetty, also at a right angle to the shore. The outer end of the jetty was submerged but with sufficient water over it at that stage of the tide to permit passage by the yachts if they raised their boards slightly. Presently *B* called for room and hailed *A* about. *A* replied "Lift up your centreboard!," and refused to tack. *B's* centreboard scraped the submerged portion of the jetty lightly. She hauled up her board a trifle, luffed and passed over the obstruction. *B's* protest of *A* was sustained.

"The Council decided:

1. That *A* had no right to hail *B* to lift her centreboard to pass the obstruction.
2. *B's* neglect to go about immediately she hailed for water does *not* affect the issue of this case without having regard to what *A* did or did not do."[15]

At the International Conference in London in November, 1929, a new clause was inserted to the effect that if the leeward yacht is obliged to alter course to clear the obstruction but elects to pass to leeward of it, she must permit the windward yacht to do likewise if she so desires.

[14]*No. 1 O. D. Dinghy* v. *No. 2 O. D. Dinghy.* Y. R. A., 1926, page 151.
[15]*Gwen* v. *Fulmar.* Y. R. A., 1903, page 109.

THE SAILING RULES

Diagram 46.

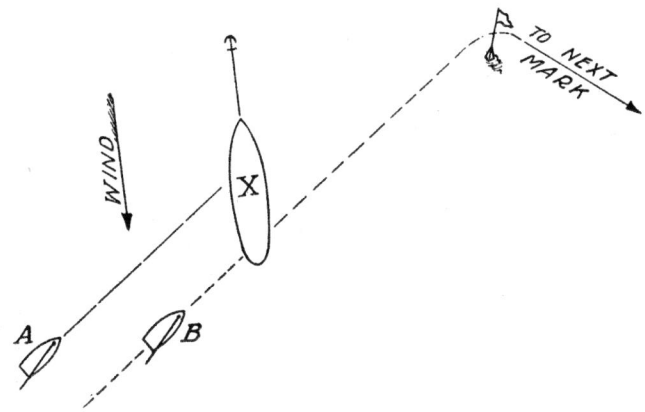

In Diagram 46, *B* may hail *A* about, but if *B* elects to bear away and pass to leeward of *X* she must allow *A* "room to do the same if she desires."

We now come to the last sentence of the first paragraph of the rule, already referred to at the beginning of this Chapter. For many years prior to 1895 a part of the British Y. R. A. Sailing Rules, it was not added to the Racing Rules of the New York Yacht Club until that year when it was incorporated therein as Rule XVI—Right of Way—Section 16, as a result of the *Volunteer* v. *Gracie* foul in approaching a weather mark off Block Island in a race of the New York Yacht Club in 1891. It was not adopted by the Eastern Yacht Club of Marblehead, Massachusetts, until eleven years later, when it appeared in the Racing Rules of that Club as Rule XIII—Right of Way—Section 9.

Here was the *Volunteer* v. *Gracie* situation.

Both yachts were close-hauled on the starboard tack; *Gracie* ahead but to leeward, and unable to weather the

THE SAILING RULES

Diagram 47.

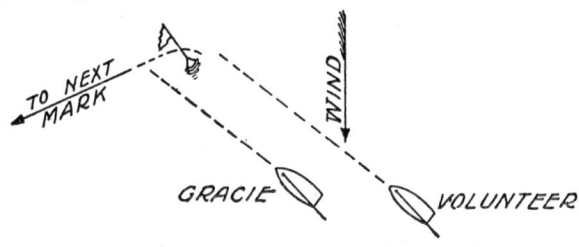

mark without tacking, *Gracie* forced *Volunteer* to tack, and on protest, was disqualified.[16]

The logic of the decision is unanswerable. Picture what would happen if the leeward yacht had the right to hail the other about merely because it was a mark which she desired to pass on the required side.

Diagram 48.

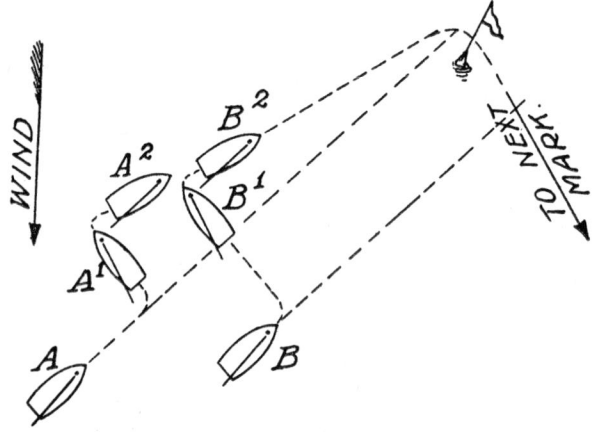

[16]*Volunteer* v. *Gracie*. N. Y. Y. C., 1891. *Decisions and Rulings, 1849–1923*, page 7.

THE SAILING RULES

Here we have two yachts close-hauled on the port tack, approaching a mark required to be left to starboard. B is ahead but to leeward. A can weather the mark without tacking, B cannot. If B could hail A about, they would assume position A^1, B^1. B would of course continue on the starboard tack until able to fetch the mark. When she again tacked to port their respective positions would be A^2, B^2. A moment later B would be around the mark with A in her wake. From a disadvantageous, leeward position, B would have become leading yacht, a most unfair climax to the battle up the wind.

Again, let us remove the mark. It resolves itself into a question either of port and starboard tack, as it would have been had both yachts originally been on the starboard tack, or a question of gathering proper way under Rule 30 (I). B was not far enough ahead to enable her to tack and gather proper way on her new tack before she would collide with A.

The object of this sentence of the rule is to protect the yacht which by superior windward work has just managed to fetch the weather mark, and to prevent her being hailed about by the yacht which has failed to fetch. In actual racing this precise situation rarely arises. It usually happens that neither can fetch, or that both can fetch, or the weather yacht fearing her competitor either will fetch or will claim that she could do so, and being aware of her own obligation as outside yacht, if overlapped, to give the leeward yacht room if she does fetch, is careful not to make her final tack for the mark until she can weather it with ease.

A rather recent case based on the last sentence of the first paragraph of Rule 32 is one which occurred at the start of the Astor Cup race on August 11, 1933. The start was to windward. At the westerly end of the long

THE SAILING RULES

starting line was Brenton Reef Lightship. At the easterly end was the Committee boat *Wilhelmina.* The direction of the first leg of the course was E x S, and the starting line was at right angles to the first leg. Let us quote from the Race Committee Report:

"Shortly before the starting signal *Cantitoe,* (*A*), on the starboard tack, was sailing on the leeward side of the starting line with the wind slightly free and toward the Committee boat. *Weetamoe,* (*B*), was to leeward of *A,* also sailing slightly off the wind and was the overtaking yacht. Both yachts started to cross the starting line hard on the starboard tack after the starting signal, *B* crossing some seconds after *A,* and *B* luffed and crossed the bow of the Committee boat by a narrow margin."

The facts further showed that when the yachts hardened on the wind *A* could just clear the bow of the Committee boat but that *B,* still overtaking *A* to leeward, could not. *B* "called for room to tack, the right to do which was denied by *A.* In spite of which *B* tacked to port and forced *A* about in order to avoid a serious collision." (Quoted from *A's* protest.)

The Race Committee disqualified *Weetamoe* (*B*), for forcing *A* about in violation of Rule 32, first paragraph, last sentence.[17]

On all fours with *Cantitoe* v. *Weetamoe* but with the sole exception that it occurred just before the finish instead of at the start is a very recent decision. The boats were dinghies. The northerly end of a breakwater marked the southerly end of the finish line which ran approximately north and south. The wind was N.E. *B* was a couple of boat-lengths ahead of *A* and about the same distance to leeward. Both boats were close-hauled on the

[17]*Cantitoe* v. *Weetamoe.* N. Y. Y. C. 1933 Report of Race Committee, page 4.

THE SAILING RULES

port tack. *A* could safely weather the end of the breakwater; *B* could not. The Race Committee found that there was no way in which *A* could have avoided the collision when *B* suddenly flung about on the starboard tack without hailing. *B* was disqualified under Rule 30 (I). The Executive Committee remarked that in view of the last sentence of the first paragraph of Rule 32, *B* had not the right to hail *A* about.[18]

Now take this case.

Diagram 49.

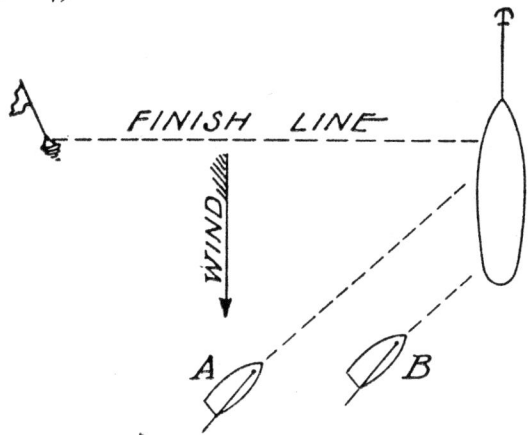

At one end of the finish line is a flag mark. At the other is a large Committee boat which neither yacht can weather without tacking. In this situation, *B* may hail *A* about as *A*, herself, must tack in order to clear the obstruction and cross the finish line.

The next and last situation to be discussed under Rule 32 is one involving two divisions of yachts on opposite tacks, and about to meet as shown in the following diagram.

[18]*Jake* v. *Kittiwake*. N. A. Y. R. U. Appeal No. 8, February 6, 1939.

THE SAILING RULES

Diagram 50.

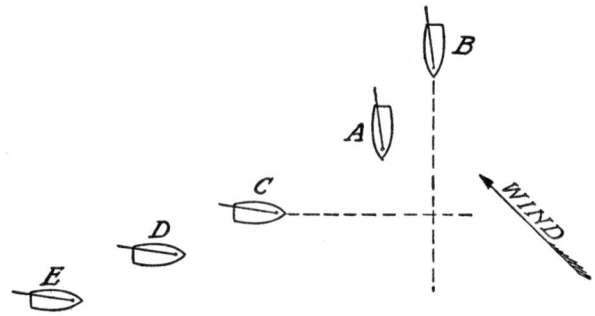

A and *B*, close-hauled on the port tack but not overlapped, are about to meet *C, D* and *E*, close-hauled on the starboard tack. In *A's* opinion, *B* cannot cross the starboard tack division. Rather than bear away under *E's* stern, *A* hails *B* about. *B* thinks she can safely cross *C* and refuses to tack. The question is whose judgment should be paramount? It would seem that the judgment of *A* should govern, and that if *B* refuses to tack in response to the hail, and a moment later her skipper changes his mind and concludes he cannot cross *C*, and *then* tacks, *A's* protest under Rule 32 should be sustained.

By the terms of the last sentence of the first paragraph of Rule 31, *C, D* and *E* rank as obstructions to *A*. Under present Rule 32, *A* may elect whether to bear away under the stern of the starboard tack yachts, in which case she must permit *B* "to do the same if she so desires" or she may hail *B* about.

In Chapter VI we briefly touched upon the ethics of a hail before making a sudden luff. Rule 32 is the only rule under which a situation can arise which *requires* a hail before altering course. Under no other rule is a hail for buoy room, for right of way or for what-not, required.

THE SAILING RULES

The second and last paragraph of the rule seems quite significant. It would seem strongly to imply that it is good sportsmanship to warn a competitor before an alteration of course is made which he cannot reasonably foresee or which he has every reasonable right to assume will not be made. Surely this is the implication which may be read between the lines of the last paragraph of Rule 32.

CHAPTER XV

RULES 33, 34 and 35

Rule 33

FOULING OR IMPROPERLY ROUNDING MARKS

A yacht must go fairly around the course, rounding the series of marks as specified in the instructions, and in rounding each specified mark her track from the preceding to the following mark must enclose it on the required side. A yacht shall not touch a mark of the course unless wrongfully compelled to do so by another yacht. A yacht which has touched a mark of the course must immediately either abandon the race or hoist a protest signal. Every essential or ordinary above-water part of any object named as a mark, counts as a mark, but no part below water, nor any object accidentally or temporarily attached to the mark.

Unless so designated in the sailing instructions for the race, the Committee boat is *not* a mark of the course in the sense that it must be enclosed by the yacht's track. Accordingly it should be shifted so that at the finish the flag mark will be left by the yachts, on the same side as it was passed when starting. See Diagram 51. If this is not done and the race circular does not prescribe how it shall be left at the finish, the flag mark at the other end of the starting line will *not* be enclosed by the yacht's track around the course. See Diagram 52. The Committee boat merely limits one end of the starting and finishing lines, and is a mark for these lines only. It is not a mark to be rounded unless specially mentioned in the instructions.

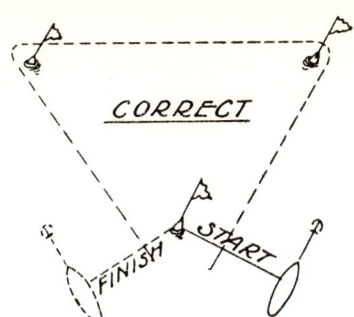

Diagram 51.

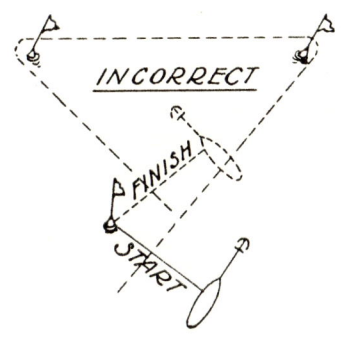

Diagram 52.

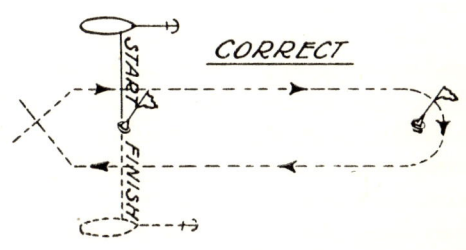

Diagram 53.

THE SAILING RULES

The same is true for windward, or leeward races and return, as shown in Diagram 53.

Now what is the meaning of the phrase *"her track from the preceding to the following mark must enclose it on the required side"?*

First let us consult the dictionary. "Track" is defined as "mark left by the passage of anything"; "line drawn." "Enclose" is defined as "to surround, as with a fence."

Let us consider the case illustrated in Diagram 54 (*A*), (*B*) and (*C*).

Diagram 54 (A), (B) and (C).

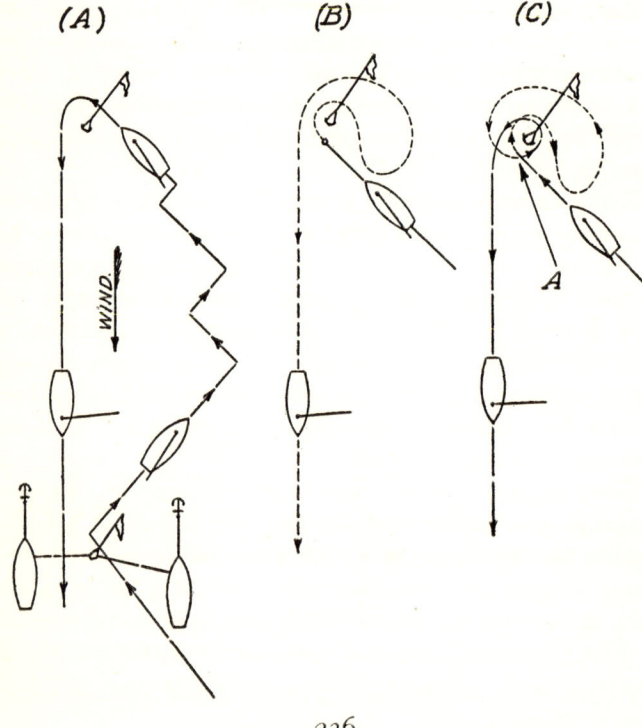

THE SAILING RULES

The course is windward and leeward; the windward mark to be left to port. Diagram 54 (*A*) "illustrates the proper 'track' according to Rule 33."[1] Diagram 54 (*B*) depicts the course actually sailed in the "improper attempt to leave the mark to PORT."[1] Diagram 54 (*C*) portrays the course the yacht "should have taken to correct error."[1] In Diagram 54 (*C*) " '*A*' indicates intersection of IMPROPER course with *correct* course incident to leaving the windward mark on the port hand."[1] To the same effect as to Diagram 54 (*B*), is *Queenstown People's Regatta Committee,* Y. R. A., 1899, page 107.

It has been argued that because a yacht returned to or actually crossed the track which she followed from the previous mark—say the starting-line flag mark—to the windward mark, her track *enclosed* the windward mark and therefore that she rounded the windward mark as required by Rule 33. This argument is illustrated by Diagram 55 (*A*).

Every yachtsman knows how difficult it is to judge from a moving vessel whether she is on the easterly side or on the westerly side of a north and south line between two stationary objects some distance apart. How often we have worried whether we were "back of" or "over" a long starting line as we counted off the final ten seconds before gunfire. A few feet one way or the other—yes, even a few inches—might mean the difference between winning or losing the race.

There is only one sure way for the yacht in Diagram 55 (*A*) to be certain that she has returned to or actually crossed her previous track. Only by anchoring and then taking accurate compass bearings of the flag mark on the starting line and also of the windward mark, can she *prove* to the Committee beyond all question of doubt and by in-

[1] *N. A. Y. R. U. Bulletin No. 26,* January 18, 1935, pages 26 and 27.

Diagram 55 (A), (B) and (C).

MARK TO BE LEFT TO STARBOARD.

(A)

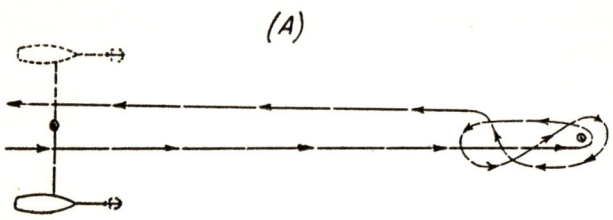

(B)

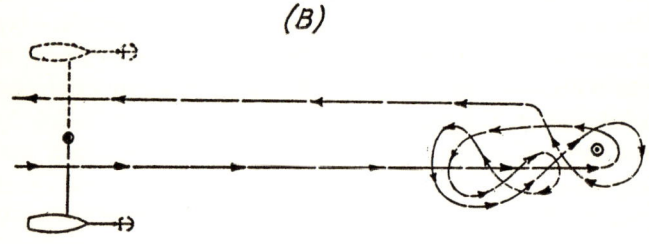

(C)

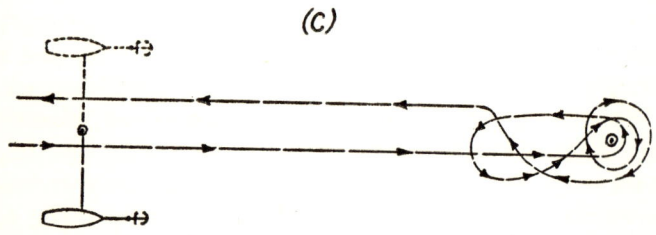

THE SAILING RULES

controvertible mathematics the correctness of her claim.

But even if she thus proves her position, has she complied with the requirements of the rule? What test can we apply to ascertain whether the rule has been obeyed?

If the rule merely means that the yacht shall pass *outside* of the mark, *i.e.,* at some time during the race leave the mark *between* herself and the preceding as well as the following mark, it might perhaps be legal to make a complete turn in each direction as shown in Diagram 55 (*A*). The last clause of the first sentence of the rule, however, contains a further requirement. It speaks of "her track from the preceding to the following mark."

We believe there should be read into the rule the figurative requirement that as the yacht proceeds in the race she pays out a log line or a board on end which has both a starboard and a port side. When the yacht crosses the finish line—which we assume has been properly established as shown in Diagrams 51, 54, and 55 (*C*)—the log line not only must pass outside of and "fence in" each turning mark but also must contact each such mark on the side of the log line, starboard or port, as specified in the race circular or instructions.

For example, if the instructions for a triangular course state that all marks shall be left to port, then the log line must enclose them all with the port side of the log line or board on end contacting the outer side of each mark when the two ends of the log line are pulled taut and a straight line is made by the log line from mark to mark.

This test is commonly termed the "string" or "thread" test. When brought together back of the starting-line flag mark and pulled taut, the two ends of the string must enclose every mark on the required side. Every turning mark, as well as the flag mark at the start and finish, must be within the "fence" made by the log line. Only if the instructions

THE SAILING RULES

designate on which side the marks of the start and finish shall be left, is it proper that the flag mark on the line of start and finish be not within the "fence."

"The track of the yacht, it should be noted, must when penciled out on the chart from the preceding to the following mark, *inclose* the mark on the required side."[2]

Of the same opinion is Dr. Manfred Curry.[3]

In September, 1934, the final races of the Women's National Yacht Racing Association were conducted by the American Yacht Club at Rye, N. Y. The Judges were George E. Roosevelt, then Vice-Commodore of the Cruising Club of America and Secretary of the N. A. Y. R. U., and now Vice-Commodore of the New York Yacht Club, John B. Shethar, then Commodore of the American Yacht Club, and Leonard M. Fowle, Jr., of the Eastern Yacht Club.

In the seventh and final race on September 7, the course was as illustrated in Diagram 54 (*A*). One of the yachts sailed as indicated in Diagram 54 (*B*), "left the mark on the wrong hand, retraced her steps only in part and was disqualified by the Race Committee, whose action was later sustained by the Judges."[3a]

Diagram 55 (*B*) is in reality the same as 55 (*A*). The additional "gyrations" depicted in 55 (*B*) in no way alter the fundamental facts.

It seems almost unnecessary to say that if *A*, outside yacht, overlapped by *B*, forces *B* the wrong side of a turning mark, *B* must return and round the mark properly; and that *A* will be disqualified on protest.[4]

---

[2] B. Heckstall-Smith. *Yacht Racing*. 2d Ed., 1933, page 168.

[3] *Yacht Racing, Aerodynamics of Sails and Racing Tactics*, 1927, page 231. *Racing Tactics in Questions and Answers*, 1932, Diagram 53, and pages 204–205.

[3a] *N. A. Y. R. U. Bulletin No. 26*, January 18, 1935, pages 26 and 27.

[4] *Norfolk and Suffolk Yacht and Sailing Clubs Association*. Y. R. A., 1896, page 119.

THE SAILING RULES

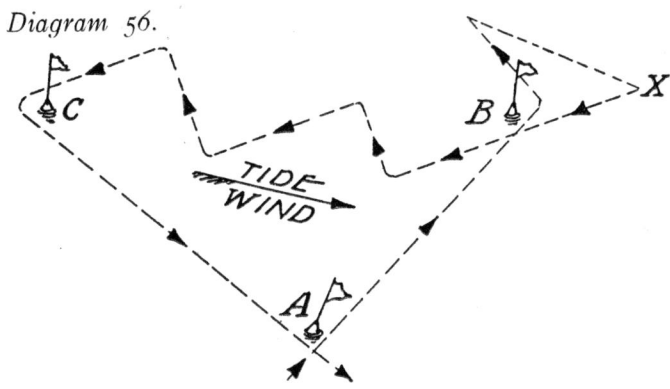

Diagram 56.

In Diagram 56 a yacht rounds mark *B;* runs into a calm; and drifts back to *X* with the tide. There she picks up a breeze and having once passed the mark to port, leaves it to starboard on again passing it on the beat to *C*. Although she has passed mark *B,* her track from the preceding mark *A* to the following mark *C* does not enclose mark *B*. If, then, the ends of the thread outlining her course are pulled taut it will be found that the thread does not enclose mark *B*.

Now consider this amusing case:

"As the boats left the Mersey on the ebb tide there was a flat calm. The yacht *Mink* came very close to a large channel buoy. The yacht or her spars did not touch, but one of the crew touched the buoy with his hand."

The Sailing Committee requested a ruling from the Y. R. A. as to whether *Mink* had contravened the second sentence of the rule and "should be disqualified through the action of the man who touched the buoy, although the yacht did not actually foul the buoy."

The Council replied: "Assuming the channel buoy to be a mark in the course, *Mink* should be disqualified."[5]

[5]*Tranmere Sailing Club.* Y. R. A., 1935, Case 7.

THE SAILING RULES

We are fortunate in being able to cite an American case to the fourth and last sentence of the rule. It occurred in a district race of the Women's National Yacht Racing Association.

"The Committee boat was moored by a hawser to one end of an eight (8) foot log or stake. This end floated slightly out of water. To the submerged end of the log was attached a hawser leading to an anchor or mooring. . . . Just as appellant's yacht was about to cross the starting line, her keel fouled the rode leading from the submerged end of the log to the anchor or mooring. This tautened the rode and caused the log to straighten up slightly and strike the port quarter topsides of appellant's yacht."

The yacht was protested for violation of Rule 33 and disqualified.

The Executive Committee sustained the appeal and reversed the decision of the Judges saying:

"The above-water part of a mooring chain or hawser of a Committee boat, other vessel or object used as a mark of the course, which is moored is an 'essential or ordinary above-water part of' an 'object used to designate the course' within the meaning of Rules 33 and 34.

"By no stretch of the imagination can the floating log, stake or buoy, to which the Committee boat was moored in the instant case be deemed an essential or ordinary above-water part of the Committee boat."[6]

Although not specifically mentioned in the rule, it seems clear that if the keel of a yacht fouls the underwater part of the anchor chain or rode of a vessel in use as a mark, so that to keep clear the crew of the mark vessel is obliged to pay out cable to avoid contact, thus causing the mark vessel to shift her position, the yacht must be

[6]*Sandy Bay Yacht Club.* N. A. Y. R. U., Appeal No. 3, November 15, 1935.

THE SAILING RULES

disqualified—protest or no protest—even if there was no abovewater contact.

Rule 34

MARKS OF THE COURSE

As we already have printed the rule in full and discussed it at length in Chapter VI, further comment would seem to be superfluous. We might add, however, that if any part of a yacht or her equipment touches a mark of the starting line during the yacht's preparatory period she will be disqualified.[7]

Rule 35

FOULING COMPETING YACHTS

If a yacht, through failure to observe any of these rules, shall foul another yacht, or cause other yachts to foul, she shall be disqualified.

Are the right-of-way rules applicable to a yacht which clearly has violated a rule but instead of withdrawing, as she should, continues in the race? Must other yachts continue to treat her as a competitor? The answer to both question is "Yes."[8]

The Bembridge Sailing Club case was cited with approval by the Council twenty-eight years later.[9]

An American decision takes the opposite viewpoint. *Lena* protested *Countess* for fouling *Raccoon*. The facts were not stated in the report of the case. The protest was not sustained. The Committee said: "*Raccoon* was disqualified for towing after the preparatory signal. She was

---

[7] *Merlin* v. *Spray*. Y. R. A., 1939, Case 9.
[8] *The Bembridge Sailing Club*. Y. R. A., 1900, page 113.
[9] *Clymene* v. *Noresca*. Y. R. A., 1927, Case 1.

therefore not in the race at all, and a foul between *Countess* and her (which *Countess* admits occurred) could not be charged against *Countess* as a breach of the Racing Rules."[10]

In the examination of many protest cases this is the only instance found of what appears to be a conflict between American and British yachting authorities of final jurisdiction.

For the purpose of these comments it will be assumed that the *Countess-Raccoon* foul involved a violation of one of the clauses of Rule 30, Right of Way, other than Clause (H), Converging Close-hauled, a situation not covered by the Rules of the Road at Sea.

With deference to the judgment of Messrs. Gherardi Davis, Clinton Mackenzie, and Oliver Iselin, who constituted the N. Y. Y. C. Race Committee in 1924, for whose experience in yacht racing and knowledge of the Racing Rules the writer has profound respect, he is frank to say that he prefers the English ruling in such a case, and for the following reasons:

1. Whether or not a yacht is racing, she is bound to observe the Rules of the Road which are binding upon all vessels navigating the high seas, as well as the inland waters of the United States. The only exception is as to other yachts competing in a race of her own club.
2. *A* may be of opinion—even may know—that *B* has made an improper start and therefore has no standing in the result of the race, but if later she collides with *B* in violation of the Yacht Racing Rules, *B's* prior disqualification will be no defense in an Admiralty Court.

[10]*Lena* v. *Countess.* N. Y. Y. C., 1924 Report of Race Committee, page 5.

THE SAILING RULES

3. To permit a yacht to violate a Sailing Rule and then hold that the occurrence is as if it had not happened, and solely because the yacht then holding right of way had been disqualified for starting improperly or for some other equally non-debatable violation of the Rules, not only denies the fact but also seems to be opening wide the door to trouble.

Suppose B, close-hauled on the port tack, attempts to cross ahead of A, close-hauled on the starboard tack. She misjudges speed and distance, and A is forced so sharply to bear away to avoid a collision that it can be said that B clearly has violated Rule 30 (E). C, close astern of A, witnesses the foul. Instead of withdrawing, as she should, B keeps on. Later in the race C fouls B in the same manner. On the doctrine of *Lena* v. *Countess*, C would go scot free. She could claim—and rightly—that from the time she fouled A, B was non-existent in the race—at least in so far as the Sailing Rules were concerned. And yet there B was—perhaps a large schooner. C, too, is a large yacht. Did they collide, much damage to property and serious injury to persons might result.

The question at issue is not specifically covered by the Racing Rules. It is entirely a question of policy. In the writer's opinion the doctrine laid down by the Council in 1899, in *The Bembridge Case*, is preferable from the point of view of safety and prevention of collision. The doctrine of *Lena* v. *Countess* permits the exercise of fallible human opinion and judgment on the part of skippers of competing yachts. The doctrine of *The Bembridge Case* removes that particular human equation. *Lena* v. *Countess* seems to establish a precedent fraught with dangerous possibilities.

THE SAILING RULES

As far as we have been able to ascertain, *Lena* v. *Countess* was not cited, even by the New York Yacht Club itself, until 1934, when the doctrine of that case was reaffirmed by the Race Committee in giving its reasons for the decision in *Endeavour* v. *Rainbow*. The Committee said: *"Endeavour's* second protest, covering the luffing incident, which occurred after rounding the first mark, could never have come before your Committee since we would have had to disqualify one of the yachts prior to the start. (See case of *Lena* v. *Countess*—Report of New York Yacht Club Race Committee—1924.)"[11]

We have reason to believe that had not the members of the Race Committee felt bound by the precedent established by their predecessors in 1924, they might not have made the remarks quoted above.

A year later, from the Cold Spring Harbor Beach Club, Long Island, N. Y., the following case was appealed to the Union:

A and *B* were involved in a foul. Each protested the other. Later in the same race, *A* close-hauled on the starboard tack, approached *C,* close-hauled on the port tack. *C,* having observed the earlier foul, and believing *A* to have been at fault, and therefore no longer entitled to her right of way, held her course. *A,* in order to avoid a collision, gave way. *A* protested *C*. A hearing was held. *A's* protest was sustained and *C* disqualified. *A* was later disqualified on *B's* protest against *A*.

C appealed upon the ground that "a boat which had committed a foul and which, after a hearing by the Committee, has been disqualified, is not entitled to the rights conferred on her by the Racing Rules if she continues as a contestant in that particular race subsequent to the occurrence of the aforesaid foul."

[11] *New York Yacht Club,* 1934 Report of Race Committee, page 15.

THE SAILING RULES

In its decision dismissing *C's* appeal and sustaining the decision of the Race Committee, the Executive Committee said:

"It will be observed that this appeal does not involve the interpretation of any existing Racing Rule.

"A yacht, involved in an alleged foul, usually does not know until the end of the race, after hearing and decision by the Race Committee, whether she has committed a foul or not. Obviously, until she has been disqualified, she is entitled to her rights of way under the Racing Rules. . . . All must, therefore, at all times accord the right of way to the yacht involved in such earlier foul as though no foul had occurred. *C* should have given way to *A*."[12]

In commenting upon the second question in the case, viz.: "Is a yacht, which, as a result of protest and hearing, has been disqualified, entitled to maintain a protest against another yacht which thereafter in the same race fouls her, the previously disqualified yacht?" the Executive Committee said:

"To deny a yacht disqualified for a foul the right to maintain a protest for a later foul may easily result in other yachts in a race, which have observed the first foul, refusing thereafter to accord the right of way to the yacht which they deem to have been in the wrong. We are clear that the best interests of yachting will be served by giving her such right."

Pilgrim v. *Maori* is in complete accord with *The Bembridge Sailing Club Case, supra,* decided by the British Y. R. A. thirty-six years previously. *Lena* v. *Countess* did not emanate from a match race between two yachts. Its doctrine, therefore, is applicable to fleet racing. On its face it would appear to be squarely in conflict with the yachting law as laid down by the yachting tribunals of final

[12]*Pilgrim* v. *Maori*. N. A. Y. R. U., Appeal No. 4, November 16, 1935.

THE SAILING RULES

jurisdiction in Great Britain and the United States, at least in so far as the overwhelming number of racing yachts is concerned.

In all fairness, however, it should be stated that in *Pilgrim* v. *Maori,* the Executive Committtee said:

"In reaching this decision this Committee has not considered, since such a case was not before it, the somewhat different situation which might arise in a Match Race between two yachts, particularly where special conditions of the match might have a bearing upon the matter, and this decision is not a determination of that question."

It is to be hoped that if and when the question comes squarely before the New York Yacht Club its then Race Committee may be able to see its way clear to overrule or at least to distinguish its 1924 decision, to the much-to-be-desired end that the yachting law of the world's three premier yachting organizations may be uniform.

Now just a word on Yachting Etiquette. In the *Bembridge Sailing Club Case* the Council said:

"If a yacht competing in a race infringes a Sailing Rule she should retire from the race; but if the owner or other person in charge is guilty of such unsportsmanlike conduct as to continue racing, other competitors are bound to treat the yacht as a competitor, and observe the Sailing Rules accordingly."

In *Pilgrim* v. *Maori,* but purely by way of *obiter dictum,* the decision concluded with this statement:

"It does seem to us, however, that this is an appropriate occasion to call attention, as we have been requested to do, to one of the well recognized, though unwritten, rules of Yachting Etiquette, viz., that a helmsman who knowingly has committed a foul should withdraw from the race forthwith, and not interfere with any other yachts competing therein. If the person in charge of a yacht involved in

THE SAILING RULES

a foul with another yacht, knowing that he has committed a foul, or if the foul is of so flagrant a nature that he should know, still continues in the race, claiming his right of way under the Rules against other competing yachts, he should be disciplined in some appropriate way, be it under the Racing Rules or otherwise, as the case in the opinion of the Race Committee merits. But even in such case, even if the first foul was so flagrant and so obvious to the other yachts as to convince them that a flagrant foul had been committed, nevertheless, to avoid the danger of collisions, the guilty yacht must thereafter be accorded its right of way under the Rules."

No comment on the ethics of yacht racing implied in Rule 35 can surpass the terse remark of Major B. Heckstall-Smith:

"A yacht breaking this rule should at once retire from the race. No other course is open to her."[13]

There is nothing more unsportsmanlike than to continue racing after a skipper *knows* or has so flagrantly contravened the rules that he *should* know that he has violated a rule.

Now, how about obeying the Sailing Rules in regard to a yacht in another class? The answer is "You must."[14]

It follows that the same is true as to a yacht in a race held by another club at the same time and in the same waters as one's own.

[13] B. Heckstall-Smith, *Yacht Racing*, 2d Ed., 1933, page 170.
[14] *Tomboy* v. *Octavia*. Y. R. A., 1913, Case 8; *The Waterwitch Case*. Y. R. A., 1932, Case 6.

Chapter XVI

RULES 36, 37, 38, 40 and 41

Rule 36

RUNNING AGROUND AND FOULING

A yacht running aground or fouling a buoy, pier, vessel or other object may use her anchors, warps, boats, and other gear to get clear, but may not receive any assistance except from the crew of a vessel fouled. Any gear used must be recovered before she continues the race.

The clear intent of this rule is that at no time during a race shall a yacht receive outside assistance except as specified in and strictly limited by the rule, viz.: "from the crew of a vessel fouled." Sound spars, standing and running rigging, steering apparatus and all other gear and equipment are as vital to success in yacht racing as are the skill of the skipper and "team work" on the part of skipper and crew.

From "way down under" came the following case:

A ran aground. She passed a line to a dinghy not her own which attempted to tow her off but was not successful. *A* recovered her line, later refloated under her own sail power and completed the course. The Sailing Committee disqualified *A* under Rule 36. "It being their opinion that she should not have received assistance, effectual or otherwise, from any source other than her own boat and crew, if her helmsman desired to continue in the race." The Council, without comment, affrmed the decision.[1]

[1]*In re Falkyre; Royal Yacht Club of Tasmania.* Y. R. A., 1934, Case 6.

THE SAILING RULES

This decision seems to be somewhat at variance with a decision in the 1928 Y. R. A. Year Book, viz.:

A yacht broke her tiller. A competitor had a spare tiller on board and loaned it to the disabled yacht which thereby was enabled to finish the race. The Council said neither yacht had violated any rule.[2]

Although we have found no American case on Rule 36, we feel sure that the 1928 British case would not be followed in this country, and for the reasons stated in the paragraph immediately following the rule. A yacht must start and finish a race "on her own." In this country the yacht that accepted the loan of the spare tiller would have been disqualified, but not the yacht which loaned it. In short, the acceptance of assistance of any sort, and whether it be effectual or not, except from the crew of a vessel fouled, contravenes the spirit and intent of Rule 36.

Rule 37

ANCHORING

A yacht may anchor, but must weigh anchor again and not slip. No yacht shall warp or kedge or make fast to any buoy, pier, vessel or other object except for the purpose mentioned in Rule 36. In weighing anchor, yachts having a power windlass as part of their regular equipment may use such power.

Numerous violations of the rule during the preparatory period were mentioned in Chapter VI.

Two other cases, however, are worthy of comment. The first is rather humorous; the second, a case of hard luck which might well have been decided the other way under Rule 1.

A yacht anchored on account of a calm and a head tide.

[2]*Naini Tal Yacht Club.* Y. R. A., 1928, Case 7.

THE SAILING RULES

Later a breeze sprang up. The crew commenced to weigh anchor and had hauled in the rode part way when the anchor fluke fouled a submerged cable. In the meantime the yacht had gathered headway. To avoid being dragged overboard the crew was obliged to let go the anchor rode which slipped overboard and was lost. The Council disqualified the yacht for violation of Rule 37.[3]

During Cowes Week in 1924 the kedge anchor cable of the King's cutter *Britannia* fouled the remains of a war casualty wreck; became chafed; parted; and the anchor was lost. The Sailing Committee was of opinion that no amount of seamanlike care or foresight could have prevented the accident and referred the case to the Y. R. A. Even these extenuating circumstances did not prevent her disqualification by the Council.[4]

The intent of the rule is, of course, that when a yacht anchors, the anchor and rode must be recovered and carried on board during the remainder of the race.

Rule 38

PROPULSION

No means of propulsion other than sails shall be employed except as provided in Rule 36.

Dropping an anchor over the bow and "walking" the hawser aft is an excellent method of propulsion in a calm but it is contrary to Rule 38.[5] So, too, is "rudder sculling,"[6] a practice we often have seen indulged in by youthful skippers in small boats. One must rely upon the sails alone. And even the sails may be manipulated in such a fashion as to violate Rule 38.

[3]*Loss of Viera's Kedge Anchor.* Y. R. A., 1906, page 120.
[4]*The Britannia.* Y. R. A., 1924, Case 8.
[5]B. Heckstall-Smith. *Yacht Racing,* 2d Ed., 1933, page 175.
[6]*Portaferry Regatta Committee.* Y. R. A., 1896, page 119; affirming a similar decision given in 1879.

THE SAILING RULES

Just before two yachts crossed the finish line the wind dropped leaving them without steerage way. The crews pushed out the main booms very slowly and then pulled them in quickly. This practice, commonly known as "fanning," caused the yachts to move ahead slowly and in time enabled them to cross the finish line. They were disqualified. We give the decision in full:

"On appeal by one of the captains involved in the disqualifications for propulsion by 'fanning' sails, the decision of the Race Committee was sustained by the Southern Massachusetts Yacht Racing Association Appeals Committee under Rule 38, PROPULSION, and Rule 1, GENERAL AUTHORITY OF RACE COMMITTEE, which prohibits a practice contrary to 'the ordinary customs of the sea.' At the time of the incident the two boats in queswere becalmed near the finish line, and by manipulating their sails back and forth they acquired way and crossed the line before several other yachts of their class. *Man power for propulsion is as unfair applied to sails as to a rudder.*"[7] (Italics—the Author.) In other words, propulsion by sails means propulsion by the normal action of the wind on the sails.

Rule 40

MAN OVERBOARD AND ACCIDENTS

Each yacht must render every possible assistance to any vessel or person in peril, and should she not render such assistance she shall be disqualified. If, in the judgment of the Race Committee, any yacht not responsible for the accident shall have thereby injured her chances of winning any prize, it shall order the race resailed between such yacht and the winner of such prize. A yacht losing a man

[7]*Edgartown, Mass., Yacht Club.* Report of Race Committee, Season of 1933, page 10.

overboard must either recover the man on board before continuing the race or give up the race.

A recent decision by the Council may be of interest to Race Committees under the jurisdiction of the British Y. R. A.

Six yachts, *A, B, C, D, E,* and *F,* started. *F* was dismasted. *C, D,* and *E* abandoned the race to render assistance. *A* and *B* were too far ahead to notice the accident, and finished in that order. The Race Committee decided that "in the circumstances, Rule 40 must apply," and ordered the race resailed.

In the re-sail, only *B* and *C* started. *B* won. On the one hand it was contended that *A* was only defending first prize against *C, D,* and *E,* and that *B* was only defending second prize, the contention being based on the second sentence of Rule 40, and that *B* could dispossess *A* of such prize. Therefore, the result must be *C,* winner, *B,* second prize.

On the other hand it was contended that the resailed race should be treated as an entirely fresh race between all competitors except *F,* dismasted in the original race, and that the previous race should have no effect. The Council said:

"The second contention is correct. The Committee were right in ordering a resail. The race was a fresh race entirely, the first prize going to *B,* the second to *C.*"[8]

We doubt if American yachting authorities would follow this decision. In commenting on the case Mr. C. Sherman Hoyt said:

"In spite of what was done I believe the Committee only had the right to order the race resailed between *C, D,* and *E* to determine who should be awarded third prize, unless they were clearly of opinion that by rendering as-

[8]*Leigh-on-Sea Sailing Club.* Y. R. A., 1932, Case 8.

sistance, any or all of these boats had 'thereby injured their chances of winning any other prize.' From the description of the event A and B were so far ahead at the time that they were unable to notice the accident, and it seems unreasonable to assume under these circumstances that C, D or E had any chance to finish first or second, and, therefore, A and B, who could in no way be considered negligent for not having gone to F's assistance, should not have been asked again to sail for prizes which they apparently had won fairly and squarely. On the other hand when the Committee had definitely ordered the race resailed, then of course the decision of the Council was correct.

"It would be most unfair to make prize winners resail a race for prizes they had honestly won, merely for the sake of one or more competitors thoroughly beaten that day. The rule was intended to apply only to cases where injury to chances of winning any prize was palpably evident. It was never intended to be invoked for the benefit of trailers in a race, and to the detriment of other competitors, when participation in attempts to render assistance by them would have been quite unnecessary or impractical."

In a race in which three prizes were offered, A, B, and C finished in the order named. D injured her chances of winning a prize by going to the rescue of a drowning person. The question submitted to the Council was whether the relative positions of A, B, and C in the original race could be disturbed if the Sailing Committee should order a resail. The Council replied that "if the Committee order the race to be resailed it must be resailed between A, B, C, and D."[9]

[9] *Royal Natal Yacht Club.* Y. R. A., 1933, Case 10.

THE SAILING RULES

Rule 41

THE FINISH

(4) A yacht which has been timed at the finish is not required to pass across the line but remains amenable to the rules so long as any part of her hull, spars or other equipment remains on the line.

It would seem unnecessary to quote other clauses of the rule.

There are, however, two situations which may be discussed.

Diagram 57.

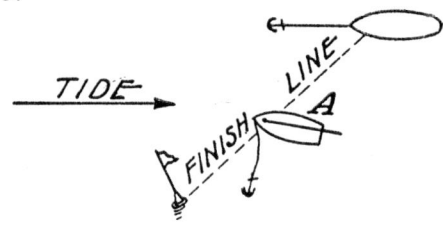

When nearly across the line, A became becalmed, and anchored. The tide caused her to veer across the line, and the Committee fired the gun, not knowing that she had anchored. The Council decided that not having again weighed anchor in accordance with Rule 37, before she crossed the line, she had not completed the race and should be disqualified.[10]

The second situation is where, after having been timed at the finish and before a yacht's hull and spars have been entirely clear of the line, she drifts back and fouls one of the finish-line marks. In such a case she will be disqualified as they still are marks of the course.[11]

[10]*Katie* v. *Hypatia.* Y. R. A., 1883.
[11]*Royal Western Yacht Club.* Y. R. A., 1928, Case 4.

Diagram 58.

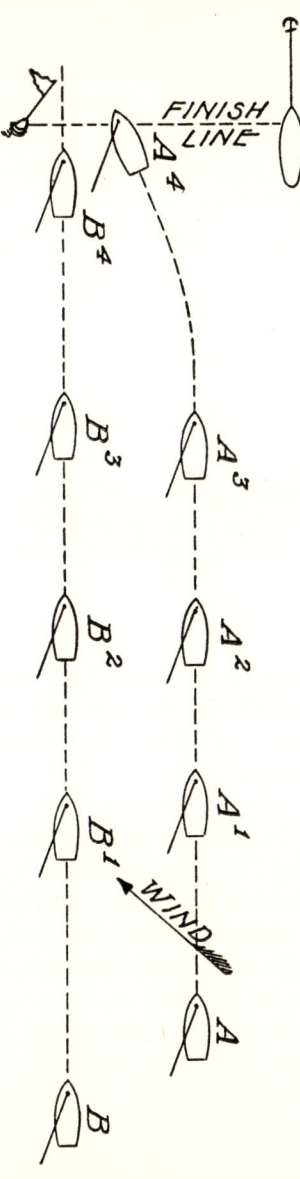

THE SAILING RULES

Let us conclude this chapter by discussing a situation which occurs occasionally just before the finish.

Both yachts, overlapped, are reaching for the finish line; B has overtaken A to leeward, and is leading by a few feet at $A^3 B^3$. B is heading for the leeward end of the line. In order to blanket B, A slacks off her sheets and bears away, but for a point sufficiently to windward of the flag mark to give B room safely to cross. A "noses out" B and is protested under Rule 30 (C).

By Rule 30 (C) "A yacht must never bear away out of her proper course to hinder an overtaking yacht passing her to leeward." In reaching for a mark, the overtaken yacht's proper course is "nothing to leeward of the next mark." The *whole* of the finish line is "the next mark." Therefore, in the case illustrated in Diagram 58, A may head for any desired point of the finish line, even though by so doing she bears down on B in order to blanket her.

A must take care that:

1. By bearing down on B, she does not cause B to alter her course below the flag mark, and
2. She allows B sufficient room to pass to windward of the flag mark.

In 1910 the Council was asked "Whether it was permissible in 'turning to windward' for a leading yacht to sail off the wind so as 'weather bow' a yacht that seems to be catching her, and, in fact, to bear away so long as she does not touch the overtaking yacht?"

The Council replied:

"There is no prohibition against bearing away except where the leeward yacht is an overtaking yacht, as per the definition of overtaking. *There is nothing in the rules en-*

THE SAILING RULES

titling a yacht to a clear wind."[12] (Italics—the Author.)

An American case is to the same effect. We quote:

"From the statements submitted it appears that *B* overhauled *A* and passing her to windward, that is, on her port hand, became leading yacht. Both the yachts were on the port tack running nearly dead before a strong wind. *B's* manœuvres, until she passed *A*, appear to the Committee to have been entirely in accordance with the Racing Rules and good seamanship. Before overhauling *A*, she bore away in an effort to kill *A's* wind, succeeded in doing so, and then passed her. There was nothing wrong in *B's* sailing up to this point from what has been submitted to the Committee."[13]

[12]*Royal Alfred Yacht Club.* Y. R. A., 1910, Case 1.
[13]*Lena* v. *Countess.* N. Y. Y. C., 1924 Report of Race Committee at page 6.

PROTESTS, DISQUALIFICATIONS AND APPEALS

Chapter XVII

RULES 43, 45, 46, 47 and 48

Rule 43

PENALTY FOR INFRINGING RULES

For a violation of the Sailing Rules there is but one penalty—Disqualification. There is no degree of guilt; guilty intent is immaterial. The Race Committee has no alternative.[1] It must make one of two "findings": "Guilty" or "Not Guilty." If "Guilty," the offender must suffer the penalty. No lesser sentence may be imposed.

Rule 45

PROTESTS

Protests must be in writing and must specify the *particular rule and clause* alleged to have been violated. A general allegation that the Sailing Rules have been violated is not sufficient.[2]

Now a word in regard to the word "promptly" in the last sentence of the rule.

"While the word 'promptly' in the last sentence of Rule 45 is not synonymous with the word 'immediately' in the next to last sentence of Rule 33, it implies that Code Flag 'B' must be displayed within a reasonably short time after a contestant has reason to believe that a competitor has breached a racing rule during a race. In fairness to such

[1] *Aito* v. *Ingane.* Y. R. A., 1925, Case 2.
[2] *Betty* v. *Sphex.* Y. R. A., 1930, Case 4.

competitor he should thus be notified promptly of his alleged breach of the rules."[3]

If Code Flag "B" is displayed promptly after the alleged foul occurs it enables all interested parties the more clearly to fix in their minds the attendant circumstances as well as the relative positions of the yachts at that particular time.

The rules are silent on the question of *jurisdiction* of a protest involving two yachts belonging to *different* clubs, each yacht sailing in a race of her own club held at the same time and in the same waters.

This question arose in Ireland a few years ago. The Council held that the protest should be heard by the Sailing Committee of the club to which the protested yacht belonged.[4]

Now a few words as to protests in general. Each competitive sport is governed by its own particular set of rules. In baseball there are umpires; in tennis, linesmen and a referee. In football, if a rule is infringed, a whistle is blown, play stops, the penalty is imposed and play is resumed. A yacht race is different; maybe it is unique. Once started, it cannot be stopped just because a rule is infringed. Action upon such an episode must be postponed until after the finish. All that can be done at the time is to display a protest flag.

Under the existing rules *yacht racing is controlled by the contestants themselves* and not by ever present officials as in other competitive sports. Protests, therefore, are of vital necessity, in fact imperative if the sport is to be kept clean. "Every rule in the rule book is there for a very good reason—either to avoid accidents at sea or to prevent some form of unfair practice. . . . If the racing rules are un-

[3] *Sandy Bay Yacht Club.* N. A. Y. R. U., Appeal No. 3, November 15, 1935; Opinion, paragraph 2.
[4] *Dublin Bay Sailing Club.* Y. R. A. 1933, Case 1.

THE SAILING RULES

just, if disqualification is too severe a punishment in certain cases, then it is up to the international body, that makes the rules, to change or modify them. Such power is not vested in the local officials who conduct the races, nor is there anything in the rules that suggests that they be disregarded in the event of extenuating circumstances. Such an interpretation would breed a complete disregard of rules in any branch of sport. The duty of any official conducting any sporting event is to establish the fact; then, if a rule has been violated, to impose the penalty provided under the code of rules that governs that sport. Sympathy, prejudice, or the friction that might be caused among certain factions, are considerations that can play no part in the decision of any honest official. To keep any sport clean, rules must be enforced, not in one case out of ten, but in every case— regardless of whether the violation was unintentional, due to ignorance, or even unavoidable.

"What people do not realize is that a skipper who takes chances, who barges the line, crosses yachts that he has no right to cross, and forces his way in at marks, gains a decided advantage. . . . Think also of the temptation to the young skipper, taught to obey the rules, who sees minor violations going on all the time and nothing being done about it. . . . *The only criticism a race committee should justly fear is that of being lax and failing to do its duty in this respect.*"[5] (Italics—the Author.)

Some people seem to have the idea that the word "protest" implies a wrongful act intentionally committed; and that the word "foul" implies "dirty" sailing. Yachtsmen know that such is not the case. Unfortunately the public does not. In the language of yachtsmen a "protest" is merely the registering of an *objection* to some act of a

[5] George W. Elder, President, International Star Class Y. R. A., *Why Glorify the Rule Breaker?*, March, 1934, *Yachting.*

friendly competitor. "Refraining from protesting is apt to be due to the false assumption that a protest implies a reflection as to a rival's good sportsmanship, and that he was guilty of unfair tactics intentionally. Others will not protest because of the sentimental reason that a race won through a protest is unsporting. . . . It should never be looked upon as a personal matter but merely as a means of maintaining the rules. It means no more than when a referee blows his whistle to intimate that some player has infringed a rule in a game of football; *it is not the man, it is the rule, that matters.*"[6] (Italics—the Author.)

Sometimes a protest involves a difference of opinion as to the interpretation of a rule. Almost invariably it is an honest dispute. It cannot be otherwise between good sportsmen. The "game" must be played according to the rules. The only way to settle the question is to request, or if preferred to appeal to, the proper tribunal—the Race Committee—to decide the matter. Better by far, for a skipper openly and frankly to say that in his opinion his rights have been infringed, and have the question settled, than to harbor a grudge against a competitor who is not given an opportunity to present his version of the case; who may, perhaps, not even suspect that he has done something that was not "according to Hoyle." To protest, when in his opinion a rule has been seriously infringed, is the act of a sportsman. Above all, he should cheerfully abide by the fact findings of the Race Committee.

Rule 46

HEARINGS BY RACE COMMITTEE

If the Race Committee gives the owner or representative of a protested yacht reasonable notice of the time and place

[6] "F. N." *Yachting World,* September 4, 1936, page 228.

THE SAILING RULES

of the hearing, he cannot complain of an adverse decision if he does not exercise his right to be present.[7]

After the principals in the case have testified and have retired from the hearing it is improper for a Race Committee to permit a member of the Committee to "give evidence for the first time of his own observation of the incidents in question in the protest with the result that this evidence, being unknown to the principals, they had no opportunity of challenging it by questioning the witness."[8] In other words they were denied the right of cross-examination. There is nothing more sacred to Anglo-Saxon jurisprudence than the right to cross-examine an opposing witness.

Mr. Hugh M. Wharton of the Pequot Yacht Club of Southport, Connecticut, Chairman of the N. A. Y. R. U. Committee on Junior Yacht Racing, and also Chairman of the Committee of three Judges who officiate annually at the final races for the Sears "Cup"—it *really* is a bowl—emblematic of the National Junior Sailing Championship, once made a remark which we happened to overhear, a remark which it would be well for every Race Committee always to keep in mind. Said Mr. Wharton:

"A Race Committee is a Court of Inquiry, NOT a Court of Law."

How often have youthful—yes, and adult—parties to a protest entered the hearing with trepidation, to face a stern-visaged and sometimes a scowling Race Committee. The skipper and crew of the protesting yacht cannot but feel that they are doing something wrong in taking up the time of the "august" (?) members of the Committee by filing and refusing to withdraw a protest. Fortunately, however, such an attitude on the part of Committee mem-

[7]*Vivacious* v. *The Club*. Y. R. A., 1938, Case 18.
[8]*Moonfleet* v. *Ajax*. Y. R. A., 1938, Case 15.

THE SAILING RULES

bers is today a relic of the past because it is now realized almost universally that a protest is one of the most educational features of yacht racing. A skipper who is disqualified but who at the same time is painstakingly told how and why he infringed a rule is not apt to make the same mistake again.

Race Committees should remember Mr. Wharton's admonition and not be *too* technical.

"It sometimes happens that a yacht protests under one rule, while the evidence shows that some other rule was really infringed. A Committee should take cognizance of this fact, and base its decision on the testimony, since in Rule XIX, Clause 2 (now Rule 35—the Author), it is clearly stated that a yacht shall be disqualified if she neglects ANY of the rules. Failure to properly word a written protest should not be allowed to prejudice the case of a protesting yacht, and ignorance of the rules should not be accepted as an excuse."[9]

The Race Committee "should apply the rules as stringently as possible, but at the same time remember that the rules were founded upon the principle of 'fair play' only, and were not intended to be penal in their operation."[10]

Now where lies the burden of proof? In a civil action at law the term "burden of proof" is used in a double sense. In its primary meaning it imposes upon the plaintiff, the party bringing the action, the duty of establishing his case by "a fair preponderance of the evidence." In its secondary sense it concerns the burden of the introduction of evidence. This secondary meaning of the term shifts from time to time. For example: Proof of the mailing of

---

[9]Parsons, Macdonough and Spedden. *Handbook of American Yacht Racing Rules,* 2d Ed., 1923, page 147. *Dublin Bay Sailing Club.* Y. R. A., 1912, Case 2.

[10]Dixon Kemp. *An Exposition of the Yacht Racing Rules,* 1898, page 2.

THE SAILING RULES

a letter, postage prepaid, is prima facie evidence of its receipt by the person to whom it is addressed. The burden of proof thereupon shifts to the addressee to prove that he did not receive the letter; whereupon the burden of introducing additional evidence of its receipt by the addressee shifts back again to the writer of the letter.

In yachting protests, however, the burden of proof ordinarily is on the yacht accused of infringing the rule—the non-right-of-way yacht—to prove by a fair preponderance of the evidence that she did *not* infringe the rule.[11] For example: take a case under Rule 30 (E). *A,* starboard tack yacht, introduces credible testimony to the effect that she not only bore away under *B's* stern to avoid a collision, but that she had reasonable cause to believe that had she not done so a collision would have occurred. *A* has established a prima facie case. *B* must now not only go forward and rebut this presumption but she must convince the Committee by a fair preponderance of all the evidence either (1) that *A* did not bear away as alleged or (2) if she did, that she bore away unnecessarily. If *B* cannot prove herself free of fault she should be disqualified.[12]

Take a case under Rule 30 (I). *A* and *B* are closehauled on the port tack, *B* ahead but to leeward. *B* tacks to starboard. *A* alters course in order to avoid a collision and protests *B* for tacking too close, in that she had not gathered proper way on her new tack when *A* was compelled to alter course. The burden of proof that she *did* have room to tack and *did* gather proper way before she met *A* is on *B,* the yacht accused of violating the rule. The responsibility is upon the yacht which made the alteration of course complained of or did not alter course when she should have done so.

[11]*Arrow* v. *Jean.* Y. R. A., 1938, Case 1.
[12]*Flying Cloud* v. *Vagrant.* N. Y. Y. C., 1924 Report of Race Committee, page 5.

THE SAILING RULES

The same is true if *B* tacks in front of *A*. To be exonerated *B* must prove that overtaking conditions arose.[13]

In short, where there is reasonable doubt, the doubt should be resolved in favor of the right-of-way yacht.

There are only three places in the Racing Rules where this topic is mentioned, viz.:

1. Rule 29 (6) 4, Overtaking, which reads: "The obligation of proving that she has drawn clear lies upon the late overtaking yacht";

2. Rule 29 (7), Proper Course, the last clause of which specifically imposes the burden of proof upon the weather yacht to justify her more leeward course; and

3. Rule 31, last paragraph, specifically placing the burden of proof upon the late overtaking yacht.

In (1) and (3) the burden of proof is upon the non-right-of-way yacht. In (2) it is upon the right-of-way yacht.

The fact of mere numbers of witnesses all of whom testify to the same general effect is not necessarily conclusive. The Committee may be of opinion that the testimony of a single contradictory witness is more reliable than that of the multitude. If so they will find the facts to be as testified to by him.

The Committee, of itself, is a judicial court of *inquiry;* it hears, and weighs carefully, the testimony of both parties; it is mindful where lies the burden of proof; and if, as is so often the case, the testimony as to certain facts is contradictory, the Committee acts on the presumption that the witnesses are honorable sportsmen of undoubted veracity.

---

[13] *Yankee* v. *Rainbow.* N. Y. Y. C., 1936 Report of Race Committee, page 5.

THE SAILING RULES

Rule 47

DISQUALIFICATION WITHOUT PROTEST

Should it come to the knowledge of the Race Committee, or should it have reasonable grounds to believe that a competitor in a race has in any way infringed these rules, it shall have the power to disqualify such competitor without protest, but only after notice has been given as hereinafter provided and after a hearing at which the owner of the yacht involved or his representative shall have the right to be present and submit such evidence as he may deem necessary. Notice of proposed action by the Race Committee under this rule must be given to the owner of the yacht believed to have infringed these rules or to his representative, and must name the rule or rules believed to have been infringed and the time and place of the hearing thereon. Notice of proposed action, based upon an infringement of the sailing rules, must be given prior to 6 P.M. of the week-day following the race in question.

The correct interpretation of this rule presents one of our most difficult problems. What is meant by the words "come to the knowledge of the Committee," and "should it have reasonable grounds to believe" that a rule has been infringed?

We know of no American decision directly interpreting either of these questions. In fact we know of no American case bearing directly on Rule 47.

There are a number of English decisions but they are of doubtful value in America, owing to the difference in the wording of the corresponding English Rule 44. Furthermore, English Rule 43—Protests—is different from our Rule 45—Protests.

THE SAILING RULES

By English Rule 44, it is *mandatory* upon the Committee to act. By our Rule 47, its action is *optional*.

By English Rule 43, a protest once filed in writing "shall not be withdrawn, but shall be decided by the Sailing Committee." Furthermore, failure to display a protest flag *"at the first reasonable opportunity and when passing the Sailing Committee . . . will debar a yacht from bringing the incident to the notice of the Committee under Rule 44."* (Y. R. A. Rule 43.)

American Rule 45 contains no such restrictive provisions.

The words "have reasonable grounds for supposing" in English Rule 44 are, however, identical in meaning with the words "have reasonable grounds to believe" in American Rule 47.

In England, where Y. R. A. Rule 43 specifically allows *any* competitor to protest "against another," if A sees B foul C, and if A does not display a protest flag, her subsequent report of the incident to the Sailing Committee is not "independent evidence" on which the Committee is bound to act or may act under Rule 44.[14]

The English 1896 Rule 30—PROTESTS, DISQUALIFICATION WITHOUT PROTEST—contained the following provision: *"Should it come to the knowledge of a Sailing Committee, or should they have reasonable grounds for supposing that a competitor in a race has in any way infringed these rules, they shall make due inquiries and if an infringement or breach of the rules be proved, they shall disqualify the yacht accordingly."*

In August of that year in a race of *The Island Sailing Club*, "a competitor had cause for protesting but failed to display an ensign, and contended that the Committee should entertain the matter, because it had come to their

[14] *Royal Gibraltar Yacht Club.* Y. R. A., 1939, Case 5.

knowledge that a breach of the rules had been committed.

"The Committee decided not to entertain the protest on such grounds because the alleged breach of the rules had not come to them from an independent source; if they had done so, it would have removed all responsibility from the protesting party."

"The Council decided that the decision of the Sailing Committee was correct."[15]

In other words, the Sailing Committee refused to permit the complainant to evade his responsibility of bringing and proving his case by "passing the buck" to the Committee. An excellent decision.

Since the 1896 *Island Sailing Club Case,* the English decisions have been uniformly confirmatory of that case. The British interpretation of their Rule 44 seems to be as follows:

To permit a Sailing Committee to proceed on its own initiative, its "reasonable grounds for supposing" a rule to have been breached must be based on:

1. "Direct knowledge" based on the Committee's own observation of the episode or the observation of one of their agents or observers on the course or at a mark, or

2. "Independent evidence" *other* than that of a competing yacht which witnessed the incident and could have displayed a protest flag but did not do so.

In other words, skippers should not rely upon a Race Committee to protect their rights when they are unwilling to take the initiative themselves.

The rule was adopted "to prevent collusion between

[15]*The Island Sailing Club.* Y. R. A., 1897, page 106.

THE SAILING RULES

competitors, who had severally committed breaches of the rules, not to protest."[16]

English Rule 43 requires a protest to be filed with the Sailing Committee within two hours after a yacht's finish unless such time is extended by the Committee. By American Rule 45 the time limit is 6 P.M. of the week-day following the race. American Rule 47 contains a similar limitation for notice to be given by the Committee. No extension of the time limit is provided.

The second sentence of the English 1896 Rule 30—PROTESTS—contained a mandatory clause prescribing a two-hour time limit. In spite of this, Mr. Kemp in commenting upon the Disqualification Without Protest provisions of that rule said:

"The Committee is not bound under this rule, by the 'two (2) hours' clause in the rule, and would be justified in putting their prerogative in force any time before having actually disposed of the prize in dispute."[17]

American Race Committees should not be "hamstrung" by the 6 P.M.-of-the-week-day limitation in the last sentence of the rule. Suppose several days elapse before some outside and disinterested person who observed a foul happened to mention it to a member of the Race Committee. Is it fair to the other yachts in the race to permit the guilty yacht to retain her ill-gotten prize or points? The time limit in our Rule 47 should either be changed or, better yet, abolished.

Too often Race Committees see a yacht break a rule at the start of a race—barging the line for example. Some member of the Committee calls through a megaphone "You are disqualified." Such practice is absolutely unjustified.

---

[16]Dixon Kemp. *A Manual of Yacht and Boat Sailing*, 8th Ed., page 232; *An Exposition of the Yacht Racing Rules*, 1898, page 108.

[17]Dixon Kemp. *An Exposition of the Yacht Racing Rules*, 1898, page 108.

THE SAILING RULES

It is prohibited by the terms of the rule itself. The offending yacht must be notified and a hearing had as in the case of a protest by a competitor. A yacht may not be disqualified arbitrarily and "out of hand." Furthermore, she must be given the gun if she wins.[18]

Rule 48

DECISIONS OF PROTESTS

It is important that the decision in any protest case, especially in a case involving an *interpretation* of the rules, be in writing as required by Rule 48, for the reason that by Rule 49, Section 1, an appeal from a decision of the Race Committee involving *solely* the interpretation of the Racing Rules may be taken, in certain cases, to a higher tribunal.

Most protest cases involve only questions of fact. But suppose *A* protests *B* under Rule 30 (C), and the Committee says: "In our opinion *B* violated, not Rule 30 (C), but Rule 30 (K), and we disqualify her for violating the latter rule." That would be a clear case of interpretation of the rules, and *B* might have the right of appeal.

There are additional reasons why decisions in important cases should be in writing. In the first place it is only fair to both parties to announce the reasons for the decision. The second reason is educational. If we are informed of a mistake and are told what the mistake was and why it was a mistake, we are more apt to profit by that added knowledge, and what is perhaps more important, we are not so apt to repeat the error.

In any decision involving an interpretation of the rules, all the facts should be clearly stated in the decision. It should be borne in mind that the "Appellate Court" will

[18]*The Vivacious.* Y. R. A., 1928, Case 8.

THE SAILING RULES

have before it only the written record upon which to base its decision. It will not have the privilege of seeing and hearing the witnesses; of observing their behavior "under fire" so to speak.

Before concluding this chapter we will cite two English cases which may perhaps be of interest to Race Committees. The first concerns American Rule 10—WRECKING OR SHIFTING OF A MARK; the second bears on our Rule 24 —BOARDING AND LEAVING.

A turning mark consisted of a wooden float on which was a pole, to which in turn was affixed a white flag. The float capsized, submerging the flag. One half of the fleet rounded another similar mark a short distance away. The remainder of the fleet, by dint of searching, found and rounded the submerged mark. The Council held that the race should be re-sailed, saying:

"The Council wishes to explain that in this case the mark was, for the purpose of Rule 13, 'accidentally removed' by being submerged, so that the three leading boats, *A, B* and *C* could not see it; that being the case it would not be fair to award the prize to the fourth boat *D,* there being no reason why she should benefit by the accident. The Committee are allowed by Rule 13 (Removal of Mark) to order the race resailed in the case of an accident of this kind and this is the fairest thing to do. It is . . . conceivable that a case might arise when a flag being submerged did not cause the mark to disappear."[19]

American Rule 24—BOARDING AND LEAVING—has no counterpart in Great Britain where an amusing case occurred many years ago. A small yacht ran aground. The crew jumped overboard, pushed the boat off the shoal, climbed back on board and finished the race. The case was considered under the British "Running Aground and

[19]*Royal Yacht Club of Tasmania.* Y. R. A., 1936, Case 1.

THE SAILING RULES

Fouling" Rule. (Present British Rule 36.) The Council decided that no rule had been violated.[20]

British Rule 49 prohibiting an interested party from taking part in the discussion or decision upon any disputed question is worded today exactly as it was in 1927. The corresponding N. A. Y. R. U. rule is Rule 48 (1).

In an English case the Sailing Committee which heard the protest included three owners of yachts which competed in the race. The Council said: "The Council think it is most improper that an interested party should be on the Sailing Committee judging the case."[21]

[20] *Royal Cork Yacht Club.* Y. R. A., 1876.
[21] *Oola* v. *Nirvana.* Y. R. A., 1927, Case 7.

CHAPTER XVIII

COURTESY AND UNWRITTEN LAW

In concluding our discussion of the Sailing Rules we should be derelict in our duty did we not briefly amplify the title of this chapter.

The subject has been by no one better treated than by Major B. Heckstall-Smith in Chapter XII of his *Yacht Racing*, 2d Ed., 1933, pages 181–182. He says:

"Never cause a foul. Enter a protest, for to do so when in your opinion a rule is seriously infringed is the act of a sportsman. It is well to remember when you are racing, that it is your duty to observe the rules in relation to other yachts . . . precisely as though they were in your own class. . . . A yacht may protest against another yacht in a different race for breach of the rules, and in every circumstance, as Rule 42 (now Rule 43—the Author) provides, yachts in different races are to be treated as in the same race.[1]

"Gentlemanlike and generous spirit should be shown in every yacht race. Do not protest when you feel sure no benefit to the sport of yacht racing will accrue—the incident being some trivial or frivolous thing. Notwithstanding the letter of the law, as a matter of sportsmanlike spirit and courtesy it is customary for . . . a small yacht . . . to keep out of the way of a large yacht . . . if she can do so without spoiling her own chance. The yachtsman should remember the dangers of the sea, and

[1]*Kuorhaan* v. *Ancora*. Y. R. A., 1914, Case 4.

THE SAILING RULES

always try to avoid coming to unnecessarily close quarters. It is an easy thing to tack a small cutter; she can be thrown around in an instant, and without the least trouble, but this is not the case with a large schooner. Hence, let us lay down the unwritten law that, as a point of etiquette, a small yacht should endeavor, when possible, to avoid causing a large yacht in a *different* race to tack. It is an act of courtesy for small close-hauled yachts having the right of way, to avoid causing big yachts under spinnaker to alter their course, or run by the lee, if it is possible to avoid it.

"On the other hand, decidedly there is an unwritten law —and an important one, too—that a large yacht should pass to leeward of a small yacht in a *different* race and avoid blanketing her. It is the duty of the sailing master of a large yacht, as a sportsman, to cause as little trouble as possible to small yachts that are racing at the same time in other races. In considering these points of etiquette and gentlemanlike feeling, however, one must not lose sight of the original point of law. If it comes to a pinch, the letter of the law must be observed, and this is the same for great and small on the face of the waters, in different races as in the same race."

The Sailing Rules are the same for old and young, for large yachts as well as for dinghies. To earn the reputation of being a fair sailer and a true sportsman is the greatest reward the sport offers. No higher tribute can be paid a racing skipper.

APPENDIX I

N. A. Y. R. U.

CERTAIN RACING RULES

Part 1.—Management of Races

RULE 1

GENERAL AUTHORITY OF RACE COMMITTEE

All races and the yachts sailing therein shall be under the direction of the Race Committee of the Club under whose auspices the races are sailed. All matters shall be under their control, and all questions which arise respecting such races shall be subject to their decision. The decisions of the Race Committee shall be based upon these rules, so far as they apply, but as no rules can be devised capable of meeting every incident and accident of sailing, the Race Committee shall keep in view the ordinary customs of the sea, and discourage all attempts to win a race by other means than fair sailing and superior speed and skill. *[margin: General Power of R. C.]*

RULE 6

CANCELLED, POSTPONED AND RE-SAILED RACES, AND SHORTENING COURSE BEFORE THE START

(1) At any time before the starting signal of any class the Race Committee shall have power to cancel or postpone any race, or shorten the course or courses for all classes that have not started. The signal for cancellation shall be Code Flag "J." The signal for postponement

APPENDIX I

for the day shall be Code Flag "H," and such postponed race shall be considered a new race.

. . . .

Race Declared Off. (2) At any time after the starting signal and before the finish, the Race Committee shall have power to cancel or order re-sailed any race should unfavorable weather conditions render a finish improbable within the time limit, or, subject to the provisions of Rule 10, should any mark be missing or moved from its proper position during the race. The signal denoting such action shall be Code Flag "J." Attention shall be called to such signal by gun, whistle, or other proper device. New entries shall not be received for such race, if re-sailed. A yacht which has been disqualified in the original race shall not be eligible to start in the re-sailed race. A yacht which, although duly entered, did not start in the original race, may, at the discretion of the Race Committee, be allowed to compete in the re-sailed race.

RULE 7

SHORTENING THE COURSE

Shortening Course. The Race Committee may shorten the course during the race and the hoisting of Code Flag "M" and two blasts of the whistle or other proper device, or two guns fired shall show that the race is to be finished with the round about to be completed or at the mark where the Race Committee's boat is stationed when giving the signal, and the time allowance, if any, shall be proportionately reduced.

APPENDIX I

RULE 8

TIME OF RACE LIMITED

(1) Except when otherwise specified in the instructions, a race in any class in which no yacht has finished at sunset shall be deemed "no race." *(Time Limit.)*

(2) One yacht finishing within the prescribed time constitutes a race for her class, and other yachts in that class finishing later shall, in the absence of the Race Committee, take their own times upon passing the mark at the finish within such distance as may be specified in the Sailing Instructions, and report it to the Race Committee within twenty-four hours.

RULE 10

WRECKING OR SHIFTING OF A MARK

Should any mark be missing or moved from its proper position during a race, the Race Committee shall, if possible, replace it or substitute a boat displaying Code Flag "R" and if possible call attention thereto by gun, whistle or other proper device. Failing thus to re-establish the mark, the race may be ordered re-sailed or not, at the option of the Race Committee. *(Shifting Mark.)*

Part 2.—Sailing Rules

RULE 14

WHEN AMENABLE TO PART 2 OF THE RACING RULES

A yacht shall be amenable to Part 2 of the Racing Rules from the time the preparatory

APPENDIX I

signal for her class is made, and shall continue so until she has finished and her entire hull and spars are clear of the finish line.

RULE 17

CREW

DEFINITION OF CORINTHIANISM

Corinthianism.   Corinthianism in yachting is that attribute which represents participation for sport as distinct from gain, and which also involves the acquirement of nautical experience through the love of sport, rather than through necessity or the hope of gain.

RULE 24

BOARDING AND LEAVING

Boarding and Leaving.   Unless otherwise specified in the instructions no person shall board or leave a yacht except in case of accident or injury to a person on board.

RULE 25

HELMSMAN

Helmsman.   No owner shall, without the consent of the Race Committee, steer a yacht other than his own in a race in which his own yacht competes. Failure to comply with this rule shall be regarded as an infringement thereof by both yachts.

APPENDIX I

RULE 27

START AND RECALL

(1) The starting line shall be indicated by a stakeboat or other mark at one end and a white flag displayed on the Race Committee's boat or station at the other end. *Start.*

(2) The Race Committee may establish, by means of a buoy or buoys, a restricted area about the starting line, within which no yacht shall enter until the preparatory signal for her class is made. Such buoys shall not be deemed marks of the course. *Restricted Area.*

(3) Yachts whose preparatory signal has not been made must keep clear of yachts whose preparatory signal has been made. Yachts whose preparatory signal has not been made must at all times keep clear of any restricted area about the starting line established by the Race Committee.

(4) The time of the starting signal for each class shall be taken as the time of the start of each yacht in the class.

(5) If any yacht, or any part of her hull, spars or other equipment be on or across the starting line when the starting signal is made, she must return and start again. Such premature start shall be indicated by the prompt and prominent display of a white ball or cylinder bearing a red band, or such other distinctive signal, other than a flag, as may be indicated in the instructions for the race, and attention shall be called thereto by a suitable sound signal different from the starting signal. *Recall Signal.*

APPENDIX I

Should more than one yacht cross the starting line before the starting signal of her class has been made, an additional sound signal shall be given for each yacht so crossing. When practicable such yacht or yachts shall also be hailed by name, number or otherwise. Failure of the Race Committee to give the recall signals above provided for shall not relieve a yacht which has made a premature start from the necessity of returning and recrossing the line.

(6) A yacht so returning, or one working into position from the wrong side of the line after her starting signal has been made, must keep clear of and give way to all competing yachts whose starting signal has been made.

(7) A yacht starting after the signal for the start of the next class has been made, shall, in starting, keep clear of and give way to yachts starting during their specified starting intervals.

RULE 28

GOVERNMENT MARKS

Government Marks. All Government Marks and Aids to Navigation not used as turning marks shall be passed on the channel side and shall be deemed marks of the course unless the instructions specify otherwise. When used as turning marks and there is an accompanying buoy, the accompanying buoy may be disregarded and passed on either hand unless the instructions for the race specify otherwise.

APPENDIX I

RULE 29

DEFINITIONS

(1) Close-hauled and Free.
(a) Close-hauled. A yacht is close-hauled when sailing by the wind as close as she can lie with advantage in working to windward.
(b) Free. A yacht not sailing close-hauled, as defined above, and not in the wind, is sailing free.

(2) Luffing.

A yacht is luffing when she so alters her course as to sail a course more nearly into the wind.

(3) Clear Ahead and Clear Astern.

A yacht is clear astern of another when all her hull and equipment is abaft all the other yacht's hull and equipment, judged by the course which the two yachts are sailing. The other is clear ahead.

(4) Overlap.

An overlap between two yachts exists when they are sailing approximately the same course and neither has her bowsprit end (or stem if she has no bowsprit) abaft the other yacht's boom end or counter, judged by the course which the two yachts are sailing.

(5) Risk of Collision.

The phrase "Risk of Collision" is used in the widest sense, and yachts must be considered to be "approaching so as to involve risk of collision" whenever either of two cannot

Definitions.

APPENDIX I

Definitions. (*Continued*)

with perfect safety be navigated without any regard to the proximity of the other.

For example, generally speaking, two yachts cannot be navigated without any regard to each other unless either or both can at any moment turn a complete circle with helm hard over either way without fouling the other.

When there is any doubt, risk of collision is to be presumed to exist.

(6) Overtaking.

Of two yachts sailing the same or nearly the same course one which is clear astern of the other begins to rank as overtaking yacht as soon as she comes anywhere within range of risk of collision and continues so to rank until she either—

1. Draws clear ahead; and then she begins to rank as overtaken yacht.
2. Draws clear abreast by widening out beyond range of risk of collision.
3. Falls astern beyond range of risk of collision.
4. One or both of the yachts tack.

The obligation of proving that she has drawn clear lies on the late overtaking yacht.

No question of overtaking can arise unless the yachts are sailing approximately the same course (A luff by one of the yachts under Rule 30, clause (B), does not count as a difference of course in this connection).

(7) Proper Course.

During the existence of overtaking conditions the proper course is prima facie nothing to leeward of full and by if on a wind, or of the

APPENDIX I

next mark if the wind be free; but there may be conditions of tide or circumstances, other than the desire to hinder the competitor overtaking to leeward, which justify a more leeward course; in this case the responsibility for proving the justification for such a leeward course would lie upon the weather yacht.

Definitions. (Continued)

RULE 30

RIGHT OF WAY

When one yacht is approaching another yacht, so as to involve risk of collision, one of them shall keep clear of the other as follows:

Right of way.

OVERTAKING

(A) A yacht overtaking another shall keep out of the way of the overtaken yacht.

(B) If the overtaking yacht steers a course to pass the overtaken yacht on the side opposite to that on which the latter then carries her main boom, the latter may luff from her course, head to wind if she pleases, to prevent the former passing her to windward, until she is in such a position that her bowsprit end, or stem if she has no bowsprit, would strike the overtaking yacht abaft the main shrouds, after which she may maintain her course, but may luff no further.

APPENDIX I

Right of Way.
(Continued)

In cases of doubt as to the right of the leeward yacht to luff, the windward yacht must respond to the luff, and protest if she thinks fit.

> (C) A yacht must never bear away out of her proper course to hinder an overtaking yacht passing her to leeward. The overtaking yacht, if to leeward, must not luff so as to interfere* with the windward yacht or cause her to alter her course, until she ranks as an overtaken yacht. The lee side shall be considered that on which the leading yacht of the two carries her main boom at the time she ceases to be clear ahead.

MEETING, CROSSING AND CONVERGING

These clauses are framed particularly to avoid collision and the yacht which by rule has to keep out of the way must always do so (see clause [K]).

Before the starting signal is given there are no restrictions upon the manœuvring of the yachts other than the provisions of Rules 30, 31 and 32, and the yacht holding right of way may alter course in any reasonable manner (but a luff so sudden that it cannot be easily responded to would not be considered reasonable).

As soon as the starting signal is given, yachts must sail a course consistent with the intention

---

*"interfere" is used in the sense of interference through actual contact.

APPENDIX I

of crossing the line, but in all other respects the only restrictions on manœuvring are those provided in Rules 30, 31 and 32. After crossing the line the only restrictions upon manœuvring are those provided in Rules 30, 31 and 32.

Right of Way. *(Continued)*

(D) A yacht which has the wind free shall keep out of the way of one which is close-hauled.

(E) A yacht which is close-hauled on the port tack shall keep out of the way of one which is close-hauled on the starboard tack.

(F) When both yachts have the wind free on different sides, and neither can claim the rights of a yacht being overtaken, the yacht which has the wind on the port side shall keep out of the way of the other.*

(G) When both yachts have the wind free on the same side, and neither can claim the rights of a yacht being overtaken, the yacht to windward shall keep out of the way of the yacht to leeward.

(H) When two yachts, both close-hauled on the same tack, are converging by reason of the leeward yacht holding a better wind, and neither can claim the rights of a yacht being overtaken,

---

* A yacht is deemed to have the wind on the side opposite to that on which she is carrying her main-boom.

APPENDIX I

Right of Way. (*Continued*)

then the yacht to windward shall keep out of the way.

ALTERING COURSE

(I) A yacht may not tack so as to involve probability of collision with another yacht unless she can gather proper way on her new tack before a collision would occur; nor so as to involve probability of collision with another yacht which, owing to her position, cannot keep out of the way. A yacht which tacks so close in front of another as to cause the latter to alter course to avoid a collision before the former has gathered proper way must be disqualified.*

*INTERPRETATION OF "PROPER WAY"

In reference to the words "proper way" of Rule 30 (I) the following Resolution was enacted at the Annual Meeting of the North American Yacht Racing Union held November 17, 1933.

"Resolved that it is the sense of this meeting that where the words 'proper way' occur in Rule 30 (I), they should be interpreted as meaning 'filled away, gathered way on her new course and is under full control.'"

(K) When by any of the above clauses one yacht has to keep out of the way of another, the latter (subject to clause [B]) shall not alter course so as to prevent her doing so. Although the

APPENDIX I

right-of-way yacht is not bound to hold her course, she must not so alter it as to mislead or baulk the other, in the act of keeping out of the way.

A yacht may be disqualified on a protest arising out of a breach of any of these clauses whether a collision result or not.

RULE 31

GIVING ROOM AT MARKS OR OBSTRUCTIONS TO SEA ROOM

If an overlap exists between two yachts when both of them, without tacking, are about to pass an obstruction to sea room, or a mark on the required side, the outside yacht must give room to the yacht in danger of fouling such mark or obstruction, whether she be the windward or leeward yacht, provided the yachts are overlapping on actually reaching such mark or obstruction. An overtaking yacht shall not be justified in attempting to establish an overlap, and thus force a passage between the leading yacht and the mark or obstruction, after the latter has reached it or altered her course for the purpose and in the act of rounding it. A craft under way (including another yacht racing), of which the yacht concerned has to keep out of the way, ranks as an obstruction for the purpose of this or the following rule.

Rule 31 makes exception to Rule 30 only so far as to require the outer yacht, although otherwise holding right of way under the latter

Room at Marks.

APPENDIX I

rule, to allow the inner yacht room if her overlap has been made in proper time. In all other respects Rule 30 remains in full force.

As an example, a leading yacht may tack round a mark or obstruction only when she can do so and clear the yacht astern, just as she would be required to do if she made her tack in open sea without any mark or obstruction being there.

In all protests under this rule the onus of proof that the overlap has been made in proper time rests with the yacht that previously had been astern.

RULE 32

CLOSE-HAULED, APPROACHING AN OBSTRUCTION TO SEA ROOM OR A MARK

Close-Hauled, Approaching Marks.
If two yachts are standing close-hauled on the same tack towards the shore, or an obstruction to sea room which requires the leeward yacht to alter her course to clear it, and if she is not able to tack without coming into collision with the yacht to windward; the latter shall, on being hailed by the person in charge of the leeward yacht, at once allow her room to tack. A yacht so claiming room shall be bound to tack immediately her hail is responded to. If the leeward yacht elects to clear the obstruction by bearing away she shall allow the windward yacht room to do the same if she so desires. But if the obstruction is a mark of the course the leeward yacht has not the right to so hail the other about if that other can herself pass the mark without tacking.

APPENDIX I

Although it is only in this rule that a hail is mentioned, other situations may arise in which under Rule 1 a hail should be given before making an alteration of course which may not be foreseen by the other yacht.

RULE 33

FOULING OR IMPROPERLY ROUNDING MARKS

A yacht must go fairly around the course, rounding the series of marks as specified in the instructions, and in rounding each specified mark her track from the preceding to the following mark must enclose it on the required side. A yacht shall not touch a mark of the course unless wrongfully compelled to do so by another yacht. A yacht which has touched a mark of the course must immediately either abandon the race or hoist a protest signal. Every essential or ordinary above-water part of any object named as a mark, counts as a mark, but no part below water, nor any object accidentally or temporarily attached to the mark.

Fouling Marks.

RULE 34

MARKS OF THE COURSE

A mark is any vessel, boat, buoy or other object used to indicate the course but does not become a mark of the course until the preceding mark, if any, has been rounded or passed. The marks of the starting line are marks of the course from the making of the preparatory signal for each class, but there is no required

Marks of Course.

APPENDIX I

side until after the starting signal has been made. Every mark rounded or passed remains a mark of the course until the next mark has been passed. A mark, until it becomes a mark of the course as above defined, shall be an obstruction to sea room.

RULE 35

FOULING COMPETING YACHTS

If a yacht, through failure to observe any of these rules, shall foul another yacht, or cause other yachts to foul, she shall be disqualified.

RULE 36

RUNNING AGROUND AND FOULING

Running Aground and Fouling. A yacht running aground or fouling a buoy, pier, vessel or other object may use her anchors, warps, boats, and other gear to get clear, but may not receive any assistance except from the crew of a vessel fouled. Any gear used must be recovered before she continues the race.

RULE 37

ANCHORING

Anchoring, etc. A yacht may anchor, but must weigh anchor again and not slip. No yacht shall warp or kedge or make fast to any buoy, pier, vessel or other object except for the purpose mentioned in Rule 36. In weighing anchor, yachts having a power windlass as part of their regular equipment may use such power.

APPENDIX I

RULE 38

PROPULSION

No means of propulsion other than sails shall be employed except as provided in Rule 36. *Propulsion.*

RULE 39

SOUNDING

No other means of sounding than a lead line shall be employed. *Sounding.*

RULE 40

MAN OVERBOARD AND ACCIDENTS

Each yacht must render every possible asistance to any vessel or person in peril, and should she not render such assistance she shall be disqualified. If, in the judgment of the Race Committee, any yacht not responsible for the accident shall have thereby injured her chances of winning any prize, it shall order the race resailed between such yacht and the winner of such prize. A yacht losing a man overboard must either recover the man on board before continuing the race or give up the race. *Accidents.*

RULE 41

THE FINISH

(1) The finish line shall be indicated by a stakeboat or other mark at one end and a white flag displayed on the Race Committee's boat or station at the other end. *The Finish.*

(2) The Race Committee's boat or station at the finish line shall fly the Race Committee's

APPENDIX I

flag and after sunset shall show either the Club's night signal or two red lights.

(3) The time of a yacht at the finish shall be taken when first any part of her hull or spars is on the finish line.

(4) A yacht which has been timed at the finish is not required to pass across the line but remains amenable to the rules so long as any part of her hull, spars or other equipment remains on the line.

(5) After finishing, yachts must keep clear of the line and of other yachts which are still racing.

RULE 42

THE CASE OF A DEAD HEAT

In the case of a dead heat, the race shall either be resailed by the yachts having made the dead heat, or, if ordered by the Race Committee, the prize shall be decided by the spin of a coin.

Part 3.—Protests, Disqualifications and Appeals

RULE 43

PENALTY FOR INFRINGING RULES

Protest and Appeal.

A yacht infringing any of these rules, which shall apply to all yachts whether sailing in the same or different classes, or shall attempt to win a race by other means than fair sailing and superior speed and skill, shall be disqualified.

Any yacht which has violated any of the foregoing Racing Rules 1 to 42 inclusive, in a man-

APPENDIX I

ner which she knows would cause her disqualification, whether the foul involves a yacht in her own class or in any other class, shall immediately withdraw from the race. The owner of a yacht which infringes these rules shall pay all damages caused thereby to another yacht.

RULE 44

PENALTY FOR GROSS BREACH OF RULES

Should a gross breach of these rules be proved against any sailing master, the Race Committee may disqualify him from sailing in any race held by the Club for such time as they may deem fit.

RULE 45

PROTESTS

All protests must be made in writing, signed by the owner or his representative, and must name the rule or rules alleged to have been infringed, and contain a statement of the facts. They must be filed with the Race Committee before 6 P.M. of the week-day following the race. A yacht having cause to protest another yacht for infringement of these rules occurring during a race must promptly display Code Flag "B" and keep such flag flying until she has finished the race, unless her owner or his representative has no knowledge of the facts justifying the protest until after the conclusion of the race.

Protests.

APPENDIX I

RULE 46

HEARINGS BY RACE COMMITTEE

Hearings by Race Committee.

(1) The Race Committee shall promptly notify the owner of a protested yacht or his representative of the receipt of a protest and the rule or rules alleged to have been violated, and shall arrange for a hearing thereon as soon as possible. Due notice of such hearing shall be given to the owners of the yachts involved or their representatives.

(2) The Race Committee shall take the evidence presented by the parties to the protest and such other evidence as the Race Committee may consider necessary, and the owners of the yachts involved in a protest, or a representative of each owner, shall have the right to be present during the taking of evidence by the Race Committee.

RULE 47

DISQUALIFICATION WITHOUT PROTEST

Disqualification without Protest.

Should it come to the knowledge of the Race Committee, or should it have reasonable grounds to believe that a competitor in a race has in any way infringed these rules, it shall have the power to disqualify such competitor without protest, but only after notice has been given as hereinafter provided and after a hearing at which the owner of the yacht involved or his representative shall have the right to be present and submit such evidence as he may deem necessary. Notice of proposed action by

APPENDIX I

the Race Committee under this rule must be given to the owner of the yacht believed to have infringed these rules or to his representative, and must name the rule or rules believed to have been infringed and the time and place of the hearing thereon. Notice of proposed action, based upon an infringement of the sailing rules, must be given prior to 6 P.M. of the week-day following the race in question.

RULE 48

DECISIONS OF PROTESTS

(1) All decisions of the Race Committee shall be in writing, and shall be communicated to the parties involved. The facts found by the Race Committee and the grounds of each decision shall be specified therein, and the determination of the Race Committee as to the facts involved in any protest shall be final. A member of the Race Committee, who is the owner, in whole or in part, of a yacht sailing in a race, shall not act upon the Committee on any question which concerns the class in which his yacht is competing.

Decisions of Protests.

RULE 49

APPEALS

(1) Appeals involving solely the interpretation of the Racing Rules may be taken from the decisions of the Race Committee of a club which is a member of a yacht racing association, either (1) to the Executive or other appropriate Committee of the association, or (2)

Appeals.

APPENDIX I

Appeals (*Continued*)

directly to the Executive Committee of the Union, provided the consent of such yacht racing association is first obtained. When such appeals are taken to the Executive or other appropriate Committee of the yacht racing association, they shall be taken in accordance with its rules. An appeal may be taken by the Race Committee or by any of the parties to the protest from the decision of such Committee of the Yacht Racing Association to the Executive Committee of the Union, provided the consent of such yacht racing association is first obtained.

The Executive Committee of the Union shall have the right to refuse to hear any appeal from a decision in which the Race Committee and the Executive Committee or other appropriate Committee of the Association, concur.

(2) Appeals involving solely the interpretation of the Racing Rules may be taken from the decisions of the Race Committee of a club which is not a member of a yacht racing association, provided the consent of such Race Committee is first obtained. Such appeals shall be taken directly to the Executive Committee of the Union.

(3) All appeals must be in writing setting forth the grounds of the appeal and signed by the owner or his representative. They must be filed with the Secretary of the Union within thirty days after the receipt by the appellant of the decision appealed from and must be accompanied by the written consent provided for in Sections (1) and (2) of this Rule.

APPENDIX I

(4) Upon an appeal being taken, the Committee whose decision is appealed from shall promptly file with the Secretary of the Union:

1. A copy of the protest, or where action has been taken upon the initiative of the Race Committee, a copy of the notice given pursuant to Rule 47.
2. A plan showing:

   a. the course
   b. the direction and velocity of the wind
   c. the set of the current, and
   d. the positions and tracks of the yachts involved in the protest.

3. A copy of the instructions for the race.
4. A copy of the decision of the Race Committee containing the facts found by it.
5. A copy of the decision of the Committee of the local yacht racing association, if the appeal is taken under Section (1) of this rule.

(5) The decisions of the Executive Committee shall be in writing and the grounds of each decision shall be specified therein. All decisions of the Executive Committee shall be filed with the Secretary of the Union, who shall communicate the result thereof, with a copy of the decision, to the parties interested and to the Secretary of the Committee whose decision has been appealed from.

APPENDIX II

SUGGESTED CHANGES IN THE RACING RULES

INTRODUCTION

In June, 1936, Mr. Harold S. Vanderbilt in collaboration with three other well-known American yachtsmen published "A Suggested Revision of the International Yacht Racing Right of Way Rules." Part V of Commodore Vanderbilt's *On the Wind's Highway,* published three years later, contains a further and simplified revision of his 1936 "Suggested Revision."

That the existing Sailing Rules—The Right of Way Rules—adopted at the International Conference in London on November 4–5, 1929, can be improved in form as well as in substance cannot seriously be denied. As Mr. Vanderbilt truly says, "the main defect in the existing rules is that facts which determine right of way and manœuvring rights are often so difficult to agree upon that honest differences of opinion as to which rule (if any) to apply arise far too frequently." The fact should not be overlooked, however, that the code of Sailing Rules adopted at London in November, 1929, was the culmination of many years of earnest and laborious effort on the part of yachtsmen in many parts of the world to bring about uniform right-of-way rules in yacht racing. Imperfect as the present code may be, its adoption was a great step in furthering the cause of international yacht racing.

While the present rules may be far from perfect and show unmistakable signs of being a compilation and revision of earlier amendments, it must be remembered that during the past ten years they have become so firmly in-

APPENDIX II

grained in the minds of so many thousands of yachtsmen both young and old that it would be difficult to uproot the old rules from their minds and implant a new set based upon new and in many respects very different right-of-way determinatives. It is easier to learn something new than to "unlearn" something that has become almost instinctive.

Whether one agrees with Mr. Vanderbilt in whole or only in part, it is indisputable that in endeavoring to eliminate the uncertainties in the present rules he has found it necessary to introduce some new and radically different right-of-way determinatives. We believe that there is a strong feeling on the part of many of the men who were most active in bringing about the adoption of the present Sailing Rules that there would be grave danger of undoing that work if any attempt were made at this time to make drastic changes in those rules.

It seems to us, therefore, that the likelihood of the adoption of clarifying changes in the Sailing Rules might be rendered less difficult if the familiar numbering, sequence and general basic principles of the present rules were adhered to. Nor should there be overlooked the difficulty of translating the official English text into many foreign languages to the end that the English meaning and intent of a given choice of words shall, so far as possible, have the same meaning and intent in each language into which it later may be translated. That is an additional reason why we have refrained so far as possible from changing the existing English text.

We wish to give credit to Mr. Vanderbilt and his collaborators for many of the ideas incorporated in this suggested revision. Some of their suggestions have been incorporated almost verbatim. We have no desire to be given credit for any changes which may perhaps be adopted by reason of what we may suggest herein. We are concerned

APPENDIX II

only with the hope that somehow, sometime, even if we may not live to see it, the Sailing Rules may be amended for the betterment of the sport of yacht racing.

SET-UP OF THIS SUGGESTED REVISION

For the sake of brevity and, we hope, clarity we shall merely indicate the suggested changes. Some of the changes are too obvious to require comment. Where comment has been deemed necessary, we have tried to be as brief as possible.

The suggested changes and additions are in italics. The Author's comments thereon are in brackets immediately following each suggested change.

RULE 29

DEFINITIONS

(1) Close-hauled and Free.
   (a) Close-hauled (*Full and By*). *The course the yacht under existing conditions would normally sail beating to windward.*
   [This change should remove all doubt as to the meaning of this subsection.]

(3) Clear Ahead and Clear Astern.
   A yacht is clear astern of another when all her hull and equipment is *astern of* all the other yacht's hull and equipment, *as determined by a line drawn at right angles to the mean of the courses* which the two yachts are sailing. The other is clear ahead.
   [The word "abaft" pertains to the relative positions of two objects on board of *a* vessel. It should not be used to designate the relative positions of *two* vessels.]

(5) Risk of Collision.
   Second paragraph to read as follows:
   "Risk of Collision" exists between two yachts unless either one, with helm hard over, can turn toward and inside of the other and clear her, despite the other's best effort to prevent said manœuvre.
   [This wording covers the case of a small yacht following

APPENDIX II

close aboard a large yacht, a situation not covered by the present second paragraph. It does not materially alter, in fact it may slightly extend, the existing range of risk of collision.]

(6) Overtaking.

Of two yachts sailing *approximately* the same course the one clear astern begins to rank as overtaking yacht as soon as she comes within range of risk of collision and continues so to rank *until Overtaking terminates.*

Overtaking terminates if:

1. The overtaking yacht draws clear ahead;

2. The overtaking yacht falls astern beyond *the* range of risk of collision;

3. The yachts widen out abeam beyond *the* range of risk of collision;

Note: The obligation of proving that she has drawn clear lies on the late overtaking yacht.

4. One or both of the yachts tack;

5. *While overlapped, both yachts (1) jibe around an obstruction to sea room, a government buoy or a mark of the course, or (2) jibe and make a material alteration of course.*

No question of Overtaking can arise *or continue to exist* unless the yachts are sailing approximately the same course. A luff by one of the yachts under Rule 30, Clause (B), does not count as a difference of course in this connection.

[The only material change is the addition of a fifth state of facts which terminates Overtaking. It covers a situation where one yacht overtakes and overlaps another either to windward or to leeward, and thereafter both yachts jibe around an obstruction, a government buoy or a mark, or jibe and make a material alteration of course, and after completing the manœuvre still are overlapped; as in The Florida Case for example. Under the existing rule the jibe does not necessarily terminate Overtaking; the clause of the overtaking rule in effect prior to jibing technically is still in force; and the result may be an anomalous and "impossible" situation.]

(8) *Mast Line.*

An imaginary line drawn through the center of the mainmast of the leeward yacht at right angles to her fore and aft center line.

[The purpose of this new definition will become apparent later on.]

APPENDIX II

(9) *Obstructions.*

Craft under way (including another yacht racing), of which the yacht concerned has to keep out of the way, *and is in danger of fouling, other objects necessitating an alteration of course, and shoals over which the yacht in question may not be safely piloted* are "obstructions." *A government buoy is not an "obstruction" unless it marks such a shoal.*

[No. 9 is the second new definition. The words not in italics are taken verbatim from the last sentence of the first paragraph of Rule 31. The existing rules contain no definition as to what does or does not constitute an obstruction within the meaning of Rules 31 and 32. Is not such a definition advisable in order to remove all doubt?]

(10) *Approximately the Same Course* ⎫
    Nearly the Same Course ⎭

Wherever used in Rule 29—Definitions—these phrases signify a divergence of course of not more than one compass point ($11\frac{1}{4}°$).

RULE 30

RIGHT OF WAY

After the first paragraph and immediately before the heading OVERTAKING insert the following:

Before the starting signal is made:

(1) A yacht holding right of way may alter course in any reasonable manner, but a luff, a bearing away or a jibe so sudden that it cannot be easily responded to would not be considered reasonable;

(2) A yacht on the port tack shall keep out of the way of a yacht on the starboard tack;

(3) A yacht approaching from clear astern and establishing an overlap to windward shall keep out of the way of the leeward yacht;

(4) A yacht approaching from clear astern and establishing an overlap to leeward shall have right of way over the windward yacht and may luff in a manner to which the other can easily respond even to the extent of forcing the windward yacht to start prematurely.

During the preparatory period the foregoing four (4) provisions OVERRIDE any provisions of Clauses (A) to (H) inclusive, which may be inconsistent therewith.

APPENDIX II

[We stated in Chapter VII that as interpreted by the Council of the Y. R. A., and by the N. A. Y. R. U., the third paragraph of Meeting, Crossing and Converging "did not interfere with the Clauses of Rule 30, beyond prohibiting a leeward yacht after gunfire, deliberately luffing a windward yacht so that the latter could not cross the line." (Y. R. A., 1931, page 173.)

Even without this contentious third paragraph in regard to sailing a course consistent with the intention of crossing the line, a leeward yacht could not luff a windward yacht the wrong side of a starting line mark *after* gunfire unless she went with her. Except in a match race between two yachts, as is permitted by the Racing Rules of the New York Yacht Club, such a manœuvre would be little short of ridiculous.

Before the start the only limitation on manœuvring contained in Rules 30, 31 and 32 is to be found in the second paragraph of Meeting, Crossing and Converging, and is to the effect that a right-of-way yacht may alter course only in a reasonable manner, *i.e.*, in a manner to which the other can easily respond. This limitation we have retained intact. The remainder of the second paragraph together with the entire third paragraph is valueless. Why, therefore, not delete them both?

To quote Mr. Vanderbilt, "simplicity in the starting rules is of paramount importance." He is of opinion that the separate set of starting rules contained in his revision "constitute the greatest suggested improvement in the existing rules."

The adoption of our suggested changes would mean that *before* the start:
(1) "Overtaking" would be abolished.
(2) The only rules applicable would be:
   (a) Port tack yacht keeps clear.
   (b) Windward yacht keeps clear.]

(B) If the overtaking yacht steers a course to pass the overtaken yacht on the side opposite to that on which the latter then carries her main boom, the latter may luff from her course, head to wind if she pleases, to prevent the former passing her to windward, *until the helmsman of the windward yacht is forward of the mast line. Thereafter, while the overlap lasts, the leeward yacht shall not sail higher than full and by, and shall not luff so as to force the windward yacht to luff in order to keep clear.*

The member in charge of the windward yacht is prima facie the

APPENDIX II

judge as to when her helmsman reaches the mast line position.
While a hail by the member in charge—"mast in line" or words to that effect—is not mandatory; yet until one is made, and if there is reasonable doubt, the leeward yacht may assume that the relative position of the two yachts does not (or did not) warrant such a hail. The leeward yacht, when so hailed, must be governed accordingly; her only remedy lies in a protest if she deems the hail improper.

[One of the greatest difficulties in the present rules is to determine when the luffing rights of the overtaken-to-windward yacht terminate. As is so clearly pointed out by Mr. Vanderbilt in his discussion of the *Endeavour* v. *Rainbow* protest on page 213 of *On The Wind's Highway,* "it is impossible to know when the existing determinative becomes operative, because (1) it is necessary to visualize an imaginary future luff to determine where the bow of the leeward yacht would hit the other yacht; (2) it is impossible accurately to estimate the distance the leeward yacht would lose in making her imaginary future luff because yachts narrow rapidly as they near the bow, and because the leeward yacht would often be retarded by backwind.

"The difficulty of applying the present yardstick is further enhanced by the fact that 'the member in charge'" of the leeward yacht, "is usually, during such manœuvre, at or near the helm, a poor place to judge the operation of the present yardstick."

We have adopted Mr. Vanderbilt's suggestion that the member in charge of the windward yacht be constituted the judge, prima facie, of when her helmsman has reached the mast line position, because almost always he is at the helm during a luffing match. It also avoids having more than one judge, and therefore lessens the chance for argument. It is unthinkable that he would cheat.

As soon as the helmsman of the windward yacht is forward of the mast line of the leeward yacht the latter, if then heading above full and by, must bear away to not less than full and by even though such bearing away is not necessary to avoid a collision.

The suggested substitute rule does three things therefore:

First: It establishes an easily determined point at which the right of the overtaken yacht to luff terminates;

Second: It defines the maximum windward course she may sail thereafter; and

Third: It protects the windward yacht after she has won the luffing match.]

APPENDIX II

MEETING, CROSSING AND CONVERGING

[As stated above, we suggest that the second and third paragraphs of Meeting, Crossing and Converging be deleted.]

(G) When two yachts *with* the wind on the same side *are approaching each other* by reason of the leeward yacht holding a *higher course,* the windward yacht shall keep out of the way.

If when the yachts no longer are clear of each other as defined in Rule 29 (3), the helmsman of the windward yacht is aft of the mast line, the leeward yacht may luff even head to wind but in a manner to which the windward yacht may easily respond, until the helmsman of the windward yacht is forward of the mast line. Thereafter, while the overlap lasts, the leeward yacht shall not sail higher than full and by, and shall not luff so as to force the windward yacht to keep clear.

The member in charge of the windward yacht is prima facie the judge as to when her helmsman reaches the mast line position.

While a hail by the member in charge—"mast in line" or words to that effect—is not mandatory; yet until one is made, and if there is reasonable doubt, the leeward yacht may assume that the relative position of the two yachts does not (or did not) warrant such a hail. The leeward yacht, when so hailed, must be governed accordingly; her only remedy lies in a protest if she deems the hail improper.

If there is doubt under which of the two rules, overtaking or converging, the yachts rank, overtaking conditions shall be presumed to exist. The burden of proof that converging conditions exist shall be upon the yacht making such claim.

[The only real difference between existing Clauses (G) and (H) is that (G) applies to yachts sailing free, and (H) to yachts sailing close-hauled. The words "by reason of the leeward yacht holding a better wind" in Clause (H) are meaningless. What they are meant to imply is "holding a higher course." Two yachts close-hauled may be pointing equally high, and yet the windward yacht may be sagging down on her opponent. The leeward yacht is not "holding a better wind." She is, however, holding a higher course. Is it not advisable, therefore, to simplify the two existing clauses by combining them into one?

It should be noted that the same determinatives as to luffing

APPENDIX II

rights are included in suggested Clause (G) as were set forth in suggested Clause (B). In other words, with the exception of the right of sharp luffing given to an overtaken-to-windward yacht by Clause (B) the two luffing rules may be said to be identical; a result much to be desired.

The last paragraph was added in order to make as small as possible the "twilight zone" between "Overtaking" and "Converging" in the existing rules. After the start, except on windward legs, the yachts are sailing in the same general direction. We feel that in case of doubt the presumption should be in favor of the existence of overtaking conditions and that the burden of proof should be on the yacht which claims that converging conditions existed to rebut the presumption that they did *not* exist. In other words, she must prove by a fair preponderance of all the evidence that after the yachts came within the range of risk of collision one yacht was neither (1) clear astern of nor (2) sailing approximately the same course as the other.]

ALTERING COURSE

(I) *A yacht shall not tack within the range of risk of collision, as defined in Rule 29 (5), (1) so as to cause another yacht to alter course to avoid a collision; or (2)* so as to involve probability of collision with another yacht which, owing to her position *or her size,* cannot keep out of the way.

[There is, we believe, practically unanimity of opinion on the part of racing yachtsmen and Race Committee members that the phrase "proper way" is too indefinite to be of much help in determining what speed or what degree of manœuvrability a yacht must have attained after tacking, and before she can be held to have gathered proper way on her new course, in the two situations specified in existing Clause (I) viz.: As enumerated in the first clause of the first sentence, and in the last sentence of the rule.

On May 10, 1933, the Council of the Y. R. A. debated the suggested change of "full way" to "proper way." Sir Charles MacIver said that the Council had always interpreted the term "full way" as follows:

"A yacht must not tack so as to involve probability of collision with another yacht and if a yacht made a tack so that she did involve any probability of collision, she would be liable to disquali-

APPENDIX II

fication, and if there was any doubt about it, the onus was upon the yacht which made the tack. That was the principle from which the Y. R. A. should not depart." The records of the meeting, Y. R. A., 1934, page 166, state that "The Council concurred."

We do not believe that the suggested changes in the rule in any way alter the fundamental intent of prohibiting "tacking in another yacht's 'water.' "

The words *"or her size"* in Clause (2) were inserted in order to cover a situation where a small yacht beating to windward tacks to starboard so close aboard a large yacht on the port tack, also beating to windward, that the latter is unable to keep clear, not because of her position but because of her size.]

RULE 31

GIVING ROOM AT MARKS OR OBSTRUCTIONS TO SEA ROOM

(1) *If, under conditions other than those of overtaking,* an overlap exists between two yachts when both of them, without tacking, are about to pass an obstruction to sea room or a mark on the required side, the outside yacht must give room to the yacht in danger of fouling such mark or obstruction, whether she be the windward or the leeward yacht, provided *that the overlap has been made at a distance from the mark or obstruction great enough to allow the outside yacht ample time to give room under the prevailing conditions of wind, tide and sea. Under no conditions shall such distance be less than three times the overall length of the larger yacht, including bowsprit and overhang of boom as trimmed and/or boomkin.* A craft under way (including another yacht racing), of which the yacht concerned has to keep out of the way, ranks as an obstruction for the purposes of this or the following rule.

(2) *Under overtaking conditions a* yacht shall not be justified in attempting to establish an overlap, and thus force a passage between the leading yacht and the mark or obstruction, after the latter has reached it or *has* altered her course for the purpose of and *is* in the act of rounding it.

(3) *In other words,* Rule 31 makes exception to Rule 30 only so far as to require the outer yacht, although otherwise holding right of way under the latter rule, to allow the inner yacht room if her overlap has been made in *accordance with the above requirements.*

APPENDIX II

As an example, a leading yacht may tack around a mark or obstruction only when she can do so and clear the yacht astern, just as she would be required to do if she made her tack in open sea without any mark or obstruction being there.

(4) *A government buoy is not an obstruction unless it marks a shoal over which the yacht concerned may not be safely piloted.*

(5) In all protests under this rule the onus of proof that the overlap *was legally established* rests with the yacht making such claim.

[If new definition Number 9 should be adopted, the last sentence of paragraph (1) and the whole of paragraph (4) should be deleted. Paragraph (5) would then become paragraph (4).

In Chapter XII we endeavored to demonstrate that barging at the start is not prohibited by Rule 31 as now worded. Also that the phrase "overlap made in proper time" is a most unsatisfactory determinative in so far as stamping out that unfair and almost unanimously frowned-upon practice. Our aim in the suggested revision of Rule 31 is (1) to prohibit that unsportsmanlike manœuvre, and (2) to clarify the rule in a few other minor aspects.]

RULE 32

CLOSE-HAULED, APPROACHING AN OBSTRUCTION TO SEA ROOM OR A MARK

Amend the second paragraph to reflect the suggested changes in Rules 30 (B) and (G), so that the second paragraph will read as follows:

Although it is only in this Rule *and in Rule 30, Clauses (B) and (G),* that a hail is mentioned, other situations may arise in which under Rule 1 a hail should be given before making an alteration of course which may not *reasonably* be foreseen by the other yacht.

RULE 34

MARKS OF THE COURSE

(1) A mark is any vessel, boat, buoy or other object used to indicate the course but does not become a mark of the course until the preceding mark, if any, has been rounded or passed. Every mark rounded or passed remains a mark of the course until

APPENDIX II

the next mark has been *rounded or* passed. A mark, *other than a government buoy, when not* a mark of the course as above defined, shall be an obstruction to sea room.

(2) Marks *used in connection with* the starting line are marks of the course from the making of the preparatory signal for each class. *They do not rank as obstructions to sea room within the meaning of Rules 31 and 32 nor have they* a required side until after the starting signal has been made.

[The reasons for the rearrangement of Rule 34 have been fully discussed in Chapter V. Separating the Rule into two paragraphs makes for clarity.]

RULE 35

FOULING COMPETING YACHTS

(1) If a yacht, through failure to observe any of these rules, shall foul another yacht, or cause other yachts to foul, she shall be disqualified.

(2) *A protested yacht or one which is disqualified later, which continues in the race shall be granted full rights under these rules until she (1) withdraws from the race or (2) completes the course.*

[Paragraph (2) merely incorporates as part of the rule the effect of the decision in *Pilgrim* v. *Maori,* N. A. Y. R. U., Appeal No. 4, November 16, 1935.]

RULE 47

DISQUALIFICATION WITHOUT PROTEST

In place of the last sentence of the rule insert the following:

Notice of proposed action, based upon an infringement of the Sailing Rules, must be given *within a reasonable time* following the race in question.

[The present limitation of "6 P.M. of the week-day following the race in question." "ham-strings" Race Committees and may easily redound to the advantage of a rule breaker.]

CITATIONS AND REFERENCES

ARRANGED BY RULE NUMBER

KEY TO ABBREVIATIONS

N. A. Y. R. U. = North American Yacht Racing Union.

Y. R. A. = Yacht Racing Association of Great Britain.

N. Y. Y. C. = New York Yacht Club; Reports of Race Committee.

Y. R. A. of L. I. S. = Yacht Racing Association of Long Island Sound, New York.

RULE	SUBJECT	REFERENCE	PAGE
1.	General Authority of Race Committee.	*Ace* v. *Whitecap*	15
		Yachting World, Jan. 1, 1937, page 9	17
		Marjorie v. *Sheila*	17–18
		Lady Dainty	18
		Yachting World, Oct. 28, 1938, page 433	18
		Jade v. *Bluebell*	18
		Tringa v. *Susette*	18
		Yachting World, May 26, 1939, page 521	19
		Southern Mass. Y. R. A., Appeals Committee	253
		B. Heckstall-Smith	175–176
10.	Wrecking or Shifting of a Mark	Royal Yacht Club of Tasmania, Y. R. A., 1936, Case 1	276
14.	When Amenable to Sailing Rules.		
	What Constitutes a Part of a Yacht	*Yare and Bure Sailing Club*	23
	Yacht Racing Rules Supersede Board of Trade Rules (English)	*The Satanita*	25
		Royal Singapore Yacht Club	26
	Rules of the Road at Sea (U. S. A.)	*Clark* v. *Thayer*	25
	Fouling Starting Line Mark During Preparatory Period	*Tranmere Sailing Club*	241

CITATIONS AND REFERENCES

RULE	SUBJECT	REFERENCE	PAGE
24.	Boarding and Leaving. Yacht Pushed off Shoal by Crew	*Royal Cork Yacht Club*, Y. R. A., 1876	277
27.	Start and Recall. Winner though later disqualified entitled to winner's gun	*The Vivacious*	44
" § 5.	Premature Start	*Jane* v. *Daphne*	44
		Clymene v. *Noresca*	44
		But see *Lena* v. *Countess*	44
		and *Pilgrim* v. *Maori*	44
		Girleen v. *Piccolo*	44
" § 6.	Wrong Side of Starting Line	*B. Heckstall-Smith*	46
" § 7.	Delayed Start	*Crouch Yacht Club*	47
29.	Definitions.		
" § 5.	Range of Risk of Collison	*Surinam* v. *Elva*	51
" § 6.	Overtaking: Widen Out Abeam	*Prestige* v. *Carolina*	53
	Terminated by:		
	Tacking	{ *Ananké* v. *Banshee* / *Talisman* v. *Ivanhoe* }	57–58
	No Longer Sailing Same Course	"*On the Wind's Highway*"	90
	Not Necessarily Terminated by a Jibe	*Forelle* v. *Seagull*	57
" § 7.	Proper Course: None Prior to Start	*Gleam* v. *Seven Seas*	30, 58
		Alerte v. *Freida*	58
		Council, Y. R. A.	58
		Sir William Burton	58
		C. Sherman Hoyt	60
30. 1st Par.	Right of Way. "Shall Keep Clear"	*Yachting World*, Mar. 20, 1936, page 243	152
" (A).	Overtaking:	*Tringa* v. *Ceres*	68–70
		Shamrock v. *White Heather*	70
		Mignonette v. *Pariah*	70
		Indra v. *Nike*	70
		Viola v. *Camelia*	81–82
		June Mary v.*Flying Cloud*	82–83
		Aileen v. *Canvasback*	82–85
	Not Necessarily Terminated by Jibing	*Forelle* v. *Seagull*	57, 77
		Rainbow v. *Yankee*	77–79

CITATIONS AND REFERENCES

RULE	SUBJECT	REFERENCE	PAGE
30. (B).	Overtaking to Windward	Royal Dart Yacht Club	73
		Moonfleet v. Ajax	73
		Yachting World, Nov. 29, 1929	75
" (C).	Overtaking to Leeward:	Juno v. Zoe	76
	Luffing Illegal	Thistle v. Felma	77, 104
	Jibing and Luffing	Nyria v. White Heather	81, 104
		Su Su v. Endrick	81, 104
		{ The Florida Case / Doris v. Seagull }	92–103
		Widgeon v. Chittabob	87, 104
	Jibing Twice	Lurcher v. Kaga	104
	Meeting, Crossing and Converging:		
	Manœuvring:		
	2d Paragraph; Before the Start	Alerte v. Freida	58
		Gleam v. Seven Seas	27
		The Satanita	25
	3d Paragraph; After the Start	{ Italia v. Nutmeg III / Stranger v. Nutmeg III / Y. R. A. Annual General Meeting, Feb. 18, 1931 }	49
		C. Sherman Hoyt, N. A. Y. R. U. Bull. No. 21, Jan. 28, 1933, page 19	50
	After the Finish	Clark v. Thayer	25
" (D).	Free and Close-hauled	Tramontana v. Triphon	109
" (E).	Starboard and Port Tack: Close-hauled	Breeze v. Ultra	110
		Egeria v. Olga	110
		Flying Cloud v. Vagrant	110–111
		British Boat Club, Alexandria, Egypt	111
		Girleen v. Piccolo	111–112
		Rainbow v. Yankee	112–113
		Istalena v. Avatar	115
" (F).	Free on Opposite Tacks, No Overtaking	Endeavour v. Rainbow	116–120
		Marilee v. Shawara	121–122
" (G).	Converging, Free, Neither Overtaken	Prestige v. Carolina	106
		Fortuna v. Circus Girl	144
	Luffing Head to Wind Illegal	B. Heckstall-Smith	124
" (I).	Gather Proper Way:	Indra v. Nike	131–134
		Yankee v. Rainbow	134–135
		No. 11 Dinghy v. No. 13 Dinghy	136
		Beryl v. Zmoya	136
		Fintra v. Coral	136
		Mustang v. Frothblower	137

CITATIONS AND REFERENCES

RULE	SUBJECT	REFERENCE	PAGE
30. (I).	Owing to Position Cannot Keep Clear	*Ibis* v. *Resolute*	138
" (K).	Altering Course: Balk	*Gleam* v. *Seven Seas*	31–32
		Istalena v. *Avatar*	115
		Star Dust II v. *Queen Mary*	145
		Tramontana v. *Triphon*	146
	Balk, Jibing Twice	*Lurcher* v. *Kaga*	146

Rule 30 Not Affected by the Presence of Marks:
As to:

(E).	Port and Starboard Tack	*Rosalind* v. *Lassie*	147
		Gracie v. *L'Amoureuse*	148
		Gladys v. *Mosquito*	154
(I).	Tacking Too Close	*Satanita Too* v. *Mallard II*	149
(K).	Hold Course	*Larkspur* v. *Rosalind*	154
31.	Giving Room at Marks or Obstructions to Sea Room.		
"	Temporarily Supersedes Rule 30	Editor, *Yachting World*, Sept. 15, 1933, page 225	157
"	Obstruction, Definition of	B. Heckstall-Smith, *Yachting World*, Sept. 15, 1933, page 386	157
		Capt. R. T. Dixon, *Yachting World*, Mar. 20, 1936, page 243	157
"	Government Buoy, Entitled to Pass on Channel Side of	*Flying Cloud* v. *Advance*	158
"	No Material Alteration of Course	*Arcadian* v. *Margitta*	158–159
"	Rounding, Act of	B. Heckstall-Smith and E. Du Boulay, *The Complete Yachtsman*, page 185	162
"	Overlap Made in Proper Time	B. Heckstall-Smith, *Yacht Racing*, 2d Ed., 1933, page 123	163
"	Forcing a Passage	B. Heckstall-Smith, *Yacht Racing*, 2d Ed., 1933, page 124	164
"	Burden of Proof	*Saga* v. *Finetta*	164
"	Overlap Before Mark Is Reached	Parsons, Macdonough and Spedden, *Handbook on American Yacht Racing Rules*, 2d Ed., 1923, pages 96–97	165–166

CITATIONS AND REFERENCES

RULE	SUBJECT	REFERENCE	PAGE
31.	Rounding Mark, "Follow My Leader"	B. Heckstall-Smith, *Yachting World*, Jan. 15, 1937, page 58	168
"	"Cutting in" at a Mark	*Harmony* v. *Sealark*	167–168
		Alouette v. *Una*	168
"	Overlap at Marks	*Rosalind* v. *Newt*	169–170
		Circe v. *Fantasy*	170
"	Rounding Mark, Manner of	B. Heckstall-Smith, *Yachting World*, Dec. 8, 1933, page 475	171
"	"To Pass" Means "To Sail By" not "To Round"	*Dinghy No. 33* v. *Dinghy No. 16*, N. A. Y. R. U. Appeal No. 7, Dec. 14, 1936	172
"	Converging at the Start	*Georgia* v. *Grey Dawn*	175
"	Barging at the Start: Windward Yacht Must Pass Astern of Leeward Yacht if Possible	B. Heckstall-Smith, *Yachting World*, Nov. 20, 1936, page 474	175–176
		Royal Albert Yacht Club	176
"	Squeezing the Inside Yacht	*Pyxie* v. *Sylvia*	177
"	Another Yacht Racing	*Moana* v. *Victory*	177–181
"	Lay Mark Without Tacking	{ *Lackagh* v. *Laragh* *Glynn* v. *Lackagh* }	182
"	Luffing and Forereaching Past a Mark	*Decisions and Rulings*, N.Y. Y. C., 1849–1923, pages 9–14	185
	Weather Shore, Whole of, ning of	B. Heckstall-Smith, *Yacht Racing*, 2d Ed., 1933, page 75	187
"	"Without Tacking" Means Cannot "Lay" the Mark	*Dinghy 33* v. *Dinghy 16*	188
"	Weather Shore, Whole of, an Obstruction	B. Heckstall-Smith, *Yacht Racing*, 2d Ed., 1933, page 132	188
"	Weather Shore an Obstruction	*Sankuntala* v. *Polynia*	189
"	Shoaler Draft, May Take Advantage of	*Watersprite* v. *Susan*	190
"	Obstruction, Shoal	*Jeanette* v. *Beryl*	190
"	Lee Shore, Forcing Passage	*Eelin* v. *Astrild*	192
"	Narrow River, Foul Tide	*Sapphire* v. *Ruby*	193

CITATIONS AND REFERENCES

RULE	SUBJECT	REFERENCE	PAGE
31.	Word "Tack" in 3d Paragraph Does Not Include Jibing	*Aileen* v. *Canvasback*	85–86
		B. Heckstall-Smith, *Yachting World*, June 12, 1931, page 564	195
30 & 31.	Overtaking; Another Yacht Racing; Obstruction	*Dinghy No. 33* v. *Dinghy No. 16*	198, 207
		Humming Bird v. *Dolphin*	198
		{ *Nancy* v. *Redshank* *Wraith* v. *Redshank* }	202
		Dixon Kemp, *A Manual of Yacht and Boat Sailing*, 8th Ed., 1895, page 215	200
32.	Close-hauled, Approaching an Obstruction or a Mark.		
"	Tacking Simultaneously	*Elmina* v. *Queen*	219
		Dixon Kemp, *A Manual of Yacht and Boat Sailing*, 8th Ed., 1895, page 222	219
		Blue Bird v. *Fay*	221
"	A Call for Room Is Not a Demand to Tack	*Jade* v. *Bluebell*	219
"	Hail to be Seasonable	*Red Jacket* v. *Blue Bell*	221
"	Leeward Yacht the Judge of Her Own Peril	Dixon Kemp, *An Exposition of the Yacht Racing Rules*, 1898, page 92	222
"	Interpreted by Ordinary Customs of Prudence and Careful Navigation	Dixon Kemp, *A Manual*, etc., ubi supra, page 222	222
"	Hailing Yacht Responsible for Her Hail	*Character of a Mark, Decisions and Rulings*	222
"	Entitled to Pass on Channel Side of Government Buoy	*Flying Cloud* v. *Advance*	222
"	That "Familiar With Waters" No Excuse for Failure to Respond to Hail	*Coomara* v. *Pixie*	222–223
"	Not Approaching Shore	*Halcyone* v. *Bedouin*	225
		Princess v. *Elena*	225
"	Must be Approaching Shore	*Flying Cloud* v. *Advance*	225
"	Distance Apart	*Emerald* v. *Nona*	225
		No. 1 O. D. Dinghy v. *No. 2 O. D. Dinghy*	226

CITATIONS AND REFERENCES

RULE	SUBJECT	REFERENCE	PAGE
32.	Leeward Yacht Not Bound to Lift Centreboard Slightly	*Gwen* v. *Fulmar*	226
"	Mark of Course, Exception	*Volunteer* v. *Gracie* *Cantitoe* v. *Weetamoe* *Jake* v. *Kittiwake*	228 230 231
"	Obstruction, Another Yacht Racing (Rule 31, Par. 1, last sentence)	*Moana* v. *Victory*	177–181
33.	Fouling or Improperly Rounding Marks.		
"	Improper Rounding, Track of Yacht	N. A. Y. R. U. Bull. No. 26, Jan. 18, 1935, page 27 *Queenstown People's Regatta Committee* B. Heckstall-Smith, Yacht Racing, 2d Ed., 1933, page 168 Dr. Manfred Curry, Aerodynamics of Sails and Racing Tactics, 1927, page 231 Ditto, *Racing Tactics in Questions and Answers*, 1932, Diagram 53, and pages 204–205	237, 240 237 240 240 240
"	Forced the Wrong Side of Turning Mark	*Norfolk and Suffolk Yacht and Sailing Clubs Association*	240
"	Fouling Starting Line Mark, Preparatory Period	*Merlin* v. *Spray*	243
"	Crew Touched Government Buoy	*Tranmere Sailing Club*, Yacht "*Mink*"	241
"	Floating Starting-Line-Stake Not Part of Mark	*Sandy Bay Yacht Club*, N. A. Y. R. U. Appeal No. 3, Nov. 15, 1935	242
34.	Marks of the Course.		
"	Preparatory Period, Fouling Starting Line Mark During	*Merlin* v. *Spray*	42, 243
"	No Required Side, Starting Line Mark, Obstruction, Rule 31	*Cutty* v. *Nona* *Riptide* v. *Stella*	38–39 40–41
35.	Fouling Competing Yachts.		

CITATIONS AND REFERENCES

RULE	SUBJECT	REFERENCE	PAGE
35.	Entitled to Rights of Way Despite Previous Foul	*The Bembridge Sailing Club*	243
		Clymene v. *Noresca*	243
		Lena v. *Countess*	244
		Endeavour v. *Rainbow*, N. Y. Y. C., *1934 Report of Race Committee*, page 15	246
		Pilgrim v. *Maori*	246–247
"	Yachting Etiquette, Withdraw After Foul	*Pilgrim* v. *Maori*	248
		B. Heckstall-Smith, *Yacht Racing*, 2d Ed., 1933, page 170	249
"	Yacht in Another Class	*Tomboy* v. *Octavia*	249
		The Waterwitch Case	249
36.	Running Aground and Fouling.		
"	Assistance Other Than From Crew of Vessel Fouled	*In Re Falkyre, Royal Yacht Club of Tasmania*	250
		Naini Tal Yacht Club	251
37.	Anchoring.		
"	Remaining at Mooring	*Pelican* v. *Polly*	32
"	Made Fast to a Pier, Float, Shore, or Other Object	*Great Yarmouth Yacht Club*	32
"	Cannot Slip or Buoy Anchor Cable	*Royal Sidney Yacht Club*	33
"	Not Even to Prevent Crew Being Pulled Overboard	*Loss of Viera's Kedge Anchor*	252
"	Nor If Anchor Fluke Caught in War Wreckage	*The Britannia*	252
"	Veering Across Finish Line While Anchored	*Katie* v. *Hypatia*	256
38.	Propulsion.		
"	"Walking" Aft With Anchor Cable	B. Heckstall-Smith, *Yacht Racing*, 2d Ed., 1933, page 175	252
"	"Fanning" Sails	*Edgartown Yacht Club, Southern Mass. Y. R. A., Appeals Committee*	253
"	"Rudder Sculling"	*Portaferry Regatta Committee*	252
40.	Man Overboard and Accidents.		
"	Resail of Race	*Leigh-On-Sea Sailing Club*	254
		Royal Natal Yacht Club	255

CITATIONS AND REFERENCES

RULE	SUBJECT	REFERENCE	PAGE
41.	The Finish.		
"	Timed at Finish but Drifts Back and Fouls Mark	*Royal Western Yacht Club*	256
"	Veering Across Finish Line While Anchored	*Katie* v. *Hypatia*	256
43.	Penalty for Infringing Rules.		
"	Only Penalty Is Disqualification	*Aito* v. *Ingane*	263
45.	Protests.		
"	Necessary Allegations	*Betty* v. *Sphex*	263
"	Displaying Code Flag "B"	*Sandy Bay Yacht Club* *Endeavour* v. *Rainbow*	264 116, 118
"	Jurisdiction of Protest	*Dublin Bay Sailing Club* (Y. R. A., 1933, Case 1)	264
"	Rules to be Enforced	*George W. Elder, Yachting,* March, 1934	264–265
"	Words "Foul Another Yacht" Do Not Imply "Dirty" or "Unfair" Sailing	"*F. N.*" *Yachting World,* Sept. 4, 1936, page 228	266
"	Protest Merely a Means to Maintain Rules	"*F. N.*" ubi supra	266
46.	Hearings by Race Committee.		
"	No Cause for Complaint by Owner if Fails to Attend After Due Notice Given	*Vivacious* v. *The Club*	267
"	Testimony Improperly Admitted	*Moonfleet* v. *Ajax*	268
"	Right to Cross-Examine Witness		
"	Race Committee a Court of Inquiry, Not a Court of Law	*Hugh M. Wharton*	267
"	It Should Not be Too Technical	*Handbook of American Yacht Racing Rules,* 2d Ed., 1923, page 147	268
"	Racing Rules Not Penal	*Dixon Kemp, An Exposition of the Yacht Racing Rules,* 1898, page 2	268
"	Burden of Proof: In General on Non-Right-of-Way Yacht	*Arrow* v. *Jean*	269
"	Rule 30 (A)	*Yankee* v. *Rainbow,* Race of July 21, 1936	270

CITATIONS AND REFERENCES

RULE	SUBJECT	REFERENCE	PAGE
46	Rule 30 (E)	*Flying Cloud* v. *Vagrant*	110–111, 269
		British Boat Club, Alexandria, Egypt	111
"	Rule 30 (I)	*Yankee* v. *Rainbow*, Race of July 21, 1936	270
"	Rule 32	Dixon Kemp, *An Exposition of the Yacht Racing Rules*, 1898, page 92	221–222
"	Exceptions to General Rule: Rules 29 (7) and 30 (C)		270
47.	Disqualification Without Protest.		
"	Reason for Rule	Dixon Kemp, *A Manual of Yacht and Boat Sailing*, 8th Ed., 1895, page 232	274
"	Cannot Disqualify Without Notice and Hearing	*The Vivacious*	275
"	Yacht Cannot Evade and Pass to Race Committee the Right to and Responsibility of Protest	*Royal Gibraltar Yacht Club*	272
		The Island Sailing Club	273
"	Information Given to Race Committee by a Yacht Entitled to Protest Is Not "Independent Evidence" Entitling Committee to Initiate Proceedings	*Royal Gibraltar Yacht Club*	272
48.	Decisions of Protests.		
"	To be Based on Rule *Found* to Have Been Infringed, Not Necessarily on Rule *Alleged* to Have Been Infringed	*Dublin Bay Sailing Club* (Y. R. A., 1912, Case 2)	268
		Handbook of American Yacht Racing Rules, 2d Ed., 1923, page 147	268
	Interested Party Not to Sit on Protest Case	*Oola* v. *Nirvana*	277

No Particular Rule:

Right to Clear Wind	*Royal Alfred Yacht Club*	258
	Lena v. *Countess*, N. Y. Y. C., 1924 Report of Race Committee, page 6	259
Number of Starters Required by Race Circular	*Little Hampton Sailing and Motor Club*	43
	West Mersea Yacht Club	43
Loan of Gear to Disabled Yacht	*Naini Tal Yacht Club*	251

DIAGRAMS

ARRANGED BY RULE NUMBER

RULE	SUBJECT	NUMBER	PAGE
1.	General Authority of Race Committee	1	16
	General Authority of Race Committee	2	17
27.	Start and Recall:		
§ 6.	Wrong Side of Starting Line	4	45
	Premature Start, Return After	5	48
29.	Definitions:		
§ 5.	Range of Risk of Collision	6	52
§ 6.	Overtaking:		
	Overtaken Rights Lost by Tacking	7	57
	Cl. 2—Widen Out Abeam	20	105
§ 7.	Proper Course	8	59
	" "	9	61
	" "	10	62
	Proper Course, Reaching a Yacht Beyond a Mark	11	62
30.	Right of Way:		
(A).	Overtaking	12	65
"	"	13	69
"	"	15	78
"	"	17	83
"	"	18	86
"	"	25	131
(B).	Overtaking to Windward:		
	(Bluff-bow Dinghy)	14	72
(C).	Overtaking to Leeward	25	131
	Overtaking to Leeward, Jibing and Luffing	16	81
	" " " " "	17	83
	" " " " "	18	86
(C).	Overtaking to Leeward, Bearing Away	19	93
	" " " " "	58	257
	Meeting, Crossing and Converging:		
(E).	Port and Starboard Tack Close-hauled	21	113
(F).	Free, on Different Tacks	22	117
"	" " " "	23	121
(G).	Converging	20	105
"	"	24	126
(H).	"	24	126

DIAGRAMS

RULE	SUBJECT	NUMBER	PAGE
	Altering Course:		
(I).	Gather Proper Way	25	131
"	" " "	26	136
"	Cannot Invoke (E) Unless Fulfill (I)	27	137
"	Owing to Position Cannot Keep Clear	28	138
(K).	Balk, Jibing Twice	29	146
Rule 30	Not Affected by Presence of Marks:		
(E).	Starboard and Port Tack	30	147
"	Tacking Too Close	31	149
"	Starboard and Port Tack	32	150
31.	Giving Room at Marks or Obstructions to Sea Room:		
	Room at Marks	33	167
	Overlap at Marks	34	169
	Another Yacht Racing	35	178
	Obstruction in Path of One Yacht	36	182
	Weather Shore, Overtaking Along a	37	189
	" " " "	38	190
	Lee Shore, Overtaking Along a	39	191
	" " " "	40	193
30 & 31.	Overtaking, Obstruction	41	198
	" "	42	203
	" "	43	212
32.	Close-hauled, Approaching an Obstruction to Sea Room or a Mark:		
	Not Approaching the Shore	44	224
	Approaching the Shore	45	225
	Obstruction, Anchored Vessel	46	227
	Mark of the Course, Exception to Rule	47	228
	" " " "	48	228
	Obstruction (Committee Boat at Finish)	49	231
	Two Divisions of Yachts on Opposite Tacks	50	232
33.	Fouling or Improperly Rounding Marks	51	235
	" " " "	52	235
	" " " "	53	235
	" " " "	54	236
	" " " "	55	238
	" " " "	56	241
34.	Marks of the Course:		
	Starting Line Marks	3	38
37.	Anchoring:		
	Just Before the Finish	57	256
41.	The Finish:		
	Anchoring Just Before	57	256
	Overtaking, Bearing Away Just Before	58	257

INDEX

REFERENCES ARE TO PAGES

	PAGES
Accidents	253–255
Accidents (Rule 1)	18
Ace v. *Whitecap*	15
Advice, Three Bits of	11
Aileen v. *Canvasback*	82–86
Aito v. *Ingane*	263
Alerte v. *Freida*	58
Allowance for Leeway, Tide, etc.	63, 77
Alouette v. *Una*	168
Altering Course	54, 127, 158–159
Amenable to Sailing Rules, When	23
Ananké v. *Banshee*	57–58
Anchoring, etc.	18, 32–33, 252, 256
Anker, Johan	37, 174
Appeal from Protest Decision of Race Committee	275
Approaching Marks	147–150, 163–166
Arcadian v. *Margitta*	37, 158–159
Arrow v. *Jean*	269
Assistance, Other than from Crew of Vessel Fouled, Illegal	250, 251
Authority of Race Committee, General	13, 253
Balk, Mislead or	31–32, 85, 109, 115, 140–146
"Barging," Definition of	171
"Barging" at the Start	171–174, 175–176
Basic Rules, The Three	11
Bearing Away Before the Start	24, 32
Bearing Away, Jibing and Luffing May Constitute	81
Bearing Away to Hinder	76, 258
Bembridge Sailing Club, The	243, 245, 247, 248
Beryl v. *Zmoya*	136
Betty v. *Sphex*	263
Bits of Advice, Three	11
Blue Bird v. *Fay*	221
Board of Trade Regulations (English), When Superseded by Yacht Racing Rules	26
Boarding and Leaving	276

INDEX

	PAGES
Borrowing Gear from Another Yacht During Race	251
Breeze v. *Ultra*	110
British Boat Club, Alexandria, Egypt	111
Britannia, The	252

Burden of Proof:
    In General 268–269
    In General, on Non-Right-of-Way Yacht . . 269–270
    Rule 30 (A) 164, 195, 270
    Rule 30 (E) 110–111, 269
    Rule 30 (I) 269, 270
    Rule 32 221–222

Burton, Sir William, President Y. R. A. 58

Cantitoe v. *Weetamoe* 230
Cary, William Avery 124–125
"Character of a Mark" 222
Circe v. *Fantasy* 170
Citations, Arranged by Rule Number 317
Clark v. *Thayer* 25
Clear Ahead and Clear Astern, Definition of . . . 54
Clear Wind, Nothing in the Rules Entitling a Yacht to . 258, 259
Close-hauled, Approaching a Mark or an Obstruction . 218
Close-hauled, Definition of 54
Clymene v. *Noresca* 44, 243
Collision, Range of Risk of 51–53
Competing Yachts, Fouling 243–249
Complete Yachtsman, The 162
Consistent with the Intention of Crossing the (Starting) Line 49–50
Converging, Meeting, Crossing and 107
Converging, Presumption in Favor of Before the Start . 29
Coomara v. *Pixie* 222–223
Course, Altering 54, 127–139
Courtesy and Unwritten Law 278–279
Cross Examination of Witness, Right of 267
Crossing and Converging, Meeting 107
Crossing, Two Divisions of Yachts Close-hauled . . 232
Crouch Yacht Club 47

Curry, Dr. Manfred:
    Aerodynamics of Sails and Racing Tactics . . 240
    Racing Tactics in Questions and Answers . . 240

"Cutting in" at a Mark 166, 168
Cutty v. *Nona* 38–39

INDEX

	PAGES
Davis, Gherardi, Esq.	244
Decisions and Rulings, N. Y. Y. C., 1849–1923	110, 175, 185, 219, 222, 225, 228
Decisions of Protests by Race Committee	275
Definitions	51–58
Delayed Starters	47
Diagrams, Arranged by Rule Number	327
Dinghy No. 33 v. *Dinghy No. 16*	172, 188, 198, 207
Disabled by Competitor	18
Disqualification Without Protest	271
Disqualifications and Appeals	261–277

Dixon, Capt. R. T.:

"Hinder"	151–152, 157
Obstruction, Definition of	157–158
"Shall Keep Clear"—Rule 30. First Paragraph	152
Doris v. *Seagull*	92–103
Dublin Bay Sailing Club. (Y. R. A., 1912, Case 2)	268
Dublin Bay Sailing Club. (Y. R. A., 1933, Case 1)	264
Du Boulay, E., and B. Heckstall-Smith	162
Edgartown Yacht Club	253
Eelin v. *Astrild*	192
Egeria v. *Olga*	110
Elder, George W., *Why Glorify the Rule Breaker?*	264–265
Elmina v. *Queen*	218
Emerald v. *Nona*	225
Endeavour v. *Rainbow*	90, 116–120
Endeavour v. *Rainbow*, 2d "Count" of Protest	246
Evading Responsibility to Protest	272–273
Falkyre, In re (*Royal Yacht Club of Tasmania*)	250
"Fanning" Sails	253
Filing Protest	263
Finish, The	256
Finish, Bearing Away to Hinder Just Before the	258
Finish Line, Drifting Back and Fouling Mark of the	256
Fintra v. *Coral*	136
Floating Stake or Log, Not Part of Starting Line Mark	242
Florida Case, The	92–103
Flying Cloud v. *Advance*	158, 222, 225
Flying Cloud v. *Vagrant*	110–111, 269
"F. N.," *Yachting World*, Sept. 4, 1936, page 228	266
"Follow My Leader"	168

INDEX

	PAGES
Forcing a Passage	162, 164
Forelle v. *Seagull*	57, 77
Forereaching Past a Mark	185–187
Forster, Lord, British Y. R. A.	38, 39, 41
Fortuna v. *Circus Girl*	144
Foul Sailing	18
Fouling Competing Yachts	243–249
Fouling Marks	42, 84, 243
Fouling Yachts in Another Class	249
Fouling Yachts in Another Race	249
Fowle, Leonard M.	240
Free, Definition of	54
Free, No Degrees of	108
Gather Proper Way	127–137
Gem v. *Maud*	63
General Authority of Race Committee	13, 253
Georgia v. *Grey Dawn*	175
Girleen v. *Piccolo*	44, 111–112
Gladys v. *Mosquito*	154
Gleam v. *Seven Seas*	24, 27–32, 58
Glynn v. *Lackagh*	182
Gracie v. *L'Amoureuse*	148
Great Yarmouth Yacht Club	32
Gwen v. *Fulmar*	226
Hail, A, When Required	220, 232
Hail, A Yacht Is Responsible for Her	222
Halcyone v. *Bedouin*	225
Handbook on American Yacht Racing Rules, 2d Ed., 1923:	
Pages 96–97	165–166
Page 147	268
Harmony v. *Sealark*	167–168
Hearings by Race Committee:	
Burden of Proof (see that topic in Index)	
No Complaint if Owner Absent After Due Notice Given	266–267
Testimony Improperly Admitted, Right to Cross-examine Witness	267
Race Committee a Court of Inquiry, Not a Court of Law	267
Racing Rules Not Penal	268
Heckstall–Smith, Major B.:	
Barging at Start	175–176
Customs of the Sea, Fair Sailing	16–17, 19

INDEX

	PAGES
Cutting in at Marks	168
Follow My Leader	168
Forcing a Passage	164
Obstruction, Definition of	157
Overlap Made in Proper Time	163
Rounding Marks, Manner of	164, 171
Rule 30 (B)	75
Rule 30 (G)	124
Tacking, When It Begins	187
Track of Yacht Around Course	240
"Walking" Anchor Cable Aft	252
Weather Shore an Obstruction	188
"Word 'Tack' in Rule 31 Does Not Include Gybing"	195
Wrong Side of Starting Line	46
Heckstall-Smith and E. Du Boulay	162

Hoyt, C. Sherman:

Intention of Crossing Starting Line	50
Proper Course	60
Resail of Race	254–255

Humming Bird v. *Dolphin* 198

Ibis v. *Resolute*	138
"Idling" Before the Start	33
Improperly Rounding Marks	236–240
"Independent Evidence" under Rule 47	272–273
Indra v. *Nike*	70, 131–135
Infringing Rules, Penalty for	263
Intention of Crossing the (Starting) Line, Course Consistent with the	49–50
Interested Party Disqualified to Judge Protest	277
International Star Class Y. R. A.	15
Iselin, C. Oliver	244
Island Sailing Club, The	273
Istalena v. *Avatar*	115
Italia v. *Nutmeg III*	49

Jade v. *Bluebell*	18, 219
Jake v. *Kittiwake*	231
Jane v. *Daphne*	44
Jeanette v. *Beryl*	190
Jibing and Luffing by Overtaken Yacht	77–104
Jibing by Overtaken Yacht	57, 77, 79, 81, 82

INDEX

PAGES

Jibing and Subsequent Luffing by Overtaken Yacht May Constitute Bearing Away 81
Jibing Not Included in Word "Tack" . . . 85–86, 195
Jibing Twice in Front of Overtaking Yacht . . . 104, 146
June Mary v. *Flying Cloud* 82–83
Juno v. *Zoe* 76
Jurisdiction of Protest 264

Kampen, H. C. A. van 68, 88, 89
Katie v. *Hypatia* 256
Kedge Anchor, Loss of 252
Kemp, Dixon:
  A Manual of Yacht and Boat Sailing, 8th Ed., 1895:
    Page 215 200
    " 222 . . . . 219, 222
    " 232 274
  An Exposition of the Yacht Racing Rules, 1898:
    Page 2 268
    " 92 222
    " 108 274
Kuorhaan v. *Ancora* 278

Lackagh v. *Laragh* 182
Lady Dainty 18
Larkspur v. *Rosalind* 154
"Laying" the Mark 188
Lee Shore, Forcing Leeward Passage when Allowed . . 191–192
Leeway and Tide, etc., Allowance for 63, 77
Leigh-On-Sea Sailing Club 254
Lena v. *Countess* 44, 244–245, 247, 259
Little Hampton Sailing and Motor Club 43
Loan of Equipment to Disabled Yacht Will Disqualify Recipient 251
Lord Forster, British Y. R. A. 38, 39, 41
Loss of *Viera's* Kedge Anchor 252
Luffing:
  Allowed by the Rules 71, 74–75
  An Alteration of Course 54
  And Forereaching Past a Mark 185–187
  By Overtaken Yacht 71, 74–75
  Contemplated by Overtaking Rule 30 (B) . . 71, 74–75
  Definition of 54
  Sudden, Without Warning 34, 74–76
Lurcher v. *Kaga* 104, 146

INDEX

	PAGES
Macdonough, Joseph M.	165
Mackenzie, Clinton	244
Maintaining Rules	264–266
Man Overboard	253
Marilee v. *Shawara*	121–122
Marjorie v. *Sheila*	17–18
"*Mark, Character of a*"	222

Marks:

Approaching	147–150, 163, 166
"Cutting in" at	166–168
Fouling	42
Improperly Rounding	236–240
Missing	276
Of the Course	34
Presence of, Does Not Affect Rule 30	147
Removal of	276
Room at	163–164, 168–169, 176
Rounding	148–149, 162–164, 166
Rounding, Act of	162
Starting Line	34, 37–41, 242
Submergence of	276
Tacking when Rounding	148–149
Wrecking of	276

Meeting, Crossing, and Converging	107
Merlin v. *Spray*	42, 243
Mignonette v. *Pariah*	70
Mink, The	241
Mislead or Balk	31–32, 85, 109, 115, 140–146
Misuse of Rules	18
Moana v. *Victory*	177–181
Moonfleet v. *Ajax*	73, 267
Mooring, Remaining at, After Preparatory Signal	32
Mustang v. *Frothblower*	137

N. A. Y. R. U. Bulletin No. 26, Track of Yacht	237, 240
Naini Tal Yacht Club	251
Nancy v. *Redshank*	202
No Required Side to Starting Line Marks During Preparatory Period	34, 37–41
Norfolk and Suffolk Yacht and Sailing Clubs Association	240
North American Yacht Racing Union, Certain Racing (Sailing) Rules, Appendix	281
Number 1 O. D. Dinghy v. *Number 2 O. D. Dinghy*	226

INDEX

	PAGES
Number 11 Dinghy v. *Number 13 Dinghy*	136
Nyria v. *White Heather*	81, 104

Obstruction to Sea Room 157–158
Obstruction to Sea Room, Definition of 157
Oddie, J. V. S. 125
On The Wind's Highway:
    Rule 29 (6) 90
    " 30 (E) 113–115
    " 30 (F) 120
Oola v. *Nirvana* 277
Overlap, Definition of 55
Overlap, Explanation of 55–56
Overlap Made in Proper Time 163
Overtaken-to-Leeward Yacht, Jibing and Luffing by . . 77–104
Overtaking:
    Along a Lee Shore 190–191
    Along a Weather Shore 188–189
    Definition of 56–57
    Presumption in Favor of, After the Start . . . 29
    Rights (see Right of Way—B)
    Summary of 104
    Three Requisites 64
    To Leeward 76
Owing to Position Cannot Keep Clear 138

"Parking" on the Starting Line 33
Parsons, H. de B. 165
Part of a Yacht, What Constitutes 23
Pelican v. *Polly* 32
Penalty for Infringing Rules 263
Pilgrim v. *Maori* 44, 246–247, 248
Portaferry Regatta Committee 252
Powers of Race Committee, General 13, 253
Premature Start and Recall 43–47
Preparatory Period, Fouling Starting Line Mark During . 42, 243
Presence of Marks Does Not Affect Rule 30 . . . 147
Prestige v. *Carolina* 53, 106
Previous Foul, Entitled to Rights of Way After . 243, 246–248
Princess v. *Elena* 225
Proper Course:
    Definition of (see also Right of Way, (B) 6) . . . 58

INDEX

	PAGES
During Existence of Overtaking Conditions	58–61
No, Prior to Starting Signal	24, 31, 58
Proper Way, Gather	127–137
Propulsion, Only by Normal Action of Wind on Sails	253

Protest:
- Filing of 263
- Jurisdiction of 264
- Necessary Allegations 263
- And Appeal 275

Pyxie v. *Sylvia* 177

Queenstown People's Regatta Committee 237

Race Committee:
- A Judicial Board of Inquiry 267
- General Authority of 13, 253

Racing Rules Not Penal 268
Rainbow v. *Yankee*, Race of Aug. 15, 1936 . . 77–79, 122
Rainbow v. *Yankee*, Race of Aug. 16, 1934 . . 112–113, 115
Range of Risk of Collision 51–53
Reaching a Yacht Beyond a Mark 62
"Reasonably Experienced" Competitor 145
Recall, Premature Start and 43–47
Red Jacket v. *Blue Bell* 221
References Arranged by Rule Number 317
Remaining at Mooring After Preparatory Signal . . . 32
Removal of Mark 276
Required Number of Starters 43
Resailing a Race 254–255, 276
Responsibility to Protest 272–273
Return, Right to, and Make a Proper Start 48
Revival of Right of Way After Premature Start . . . 47

Right of Way:
- (A) Altering Course 127
- (B) Overtaking:
  1. Burden of Proof on Late Overtaking Yacht . 56, 154
  2. Jibing and Subsequent Luffing by Overtaken-to-Leeward Yacht 77–104
  3. Lee Shore, Leeward Passage when Allowed . 191–192
  4. Leeway, Wind, and Tide, Allowance for . . 63, 77
  5. Luffing Contemplated by Rule 30 (B) . . 71, 74–75
  6. Proper Course During Existence of Overtaking Conditions 58

INDEX

	PAGES
7. Rights Not Carried Over on New Tack	57
8. Three Yachts Involved, Rules 31 and 30 (A), (B), (C), (G), (K)	196
9. Weather Shore, Forcing Windward Passage Not Allowed	188
10. Conclusion and Summary	104

Right to Return and Make a Proper Start 48
Riptide v. *Stella* 40–41
Risk of Collision, Definition of Range of 52
Room at Marks 163–164, 168–169, 176
Roosevelt, George E. 240
Rosalind v. *Lassie* 147
Rosalind v. *Newt* 169–170
Rounding Marks 148–149, 162–164, 166
Royal Albert Yacht Club 176
Royal Alfred Yacht Club 258
Royal Cork Yacht Club 277
Royal Dart Yacht Club 73
Royal Gibraltar Yacht Club 272
Royal Natal Yacht Club 255
Royal Sidney Yacht Club 33
Royal Singapore Yacht Club 26
Royal Western Yacht Club 256
Royal Yacht Club of Tasmania, In Re Falkyre, Y. R. A., 1934, Case 4 250
Royal Yacht Club of Tasmania, Y. R. A., 1936, Case 1 . . 276
Rudder "Sculling" 252
Rule 31, Three Requisites to Invoke Rule 155
Rule 32, Three Requisites to Invoke Rule 218

Rules:

   1. General Authority of Race Committee 13
   10. Wrecking or Shifting of a Mark 276
   14. When Amenable to Sailing Rules 23
   24. Boarding and Leaving 276
   27. Start and Recall 43, 45
   29. Definitions:
      § 1. Close-hauled and Free 54
      § 2. Luffing 54
      § 3. Clear Ahead and Clear Astern . . . 54–55
      § 4. Overlap 55
      § 5. Risk of Collision 52
      § 6. Overtaking 56
      § 7. Proper Course 58

INDEX

		PAGES
30.	Right of Way:	
	First Paragraph, *"Shall Keep Clear"*	151
	Overtaking:	
	A. Overtaking Yacht Keeps Clear	64
	B. Luffing Rights of Yacht Overtaken to Windward	70–71
	C. Overtaking To Leeward	76
	Meeting, Crossing and Converging:	107
	D. Free and Close-hauled	108
	E. Port and Starboard Tack Close-hauled	109
	F. Free on Opposite Tacks, Neither Overtaken	116
	G. Free on Same Tack, Neither Overtaken	123
	H. Converging Close-hauled	124
	Altering Course:	
	I. Gather Proper Way	127
	Owing to Position Cannot Keep Clear	138
	Tacking Too Close	139
	K. Obligations of Yacht Holding Right of Way	140
	Mislead or Balk	31–32, 140–146
31.	Giving Room at Marks or Obstructions to Sea Room	153
32.	Close-hauled, Approaching an Obstruction to Sea Room or a Mark	218
33.	Fouling or Improperly Rounding Marks	234
34.	Marks of the Course	34
35.	Fouling Competing Yachts	243
36.	Running Aground, and Fouling	250
37.	Anchoring	251
38.	Propulsion	252
40.	Man Overboard and Accidents	253
41.	The Finish	256
43.	Penalty for Infringing Rules	263
45.	Protests	263
46.	Hearings by Race Committee	266
47.	Disqualification Without Protest	271
48.	Decisions of Protests	275
49.	Appeals	275–276
Rules of the Road at Sea (U. S. A.), When Superseded by Yacht Racing Rules		25
Rules, N. A. Y. R. U., Certain Racing (Sailing), Appendix		281
Running Aground and Fouling		250
Saga v. *Finetta*		164
Sailing Rules, Unification of		6–7
Sandy Bay Yacht Club		242, 264
Sankuntala v. *Polynia*		189

INDEX

	PAGES
Sapphire v. *Ruby*	193
Satanita, The	25
Satanita Too v. *Mallard II*	149
Shamrock v. *White Heather*	70
Shethar, John B.	240
Southern Massachusetts Y. R. A., Appeals Committee	253
Spedden, Frederic O.	165
Squeezing Inside Yacht at Marks	176
Star Class Y. R. A., International	15
Star Dust II v. *Queen Mary*	145
"Starlights"—I. S. C. Y. R. A.	15
Start and Recall	43–45
Start, "Barging" at the	171–174
Start, Right to Return and Make a Proper	48
Starters, Delayed	47
Starters, Required Number of	43

Starting Line:

Marks of	34, 37–41
"Parking" on the	33
Wrong Side of	46

Starting Line Marks:

Fouling During Preparatory Period	42, 243
No Required Side During Preparatory Period	34, 37–41

Stranger v. *Nutmeg III*	49
Submergence of Mark	276
Su Su v. *Endrick*	81, 104
Surinam v. *Elva*	51
Tack, The Word, Does Not Include Jibing	85–86, 195
Tacking Too Close	139
Tacking, When the Act of, Begins	187
Tacking When Rounding Marks	148–149
Talisman v. *Ivanhoe*	57–58
Thistle v. *Felma*	77, 104
Three Basic Rules	11
Three Bits of Advice	11
Three Yachts Involved, Overtaking, Obstruction	196
Tide, etc., Allowance for	63, 77
Tomboy v. *Octavia*	249
Touching Government Buoy by Crew	241
Track of Yacht Around Marks of the Course	236–240
Tramontana v. *Triphon*	109, 146

INDEX

	PAGES
Tranmere Sailing Club	241
Tringa v. *Ceres*	68–70
Tringa v. *Susette*	18
Two Divisions of Yachts Close-hauled on Opposite Tacks	232
Unfair Sailing	15, 17
Unification of Sailing Rules	6–7
Unwritten Law, Courtesy and	278–279

Vanderbilt, Harold S.:

Rule 29 (6)	89–90
" 30 (E)	113–115
" 30 (F)	120
Viera's Kedge Anchor, Loss of	252
Viola v. *Camelia*	81–82
Vivacious, The	44, 275
Vivacious v. *The Club*	267
Volunteer v. *Gracie*	228
"Walking" Aft with Anchor Rode	252
Watersprite v. *Susan*	190
Waterwitch Case, The	249
Weather Shore, Forcing Windward Passage Not Allowed	188
West Mersea Yacht Club	43
Wharton, Hugh M.	267
Why Glorify the Rule Breaker?	264–265
Widgeon v. *Chittabob*	87, 104
Wind, Tide, etc., Allowance for	63, 77
Withdrawal from Race After Obvious Foul	248–249
Women's National Yacht Racing Association	240
Wraith v. *Redshank*	202
Wrecking of Mark	276
Wrong Side of Starting Line, What Constitutes the	46
Yacht, What Constitutes a Part of a, for the Purpose of Overlap	23

Yachting Etiquette:

Withdrawal from Race After Obvious Foul	248, 249

Yachting World:

Accidents, Disabled by Competitor, Oct. 28, 1938, page 433	18
Customs of the Sea and Spirit of Fair Sailing, May 26, 1939, page 521	19
Proper Course, None Before Starting Signal, May 17, 1935, page 406	58

INDEX

PAGES

Rule 30 Temporarily Superseded by Rule 31, Sept. 15, 1933,
page 225 157
Unfair Sailing Before the Start, Jan. 1, 1937, page 9 . . 17

Yankee v. *Rainbow*, Race of July 21, 1936 . . 134–135, 270
Yare and Bure Sailing Club 23

Z28 v. *Z6* and *Z12*; *Z19* v. *Z12* 176